To Rona and Gia

Child of the Ghetto

Coming of Age in Fascist Italy: 1926-1946

A Memoir

Edda Servi Machlin

GIRO PRESS
Croton-on-Hudson

GiRo Press
P.O. Box 203
Croton-on-Hudson, NY 10520

GiRo Press and colophon are trademarks of
Giro Press

Manufactured in the United States of America

04 03 02 01 5 4 3 2

ISBN 1-878857-08-8

Library of Congress Cataloging-in-Publication Data

Machlin, Edda Servi, 1926-
    Child of the Ghetto : coming of age in fascist Italy, 1926-1946 :
a memoir / Edda Servi Machlin
      p. cm.
    Includes bibliographical references.
    ISBN 1-878857-08-8 (hardcover : alk. paper)
    1. Machlin, Edda Servi, 1926- . 2. Jews--Italy--Pitigliano
(Grosseto)--Biography. 3. Holocaust, Jewish (1939-1945)--Italy-
-Pitigliano (Grosseto)--Personal narratives. 4. Pitigliano
(Grosseto, Italy)--Biography. I. Title.
DS135.I9M286 1995
945'.57091'092--dc20
   [B]   95-20714
                                                   CIP

Acknowledgements

My thanks for the help I received in writing this memoir go first to my brother Gino for his willingness and ability to find much of the documentation regarding events which I did not directly witness; also to my sister Marcella, and to my brother Mario for having stimulated my memory and corroborated much of my stories; and to my two daughters, Rona and Gia, for keeping these memories alive with their curiosity and love of my *storie di Pitigliano*.

I also wish to acknowledge and offer thanks to David Markson, my Creative Writing Professor at Columbia University, for his initial encouragement. Thanks are due also to Robert Rahtz, formerly at Macmillan Company, and to Fabio Coen, formerly at Random House, both of whom have read my manuscript and provided me with valuable comments and criticism. Lawrence Groobert has been again my patient and perspicacious copy editor.

But my most heartfelt gratitude goes to my husband, Gene, my first reader and critic, who has seen me through the inevitable moments of total discouragement. Gene has with love, patience and understanding, helped me overcome the excruciating pain caused time and again by recollections of traumatic experiences, and by the mind-boggling research into the history of the most horrendous of human tragedies. Without Gene this book would not be.

Contents

Photographs on pages 26-28, 64-66, 106, 144, 182, 246-248, 307-312.

Preface

I owe my survival as a Jew in Nazi-dominated Italy to my own wits, to the good will of decent people among the Christians, and, of course, to a good measure of luck. Even though I do not underestimate the power of self-determination, and even though I could not have done it alone, it was mainly by luck that I was never in the wrong place at the wrong time. My adorable, gentle, goodhearted grandmother in Rome, Nonna Fiorina, did not have such luck when on the drizzly and chilly Saturday of October 16, 1943, Kappler's SS—armed as if they were to take an enemy fortress by storm, not an aged, frail and panic-stricken little woman—forced her out of her warm bed at 5 o'clock in the morning, stole whatever of value she was forced to take with her, and shoved her and beat her and dragged her to her miserable death together with her daughter, my aunt Rita, and more than a thousand other unarmed Roman Jews. Why was I spared? Rather, why wasn't *she* spared? Why weren't the innocent Six Million? Why and how *could* humans, created in the image of their Creator, do what they brutally and mercilessly did to fellow humans?

Why did the world remain silent?

I was in my teens when this huge human tragedy occurred, and philosophical and existential questions have been haunting me ever since. I have no answers. My principal hope in writing this memoir is to make as many people as possible aware of what can happen—and *has* happened—to decent, law-abiding citizens of a highly civilized society at the hand of other seemingly decent, law-abiding citizens of the same society when the latter, instead of listening to whatever shred of conscience they might have, blindly follow the dictates of demagogues. The former, in their innocence, cannot believe the unbelievable, cannot see the evil in its entirety until it is too late, or if they see it in time, believe that it will go away of its own accord.

This is the story of one little girl—born of Italian-Jewish parentage whose ancestry in Italy goes back at least two thousand years—as she wrestles with the difficult transition from childhood through adolescence into maturity in the midst of a Christian environment that is at times friendly, more often hostile, always alien.

I have drawn material for my early years from actual memories of my childhood and from the many tales I was told time and again by my parents.

For the period that spans the onset of the semi-official anti-Jewish campaign of the 1930s to the actual *Leggi Razziali*, the racial laws against the Jews of October 1938, in addition to my own vivid recollection of those distressing years, I have had the invaluable help of my siblings, especially my brother Gino, who is closest to me in age.

For the crucial months that preceded the end of World War II, when our family of seven was split (three taken to an Italian concentration camp while the rest of us, forced into hiding, lived moments etched into our memory for the rest of our lives), I have also had the aid of my diary of that period, which I kept mainly to record my passionately sweeping first love, but which inevitably contained very valuable historical references.

Much has been said and written, especially in the last two decades or so, on the fate of the Jews of Italy during the Holocaust by other well-qualified people.[1] However, not enough is known of the survival of those who were not deported to the German death camps, or of the decade that preceded the actual deportations and physical destruction. The incidents that occurred during those *preparatory* years, although not nearly as tragic as those that saw the systematic annihilation of a people, were nevertheless their dramatic prelude. The vexations inflicted upon innocent lives on a daily basis month after month, year after year, had different effects on different individuals. Some found easy refuge in denial (often manifested through mental derangement) or in conversion; others came out of the ordeal reinforced in their beliefs and convictions. All of us were traumatized and to a lesser or greater extent adversely affected—as have been our children.

It was for the benefit of my children that I wrote these pages, long before the compilation and publication of my two cookbooks (*The Classic Cuisine of the Italian Jews I, The Classic Cuisine of the Italian Jews II*, Giro Press, Croton-on-Hudson, New York, 1981, 1992), which inevitably make more than casual references to what has been the most poignant and unforgettable period of my life. I had no intention of publishing these memoirs then, or even to talk to strangers about them, partly because the outcome of the harrowing events that saw the destruction of so huge a number of innocent lives (among them many beloved relatives and friends) during my most impressionable years had become for me too sacred to be spoken about with the ordinary words of an ordinary vocabulary and be exposed to all sorts of people. Instead—I believed then—the catastrophe of the Holocaust should be enshrined in a mournful, respectful silence. Moreover, I felt a kind of shame—for my experiences did not match in terror and tribulation those of the deportees to the German death camps—as well as the guilt (irrational and unhealthy as it might be, but more common than it is known or imagined) that the survivors carry within them for having come out of the nightmare alive.

In time I have come to realize that shame and guilt are feelings that belong in the hearts of the perpetrators, not the victims. I also came to the conclusion that perhaps the individual accounts of personal experiences, even when not nearly as calamitous as the experiences of the silenced Six

1. For more details, see: Giuseppe Mayda - *Ebrei sotto Salò* - Feltrinelli, Milano, 1979; Luciano Tas - *Storia degli Ebrei Italiani* - Newton Company, Roma, 1987; Liliana Picciotto Fargion - *Il Libro della Memoria* - Mursia, Milano, 1991; Silvano Arieti - *The Parnas* - Basic Books, New York, 1979; Giacomo Debenedetti - *16 Ottobre 1943* - Einaudi, Milano, 1961/Sellerio, Palermo, 1993; Susan Zuccotti - *The Italians and the Holocaust* - Basic Books, New York, 1987; all the works of Primo Levi; all the works of Giorgio Bassani, and many others.

Million, add a dimension to the overall picture of those infernal events. As stated time and again in the Bible, as a Jew I am compelled to remember. And there is no better way to remember, and help people remember, than by telling one's story.

The Spanish Inquisition, for example, has come down to us as a murky history of expulsions, forced conversions, and the burning alive of tens of thousand of innocent people. We are vaguely aware that this blind hatred and destruction brought about the downfall of Spain's Golden Era (arrived at with the help of the Moors and the Jews)—a downfall from which Spain has still to recover. Don't we wish that we could learn from the written words of some of those survivors the detailed and personal accounts of what happened to *them*, and of what happened to their relatives and friends who didn't make it?

This is essentially my story. A story of pain and humiliations, of anger and frustration; but also a story of family love and high moral values, of courage and laughter, and above all a testimony of Jewish—of human— resilience. Others will write theirs. And perhaps the complex mosaic of recent history will be more encompassing, less imperfect than it is described in, and learned from, history books.

E.S.M.

Prologue

America - Summer 1970

The limousine that was to take us to Kennedy airport arrived earlier than expected, but the girls had been waiting for it outside our front door for quite some time. I watched them from the window of my sunken kitchen, my jewels, *"the Gracchis,"* as Dr. Diamond, our late dentist, used to call them. How tenderly were they saying good-bye to their kitten, one holding it close to her face, the other stroking it, her head craned to meet its eyes. At eight and six respectively, although they had the appearance of two little dolls, exquisite miniatures from another era, Rona and Gia were in fact quite mature for their age.

They were sitting on the steps that, from our house perched on the down slope, led up to the street, chatting with each other, their floral multicolored dresses bright against the dark green of the yews. Before I saw the silent stretch car approach the sidewalk, I saw their shiny curly heads, one bronze and the other black, spring up and turn first to their left and then toward me, their eyes wide with excitement. "It's here, Mamma, it's here!"

My husband and I were ready. While I gave the house the final touches, Gene gathered reading material and other small travel implements into a shoulder bag, closed the suitcases, and piled them up in the entrance hall near the door.

It was not the first time that the family was going to Europe; we had traveled there several times; but this was the first time that we had included Pitigliano, my native village, in our itinerary.

We arrived at the airport in plenty of time. We checked the luggage and relaxed. Suddenly Rona raised her head from her reading and asked me, "What do you feel about going back to Pitigliano after such a long time?"

"Yeah," echoed Gia. "How do you feel?"

The thought must have been in their minds and it was probably the subject of their confabulation on the steps in front of the house. It had been very much in my mind too, and I had discussed it at length with my husband, but coming from them it took me by surprise.

"Well, I don't know. Every return can be dangerously disappointing... Most returns are," I added, almost talking to myself.

"Meaning?"

"I mean that many people return to the places of their childhood to find the streets narrower and darker, their homes less attractive and hospitable than they had remembered them to be."

I was thinking of my return home, in the summer of 1944, after eight months of roaming the open countryside where my younger sister, two of my three brothers, and I had been hiding from the Nazi-fascists. The home we had left behind, which I remembered a spacious, luminous mansion, appeared now dingy and inhospitable. But even more than the physical condition of our home, which had been ransacked and soiled in our absence, it was the difficult readjustment and reinsertion into the society which for the most part had rejected us and had wounded our egos perhaps beyond repair that was troubling me.

"Others," I continued, "return to their long lost lovers, and the exciting gorgeous boys of their dreams have become, in most cases, fat, balding, insignificant men, and those raving beauties of girls ended up raving nags."

"How about best friends?" inquired the girls, who were not yet

16

interested in lovers.

"It can happen to them, too, as it did when my mother and her childhood best friend met again after forty years of separation."

"How about you?" insisted Rona.

"I don't expect anything, so I shouldn't be disappointed."

We were called to our gate.

After takeoff and supper the children leaned on us, one on my husband's shoulder and one on mine, and fell asleep. The lights went off, a movie was shown, and eventually everybody fell into a slumber. One light remained on all night, the light of my husband, who was *watching* over us. In reality, he had quickly become engrossed in one of the dozen mystery stories he had brought along and would not part with it until he had finished reading the very last page.

I looked at him. My companion, my best friend, my lover! The man who would do anything in his power to see my potential fulfilled. We might become fat and bald and raving nags together, perhaps, and it wouldn't matter. I admired his profile, his beautiful head of thick, black hair, his spacious forehead, the perfect design of his mouth, always illuminated by a hint of a smile, his vigorous nose... I felt a sudden surge of desire. I stretched my hand across our two children to touch his, and he turned his head and reciprocated my languid glance; widening his smile, Gene gently brought the tips of my fingers to his parted warm lips, he held them there for a moment, then returned my hand to my lap.

I could never sleep on a plane. I wondered whether I had not been too harsh in depicting returns so bleakly to my young daughters. I tried to think in more positive terms, but all the examples I reviewed in my mind were even worse—or so they seemed to me—than those I had given them.

One of these was the return of a few emigrants who had left the native village as young men to seek a fortune on faraway shores. A fortune they had not found; but they had, at the cost of sacrifices and renunciations, saved enough money to buy themselves a ticket back to the old country, and some even a small apartment in the neighborhood of their green years. These destitute and illiterate youths, who had left before the outbreak of World War I when the village was still backward with no source of employment, had returned after the end of World War II with some savings and a desire to flaunt their achievements. The sad truth was that while their perception of their native village had remained crystallized at a

17

certain juncture in history—the time of their departure—the village they had left nearly half a century earlier had evolved beyond recognition, and in most cases all their dreams of being on top of the ladder this time were shattered. Though no longer poor, they still were the ones who were backward. They were, at best, misfits in their native habitat; at worst, ghosts out of the past, belonging to an era that was forever gone, that felt, to the new breed, out of the middle ages.

When I first came to America I had none of the reasons and hopes and illusions those emigrants had. I came for a visit with a two-month visa, an elegant wardrobe, and no intention or desire to emigrate. However, circumstances worked in such a way that I stayed, got happily married, and went back to Florence, where the family had moved after the war, as often as I could.

Now that my father had died and was buried in the Jewish cemetery of his native Pitigliano, we were going to pay our respects at his grave. I had told the children that I had no particular expectations in returning to my village after so many years, but confess to having had a vague apprehension. I was a mature married woman, now, living in America—the land of many a person's dreams—but the ghosts of the past, of the anti-Jewish feelings played out by my fellow villagers against me during my childhood and adolescence, were still dancing in front of my eyes.

We landed in Milan. The few hours' trip to Florence pleasantly passed unnoticed.

A few days later, when we went to Pitigliano, Mamma came with us. As the discreet and understanding person she was, she rode unobtrusively in the back seat with the girls, gently talking with them in Italian (which they understood and spoke as natives). The girls, usually excellent, well-behaved travelers, were restless. They sensed that my vague apprehensiveness had become downright anxiety.

I had been looking out of the window all this time without really seeing, or taking pleasure in, that beautiful array of green that mantles the sober hills of Tuscany. I had not taken notice of the silvery thick-set olive trees and the contrasting dark, slender cypresses displayed in neat double rows leading to the gates of the mighty Renaissance villas, the bright green ginestra bushes,* and the dusty bluish leaves of the grape vines, all

* The longest stalks of this bush, stripped of their little stems and flowers, were used in the fields to tie the grapes to their support.

of which had always moved me.

It was time to talk to my young daughters again and warn them that all the stories of Pitigliano I had told them at bedtime every night since they were small children might have been embellished by my nostalgia of my own childhood, and that reality, now, might be a little different. I don't want you to be disappointed, I had said in the end, but what I really feared was not their but my own disappointment.

As my husband drove up and down hills through the tortuous narrow state road that leads from Orvieto to Pitigliano, I began to feel an over-whelming sensation in my chest. This time it was not anxiety but deep emotion and excitement, since we were driving through places that had been the sites of some of the eight-month-long peregrination my three siblings and I were forced to endure in order to avoid capture by the Nazi-fascists, from the fall of 1943 to the summer of 1944.

"Here, at this precise point, nearly thirty years ago, Uncle Gino met a German soldier who threatened to shoot him because... .

"Look down on the left side, now. Do you see that little round lake golden with sunshine? That's the one we crossed to go visit a fellow Jew who was hiding in a nearby grotto with his family... .

"Behind that hill, over there, we stopped one morning starved and exhausted and found a family preparing for the Communion of a child and we didn't have to beg for food, for a change... .

"Look at... . Never mind! Here is the bell tower of the Duomo ahead of us; in less than five minutes we'll be there!"

The girls began to jump up and down on their seats, echoing the pounding of my heart.

As it turned out, things worked like magic; events unfolded beauti-fully, infinitely better than I could have possibly wished for. We were quite moved by the reception we got not only from my relatives and old friends, but also from people I didn't remember having much to do with when I lived in Pitigliano. While Mamma visited with her sister-in-law, we went to take a walk in town.

As we strolled through the narrow streets of the old Jewish ghetto— the place of my birth, the theatre of my life from birth to adulthood— many of those who recognized me would offer us something to eat or to carry with us.

"Don't we have to pay for anything?" asked the children.

"No, silly girls, you don't pay when Grandma or one of your friends gives you a present, do you?"

"The children are right," intervened Gene. "Perhaps these people want to be paid."

"No, Gene. It's their excitement at seeing us that makes them act this way."

The ghetto was now occupied only by poor Christians. After their emancipation in the mid-nineteenth century, Jews began to move to better parts of town or to leave Pitigliano entirely, and after World War II, when most Jews who had survived simply abandoned their homes and their village to make a new life elsewhere, the poor took advantage of the situation and went to live where they didn't have to pay any rent.

The old public baker—whose mother and little children had come to my parents' house for alms in the past—was now retired and apparently no longer poverty-stricken. In seeing us, she drove one hand into the deep pocket of her black apron, extracted two one-hundred-lira coins, and gave one to each of my children. To my protests, she responded, addressing the children with a big grin, "Tell your mother that if she doesn't stop making a noise I will hit her on the head, so she will learn not to insult people!"

We reached the southern edge of the village where a group of old women wearing the local attire—the charcoal long full skirt with a valance topped by a dark-gray chequered short jacket gathered at the waist—were sitting outside the stoop of a house knitting and spinning and cleaning ginestra. As we came closer, they suddenly dropped their hands on their laps, then got up and deposited whatever they had been working at on their seats. They stood for a while looking at me and at my husband and children. There then was a quick consultation among them, and finally, as in a delegation, they all came to meet us with wide-open, nearly-toothless mouths, uttering first in a whisper then louder and louder, "*La figlia della Sora Sara!* The daughter of Signora Sara!" They smiled, they laughed, and wiped the corners of their eyes with the skirts of their black aprons.

One of them stood taller than the others. She was not smiling, her face almost expressionless. She shook her head and murmured, almost to herself, "The dark times we went through, when you had to leave Pitigliano in a hurry because of those damned bastards of fascists!"

I slowly nodded. I recognized Assunta, the wet-nurse of my cousin

Eugenia, the woman who had saved our heirloom jewelry for us when we had to run for our lives. I hugged her. For a long moment we remained locked in each other's arms.

On our way back toward our hotel, we stopped in front of a courtyard where an old priest was sitting alone. He looked at us for a moment, then got up and, leaning heavily on his cane, he tottered to embrace me.

"*La figlia di Azeglio!*" murmured Don Giovanni, his eyes brimming with tears.

That night, as we sat at the table of our hotel's outdoor cafe, Rona and Gia asked, "What was a priest doing among all those Jews?"

"Jews?!" I exclaimed in surprise.

Obviously the girls had assumed all these years that Pitigliano was the Italian counterpart of the *shtetl* of their father's Ashkenazic heritage. In all my tales I must never have mentioned that the Jews of Pitigliano were a small minority who had greatly contributed to the life and progress of the village. I must have said nothing of the origin and the decline of our Jewish community, perhaps because I felt frustrated that I knew a lot first hand of its demise, but very little of its origin.

During my childhood there still existed Jewish records jealously preserved in the archive room of an underground building. However, those records were dispersed and destroyed while we were in hiding, toward the end of World War II. (During our roaming the countryside in order to escape capture, we more than once found torn pages of Hebrew books and other Jewish documents which the farmers used as toilet paper.) Other documentation was scarce, and as an adult I had to rely mainly on what I had heard from my father and some of our community's elders when I was a child. The temple of my childhood was completed in 1598, as the date on its *Aaron Hakodesh,* the Holy Ark with the Torah scrolls, documented. However, an older *Aaron Hakodesh,* preserved in the old *Yeshiva*, attested to an earlier temple. In 1562, thirty-six years before the temple was completed, Cosimo I of the Medici family stipulated a "contract" (not better specified) with the Jewish community of Pitigliano,[2] which leads us to assume that by then the Community was well established and might have already built its first temple much earlier.

---

2. Roberto G Salvadori—*La Comunita' Ebraica di Pitigliano*—La Giuntina, Firenze, 1991, p. 17

According to oral tradition there were Jews in Pitigliano as early as the 1300s, mostly expelled from the Papal States. But some believe that there were settlements of Jews even much earlier than that.[3] Subsequent settlers arrived at different times, such as during the Spanish Inquisition, the Expulsions from Florence, the Destruction of Castro, etc.[4]

As for the reason why the Jews settled in Pitigliano in the first place, it is a well-known fact that whenever their lives were endangered or they were expelled from one place, they sought refuge in another that seemed more tolerant of their presence. As the first village they would have encountered outside the Papal States—where they were invited in or expelled according to the whims and interests of the various pontiffs—Pitigliano offered a measure of freedom and security. In this environment they thrived and prospered. According to the historian Roberto Salvadori, a Catholic, the Jews of Pitigliano already by the middle of the 16th century were showing "an initiative unknown to the *goyim*, the non-Jews..." [5] Not that their relative freedom and prosperity lasted forever: when the Orsini, a dynasty of at-times-benevolent tyrants from a princely Roman family who ruled the County of Pitigliano, passed their dominion to the hands of the Medici, the Jews were enclosed in a ghetto by the above-mentioned Cosimo I, and were not liberated until four centuries later by Carlo Alberto of Savoy. At this time—1848-1870—the Jewish population of Pitigliano numbered about four hundred, more than 10 percent of the entire population of a little over three thousand—the highest in any part of Italy. According to Settimio Sorani, former secretary of the Jewish Community of Rome and active member of DELASEM, an ad hoc committee that saved many European Jews, Pitigliano had hosted an even larger number of Jews. In his manuscript by the title *PITIGLIANO* of the early forties, Sorani asserts that in the two preceding centuries the Pitigliano Jews reached peaks of 15-20 percent.

3. Other sources: Carlo Agresti—*Pitigliano, la piccola Gerusalemme*, ISRAEL, LI. n. 5, p. 4, Nov. 1965, gives the presence of Jews in Pitigliano for certain around the year 1000. The Jewish scholar and philosopher Dante Lattes, in IL PENSIERO ISRAELITICO, a. I, vols. VIII and IX, 1895, hypothesizes that there were Jews in Pitigliano as early as the second century C.E.
4. Machlin, op. cit. p. 23
5. R. Salvadori, op. cit. p. 20

As already noted, from the Emancipation on, the number steadily declined, mostly due to the fact that many of the young people were now free to migrate to larger cities in pursuit of secular learning and better opportunities.

When I was a little child, there were about one hundred Jews in our Community: school teachers, civil servants, small merchants, dress-makers, embroiderers, homemakers, the village civil engineer, who was responsible for many important architectural improvements of the town (in the year I was born had brought electricity to Pitigliano, and as the story goes, on the inaugural night the mayor started his speech saying, "Glory be to Edison who made it possible to use electricity; *more* glory to Ingegner Sadun who brought it among us."), a tailor, a cabinet maker, two car mechanics, a rabbi, a chazan, and two or three dozen children. It is worth noting that in a predominantly agricultural village where illiteracy was well above ninety percent, every adult Jew could speak, read and write in at least two languages: Italian and Hebrew.

By the time the first racial laws against the Jews were promulgated and enforced in the fall of 1938, the Jewish population had further dwindled to about seventy souls. From the onset of the actual persecu-tions, and especially after the end of the conflict, many more left the village for larger cities, and by the time our family had moved to Flor-ence, the Jewish community had become numerically insignificant.

"There are no Jews left in Pitigliano," I began to explain to the children, "aside from a handful of my close relatives and friends; and even among them there are a few who have embraced the dominant religion by marriage."

"Then all those people who hugged and kissed you were all Christ-ians," said the girls, "and so must be all these people who are looking at us from their tables!"

"Indeed they are," I confirmed.

People nodded and smiled at us.

We went up to our rooms. The girls quickly got into their pajamas eager for me to start telling more stories.

Rona and Gia could both read now, but no book could compete with the stories that had fed their imagination at bedtime during their early childhood: my stories of Pitigliano.

"Where shall we start?" I asked.

"From the beginning! From the beginning!"

Surely, the wise thing to do was to stay with the beginning for the moment, and follow the path that had guided me in the past: tell only what I felt they could understand. Even though I was not like other survivors who had chosen silence to deal with the Holocaust and their difficult pasts with regard to their children (perhaps because my past had not been nearly as difficult), I'd better not be too open and specific too soon. In good time they would know.

I talked until their breathing sounded regular, a sweet smiling expression still lingering on their faces.

My stories of Pitigliano continued to be their favorites at bedtime until they were old enough to go to bed by themselves. But whenever the subject of the Holocaust was brought up in school, or whenever we went on trips together—a practice we continued throughout their high-school years—and were caught in the middle of an Italian national holiday parade celebrating an historical event of that period, their questioning started again and I would add new material or new details.

Eventually Rona and Gia begged me to put it together into a book.

Part 1

EARLY CHILDHOOD

My family at the time I was 18 months old. Gino at three and a half and Lello at five and a half years of age. As a feminist at that early age I express my anger at not being allowed to stand on the floor with the boys.

My father officiating as the Rabbi at the Bat Mitzva of Diana Lattes in the Temple of Pitigliano.

At the wedding of Cousin Angelo Servi to Emma Finzi. I am the blur between them.

In front of the carriage which transported us to the Mikva: Marcella, six; Cousin Bianca, thirteen; myself, ten; Cousins Clara and Ilda, thirteen and eleven.

A typical picnic gathering at the "Bath of the Jews", which includes my grandparents, father, uncles and aunts and some of my older cousins. Circa 1910.

Chapter One

Self and Siblings

When a family grows, the desire of the older children to retain supremacy and that of the latest addition to catch up with them often leads to a fierce competition.

My Birth

My mother was not, by any Orthodox standard, a religious woman; but the moment she became aware of her third pregnancy, she ran to Temple, sat at the far corner of the upstairs *matroneo* at a distance from all the other chatting women, and read to herself, without interruption, half of *Preghiere di un Cuore Israelita*,* the battered prayer book that had

---

* A kind of Jewish vade mecum adopted as a base for the education of a good Jew, compiled in French by the Grand Rabbi Arnaud Aron in 1849, and translated into Italian by the Rabbi of Asti, Marco Tedeschi, in 1852.

belonged to her pious and revered mother-in-law, my grandmother Debora Lattes. This was her way of asking Whoever was in charge of the selection process to send her a girl this time. There was nothing wrong with her two boys: healthy, smart, a lot of fun; but so precocious and devilish, they counted for twenty. Another one like them and she would go insane.

My father, a multitalented man with a jovial disposition, didn't care one way or the other. He enjoyed his children and educated them, but when it came to coping with sickness or mischief, he was nowhere to be found, and Mamma had to deal with the problems all by herself.

Not quite.

For sickness she sent for the family doctor; for discipline she could count on the cooperation of the maid. The trite punishment Mamma inflicted upon the boys consisted of sending them to bed without supper, but then, invariably, she sent the maid up with food and warned her, "Don't forget it's your idea, Zorama (Tonina, Santina, whoever was with us at the moment), I don't know anything about it!"

Mamma was a great story-teller and at each of our birthdays, beside cooking for us our favorite meal, she would entertain us with the detailed accounts of our births. The morning I made my appearance into this world, Mamma felt a bit sick and quite uneasy. For her first two children she had traveled all the way to her native Rome in order to avail herself of all the "advantages of modern science," and to be near her mother. But this time, with two daredevils, one of four and one of two, she resigned herself to go through the risks of giving birth to her third child in Pitigliano—a backward village which, according to her, was at least one century behind the time.

Keeping her apprehensiveness to herself, she sent her husband for the midwife (only the poorest women gave birth in a hospital at that time) and banged the heel of her shoe three times on the floor.

The apartment below ours was occupied by one of my father's brothers and his family. With no telephones in private homes, the two sisters-in-law had devised a system of communication that worked perfectly well. One bang on the ceiling with a broomstick (or with a shoe on the floor) meant, "Stick your head out of the window, I have to talk to you"; two bangs meant, "Come to see me when you have a chance"; three bangs were for emergencies.

Although the two apartments were situated one directly on top of the other, their entrances were located far apart. Ours had been the residence of the rabbi for centuries (the reason why it was occupied by our family was that Father had inherited from his father the religious leadership of our small community) and its entrance was on the side of the Temple. The apartment underneath, which in the past had been the seat of the secular elementary school—a private institution the Jews had established for their children at a time when Pitigliano had no schools at all—had its entrance through an alley parallel to the one that led to the Temple and our home.

Aunt Elda got up early on weekday mornings, before her husband and her two little girls woke up, to give orders to the maids and walk to school, where she taught third grade. She was sipping her first cup of coffee in the largeness of her still-dark kitchen when she heard the bangs. Aunt Elda, knowing that her sister-in-law Sara was a fast deliverer, didn't bother to dress. She threw a coat on top of her bathrobe and ran out into the chilly February morning, descending and climbing and descending and climbing all those steps from one alley to the other as fast as she could until she finally reached our home.

Almost out of breath, she began to scold my mother, "What are you doing out of bed?"

"I merely wanted to change the sheets," answered Mamma, intimidated by the sureness her younger sister-in-law always seemed to possess.

Aunt Elda moved fast to the closet to pick up the clean sheets, but when she saw Mamma hugging one of the ball-shaped brass knobs of the board at the foot of the bed, she dropped the sheets and ran for my head. Mamma had her panties on, so my head was saved. When Mamma learned that it was a girl, she cried with relief and gratitude. But a sneaking suspicion immediately entered her head that a creature who did things so precipitously from the start was not likely to be less mischievous than the boys.

By the time my father returned with the midwife, I was already washed and swaddled. He kissed the three women in an explosion of joy and ran out again to announce to the world that he had a daughter.

The world asked him, "What's your daughter's name?" And he answered, "I haven't thought of one."

The truth was that he and Mamma had thought of two. But they were both Hebrew names, and the fashion in Italy in those days was to name

31

children after statesmen and historical landmarks. Mazzini and Garibaldi, Goito and Lepanto, Libia and Trieste were first names. And so the Jews, who until my father's generation had only used Hebrew names such as Debora, Rachele, Salomone, Abramo, were for the first time in centuries naming their children with only secular ones. By 1926, the year of my birth, Fascism had held sway for over three years, so a fellow Jew, a fanatic fascist youth, who had been seen with a group of hoodlums brandishing the infamous club and castor oil bottle, suggested, "Why not Edda, Mussolini's daughter's name?"

Father gave in to this suggestion to mask a little his otherwise too overt anti-fascist sentiments. He was the only person I knew who, during the whole twenty years of the fascist regime, had never owned a membership card—the passport to employment—since for our livelihood he depended on the small honorarium he received from our Jewish community and on other odds and ends he pursued to round out his income. I must add to his credit that he mitigated his weakness by imposing on me also the two names he and Mamma had thought of—Debora and Raffaella, after my paternal grandmother and my mother's brother Raffaele, both of whom had died on the same day a few months earlier—which gave me an aura of distinction since everybody had only one or at most two names.

My Older Brothers

My relationship with my two brothers was an irksome one from the very beginning. It seemed to me that their uncommon brilliance and inventiveness were gifts lavished upon them so that they could excogitate ever more effective ways of tormenting me. The memory I have of them during the early years of my life is that they fought with each other as often and as harshly as little brothers do, but became the staunchest allies when it came to the common enemy—me. They indeed worked hard at trying to destroy me. I struggled for my survival—a training that would come in handy at some later day.

One of the earliest memories I have of my childhood—I was perhaps two or thereabout—is of standing on a chair in front of an open window watching, totally enchanted, hundreds of shrieking swallows dive past my eye level, obliquely plunging down the deep valley, and suddenly reappearing—a tremulous dark cloud—against the pale blue sky in an endless chase of one another.

I was so small that in order to lean on the parapet to see the swallows graze the bottom of the deep valley, I had to make leverage with my forearms and elbows to pull myself up and hang from the window sill, my rib cage pressed on the marble ridge, my feet dangling several inches from the raffia seat. When the swallows soared, I would let go and drop right back.

My four-year-old brother Gino, observing my movements, saw in my innocent pastime an opportunity for dispatching me in a hurry. During one of my suspensions, he tiptoed to my back and swiftly pulled the chair away from under my feet. I didn't move lest I might shift my precarious balance in favor of the valley side. I remained in that uncomfortable position a few eternal moments until Mamma, prompted by my brother's diabolic laughter, ran to my rescue.

My brother Lello, four years my senior, was less direct about my annihilation. His favorite game was *General Pandemonium,* of his own invention. It consisted of the three of us crawling under a bed like cats— which generated a burst of good humor in us even as we scratched and bruised ourselves against the torn naked springs. When he, the leader, shouted, "General pandemonium!" everyone was supposed to thrust kicks and blows in all direction. I always found myself unable to move between the two of them, whose kicks and blows were only thrust in my direction until I was reduced to a bundle of moaning rags. I didn't particularly like this part of the game, but did I have a say in what *they* played? I was systematically excluded from their games and indeed felt too honored to be admitted to one of them to complain when I hurt.

During violent summer storms—which were not infrequent in our hilly region—I was terrified by lightning. My two brothers explained to me that if I went around with an iron rod, I would be safe. (They had just learned that iron attracts lightning!) Armed with the cast-iron poker we used to revive the coals in the kitchen stove, I went to ask my father what was the relationship between an iron rod and safety during a storm.

"Simple," answered Father. "The rod on top of the bell tower of the Duomo (which was adjacent to our house) has been put there to *attract* lightning, so that it doesn't strike us. Eventually, running through a cable, it gets grounded without causing any damage."

Petrified, I opened my hand wide and let go of the poker. It fell on the terracotta tiles with a clang which I perceived as the thunderous response to a lightning bolt, a rush of heat invading my body.

"Don't worry, my darling," reassured my father, "lightning doesn't strike Jews!" And he let it go at that, without explaining to me that Jews, who did not own land and did not work in the fields, were less likely to be struck by lightning. (I have often wondered, as an adult, whether my tenacious attachment to Judaism did not stem from my father's reassuring statement when I was a small child!)

The pinnacle of Lello and Gino's ingenuity materialized one morning when I was not quite three. They had built a lovely doll house using pillows and quilts. When they called me to their room using all their charm to entice me to enter the air-tight construction, I resisted, presaging peril. But they finally prevailed upon me and forced me inside where I was subject to gas poisoning by their concentrated morning farts.

In order to keep up with them, I was forced to be audacious; I became fiercely competitive, and this brought about endless humiliations and defeats, like the time I tried to pee standing the way they did so skill-fully— even contending with each other at who would reach the far-thest—which only left my anklets and brand-new shoes sopping; or the time that, just to impress them, I jumped from the steps that led to the turret of the roof terrace of our uncle's house. I became aware of the rate of my heartbeat, even as I climbed the fourteen 10-inch-high steps, not from fear—I was beyond that —but from the excitement of the challenge. I reached the top, made a half pirouette, closed my eyes, and flung myself, my arms open as if they were wings...

If more than a few weeks went by without my appearing at the emergency room of the local hospital, the nuns there got worried.

But they really weren't all that bad, my two brothers. As a matter of fact they were pretty wonderful. It was my wanting to put my little nose in everything they did that induced them to act ignobly in an effort to teach me a lesson. Otherwise why would I want to risk my very life to cling to them however I could and whenever they let me? In spite of all the vexation I had to endure from them, I must have recognized that they were beautiful sensitive people: Gino—fair complexion, flaxen curly hair and sky-blue eyes—was introspective, and meditative, extremely shy and withdrawn (outside the family, that is); Lello—curly-black-haired with dark big eyes —was gregarious, dynamic, and genial, with lots of talents and superior mathematical and verbal skills. They were both at least two years younger than their classmates, having been placed a couple of years ahead of their age groups to give them a little challenge.

All appearances pointed to my being my brothers' greatest enemy; but I suspect that I also provided them with a lot of fun and fascination by my being interestingly different from them (notwithstanding my trying very hard to be *like* them).

As for me, whether at the time I did or did not recognize their good points, I didn't know any way of life other than the one that was dominated by my wonderful tormentors, who were also my teachers and mentors. I alternately hated and loved them with a passion, often the two antipodean feelings being simultaneously present in me.

In spite of all the harassment by my brothers and all the afflictions I drew upon myself, I remember that period of my childhood as a happy one, marked by travels and by plenty of fondling from amiable adults, until... my twin brother and sister were born. But by then I was four and had already enjoyed my share of wandering and merriment.

Travels

My parents, partly because they were proud of me, but mainly to assure my survival, always took me along when they went on trips. By the time I was three and a half, I had been to all of the extended family's celebrations, festive or funereal, and was beginning to get a stiff neck counting the cupolas, the gargoyles, and the pinnacles of the hundreds of Catholic churches we encountered everywhere we went.

When the eldest of my cousins from my father's side of the family got married, there were about twenty cousins and a dozen uncles and aunts scattered in various parts of Italy, but my parents and three-year-old me were the only relatives of the groom invited to the sumptuous wedding, which was celebrated by my father at the bride's villa in the outskirts of Milan.

A few days before the wedding, we got up in the dead of the night to walk to the bus that left at four o'clock in the morning to make the train connection two and a half hours later. The bus ride, a continuous jolting in all directions, thoroughly awakened us. At the bar of the train station my parents had a cappuccino and bought me a slice of panettone and a cup of boiled hot milk (the aroma of coffee made with freshly toasted and freshly ground beans teased my nostrils). Outside it was still dark.

The enormous black engine arrived puffing its dark cloud of smoke and came to a halt with a great deal of ferrous clatter. We and the few other passengers climbed hastily on the foot board and into the train, which pulled out of the station with the first shimmering of light.

It was a very long ride: I had time to sleep, time to watch the two boys across our seats, silent and immobile like statues, and time both to run around the outside corridor and to peer into the other compartments. At dusk we finally arrived at my uncle's beautiful villa with the view of Monte Rosa and the surrounding Alps in the background.

The villa was centrally heated. For the first time in my life I went to bed, in the heart of winter, without the coveted and cursed hot water bottle we had to use in Pitigliano, where the cold inside the house was such that the water in the tin bottle would freeze during the night, causing me to wake up a piece of ice myself. My crying would awaken my parents and Father would come to take the frozen bottle from my bed and wrap his warm hands around my feet until I would fall asleep again. But here at the villa, I slept comfortably all night without need of my parents' assistance.

In the morning I was presented with two new dresses expressly created for me—a white organdy one, with a big chiffon flower near one shoulder for the wedding day, and a red woolen one, elaborately hand-knitted by my aunt herself. My five cousins—from the twenty-three-year-old bridegroom to the youngest, aged six—went crazy over me. The only girl among them, a young school teacher, taught me and her little brother a song and a poem in the local dialect, to be delivered at the wedding. When it was my turn to sing, I duly performed. My cousin however—paralyzed by his shyness— began to move his lips, but remained absolutely mute. I seized the opportunity to step in and recite his poem as well. The little show aroused a storm of compliments from the family and the guests, and enthusiastic cheers from the numerous children of the neighborhood who were perched up on the cast-iron gate of the villa in order to have a glimpse of the elegant people inside and who were screaming wildly: *"Evviva i spus!,"* Long live the newlyweds!

During a trip my parents took to Florence to attend a funeral, my father, an innate lecturer who couldn't help being didactic each time he addressed us, left Mamma with her sister and took me to Piazza della Signoria to see the Loggia dei Lanzi. He first made me aware of the plasticity of forms in Gianbologna's *Rape of the Sabines,* executed in the second half of the 16th century, and then went on to contrast this upward spiraling marble composition with the more formal, exquisitely detailed bronze of Benvenuto Cellini's *Perseus and Medusa,* of a half century earlier, at the other end of the loggia. Perseus, one foot on decapitated Medusa, his right arm thrust forward holding proudly her snake-coiffured head, his left hand still firmly grasping the hilt of the bloody sabre, charmed me. An old fiacre driver, who was stationed at the foot of the loggia, took me by my hand up the steps behind the statue to show me the self-portrait of the artist—a powerful bearded face sculptured amid Perseus's ruffled locks. I had to funnel my hands to shield the light in order to descry the sculptor's features.

My father then took me to the Bargello Museum, the former House of the Mayor, to see the glass cabinet with the chiseled golden cups, also a work of Cellini. On the way to the Bargello he told me with a certain pride that Graziadio of Bologna, a Jew like us, had been one of Cellini's chisel masters. At the museum my eyes remained glued to the cups' marvelous details. (Many years later, after the war, I went back to see the things that had so fascinated me as a little child. But the cups were no longer in their place. The Germans had stolen them.)

Other trips took me to Pisa, where generous Aunt Delia lived with her husband, the *chazan* of the Temple, and their talented son Attilio; to Livorno to visit with Mamma's wealthy sister and her family in the villa where my parents had first met; to Siena, Orvieto, Porto Santo Stefano, Orbetello, and other towns in the vicinity of Pitigliano.

The majority of trips, though, were taken to Rome, Mamma's birthplace. She periodically went there to visit with her beloved stepmother,

Nonna Fiorina, the only mother she had ever known, her biological mother having died giving birth to her. Mamma liked to surprise her mother, and when the two women faced each other on the staircase landing, the endless hugs and laughs and tears of joy warmed my heart. In Pitigliano my breakfast would consist of stale pieces of saltless Tuscan bread dunked in a heavily sweetened *caffellatte,* a beverage made with ground roasted wheat grain, cut with boiled milk. In Rome Nonna Fiorina treated me to *maritozzi colla panna,* soft sweet buns filled with whipped cream, and a caffellatte made with reboiled real coffee grounds.

Mamma did not take me to see monuments and museums, as Father would, but we did make the round of her numerous relatives and friends, and I recall everyone inciting her never to forget that she came from the capital and never to lose her city manners and elegance. It paid to be harassed by my brothers in exchange for the many beautiful things I saw and the plentiful attention I received when my parents took me with them in order not to leave me at their mercy.

Birth of the Twins

The trips with my parents ended abruptly when my mother began to look like a dirigible. She had gained an enormous amount of weight, which showed not only in her abdomen, but in other parts of her body as well. Mamma's appearance and bits of conversation I heard here and there frightened me. I didn't tell anybody of my fears, but I began to have restless nights crowded with nightmares in which colossal buildings—the buildings I had seen in the big cities and especially Rome—grew larger and larger until they crumbled down and crushed me. Once in a while my dreams included such pleasures as *maritozzi colla panna* (a sweeter symbol of my mother's advanced pregnancy); but mainly I had dreams that brought me anguish and terror.

A few days after my fourth birthday, I woke up in the middle of the night in one such fright and climbed into my parents' bed for comfort. (I was sleeping in their bedroom in a single bed near their large one and often I exchanged places with my father.) It felt good and safe to fall asleep between them. But my peace didn't last long. Suddenly awake again, I saw the lights on and noticed that my father had disappeared from the room. My mother was emitting groans and moans and suffocated sobs which didn't sound like anything I had heard before. Mamma's emotionality could be excited by trifles and much too often tears flowed over her pale cheeks. But never before had I heard the utterance of any sounds to accompany her tears. This time, in fact, there were no tears, only these strange noises.

Then she stopped.

Confused and more than ever scared, I asked, "What's the matter, Mamma?"

She turned her beautiful face toward me and smiled, reassuringly, "Nothing. It is nothing, my angel. You are going to have a little brother or sister soon."

I didn't like one bit what my new brother or sister was doing to my mother.

Our maid Santina came to tear me from Mamma just as I was caressing her and making her feel better. I was carried into my brothers' room, hastily tossed on one of their beds, and told to go to sleep. My two brothers, also awakened by the excitement around the house at that unlikely hour, were out of their beds and showed no surprise to see me.

"I am going to have a little brother or sister," I proudly said in a singsong, hoping for once to be ahead of them on such a piece of news. But all I got was sneers and sarcasm: they had known of the imminent delivery for quite some time.

Of course, no one could sleep, but we kept quiet for a while. Then my older brother suggested a plan of action.

"As soon as the bustle between the kitchen and our parents' bedroom subsides," sententiously spoke eight-year-old Lello in his usual grown-up manner, "we will tiptoe to the door of our parents' room."

We soon did, and Lello managed to turn the knob just as Mamma was wailing loudest so that nobody paid any attention to what he was doing. The door was now ajar. With one eye on the crack, the three of us peered inside. Gino's chin was pressing on my head with the added weight of Lello's chin on his. I felt very uncomfortable, but couldn't bother with such trivia while so much was going on that I was witnessing.

The midwife, Aunt Elda, the maid, and a neighbor were busying themselves between our outpost and the huge bed so that I couldn't see Mamma. But I saw distinctly that an enamelled wash basin was sprinkled with alcohol and set ablaze. Then, among Mamma's moans, I heard a whine and saw my aunt place a bloody baby inside the flaming basin. (I was assured afterwards that the flames were set to sterilize the basin, and that only sterilized water, previously boiled inside a flask without its straw casing on charcoal embers, was in the basin when they bathed the baby. I guess it was wishful thinking, or lack of sleep, or the pressure on my head, or all of the above that caused my attention to falter so that I missed the transition from fire to water.)

I began to get bored and really tired. I tried to disentangle myself from my two brothers when I heard the voice of the midwife screaming, "Up with those legs! You're suffocating the other child!"

It was only then that Mamma learned that she had twins. Undoubtedly aware of our presence at the door, Mamma raised one hand and held two fingers up to let us know that there were two babies. Father, all this time, had ignored us as he stood praying in the dining room, and now he was called into the bedroom.

He seemed to understand that the arrival of two new babies instead of just one as expected might prove traumatic for us, because a couple of weeks later, on the festivity of Purim, he presented Lello and Gino with a new series of 13 juvenile books published by Bompiani, *La Collana d'Acciaio,* so called because the books were all bound in silvery covers. And for me, since I could not yet read, he bought the latest model phonograph. It was a beauty! The brass trumpet-shaped loud speaker, which in older models had been outside on the turntable, was inside an imitation mahogany cabinet in Chippendale style topped by a hinged lid, mounted on four long, curved legs, with a golden screen in front, and a removable crank on a side. It came equipped with a large box of records and a smaller box with plenty of disposable needles. The discs included a variety of recordings: several of Aesop's and La Fontaine's fables read by a male voice with a Bolognese accent; Bach's Prelude no. 1 from the well-tempered clavichord and the *Ave Maria* arranged by Gounod; two tenor arias from Puccini's *Tosca;* some American jazz; and even two Yiddish songs which no one could really appreciate since as Italian Jews we only spoke Italian and some Hebrew, and Yiddish was as alien to us as any foreign language.

Wandering and Learning

After the birth of the twins, my parents learned to relent their vigilance over me so that I, after having familiarized myself with the operation of the sound machine and completely memorized all the records—Bolognese accent, tenor pitch, nasal Yiddish and all—began to wander through the streets and alleys of Pitigliano all by myself.

This new activity proved to be at least as interesting and as instructive as my association with my older brothers and the trips with my parents. My spirit of observation had been sharpened by my early exposures to the world of city art and culture, whereas the necessity to outwit my older brothers had increased my ability to learn quickly. All this, coupled with my innate, insatiable curiosity, resulted in my becoming skilled in many arts and crafts at a very early age.

I would spend hours, forgetting hunger and other exigencies, in front of the many artisans' shops in the village, drinking in every movement, every step, every sound and smell coming from within.

One of my favorite spots was the weaving shop which an early Jewish settler, perhaps a Marrano, had established. Like most ancient Jewish-owned facilities, the shop was in a cave carved directly into the tufa—the soft volcanic rock on which the entire village was built—at the bottom end of a tortuous, steep, alley of stairs. The primitive wooden looms were manually operated. When I arrived at the shop, no matter how early in the morning, I always found that the warp was already in place and at tension at least in one of the two looms. The only operator there, Argentina, must have worked at it all night. By means of pedals, Argentina—a short, bowlegged woman who had to shift her weight on the seat from one side to the other in order to reach them—switched the warp up and down while weaving in the weft that unraveled from the spool in the shuttle she flung from side to side with perfectly synchronized movements. These looms manufactured mainly hemp sheeting, using the uneven thread hand-spun by the poor women who could not afford to buy commercial sheets. I would have given anything to be in Argentina's place.

The loom was not the only shop that fascinated me. The printing house, which at one point had belonged to Grandfather Salomone Servi; the flour and oil mills, emanating those incomparable aromas of freshly ground wheat and crushed olives; the repair shop at the bus garage, in whose pit Uncle Tranquillo, the engines' *doctor,* had broken his hip; the blacksmith where horses and donkeys were being shod with the clang of the hammer pounding the incandescent shoes on the anvil, and the acute stench of burning hoofs; the cabinet maker, where Uncle Augusto, the master of a few generations of woodworkers, taught his apprentices until late at night by the light of an acetylene lamp; and the tinker, the shoe-maker, the knife grinder... All could hold my attention almost indefini-tely.

On very cold or rainy days, when I couldn't go out, I played in the huge Hebrew schoolroom adjacent to our house. In this private play-ground I played by myself with all the school supplies that had been left unused when the school had been closed and the Jewish children had begun to attend the new public schools. When they had time, Lello and Gino joined me in the schoolroom to play, but our games never got to be as rough as they had been in the past.

I liked my new life.

Nursery School

Then one sad day my parents, at the suggestion of Aunt Elda, who always assumed an attitude of one who knows better, made an attempt to send me to nursery school. The experience turned out to be a disaster. There was only one nursery school in the village and it was run by nuns. I had always been suspicious of those ladies dressed in long black gowns with black head covers and starched white necks who went around two by two, holding their bodies stiff and gliding as if they were mounted on wheels. The nuns at the local hospital always managed to terrorize me with their stupid standard jibe, "What will happen to you if your pluck takes notice of your wounds..." But at least they were familiar to me, as I had gone to the hospital frequently to have my various bruises attended to.

After a battle that exhausted both Mamma and me, I finally grudgingly agreed to go to the much dreaded nursery school only because Mamma had finally consented to let me wear the red, hand-knitted dress which Aunt Amelia had made for me and which was associated with such lovely memories.

Father walked me to school holding my hand in one of his hands and my wicker lunch box and white smock in the other. I was too upset to be cooperative. I felt the way innocent people must feel when they are committed to jail. I kept on whimpering and dragging my feet all the way there without saying anything.

We stopped in front of the building and my father lovingly wiped my nose with his clean, white linen handkerchief. He pulled the short string that hung from a tiny hole on the right leaf of the small green door to the nursery school. From the inside came the sound of a spring bell tolling fast at a high pitch. We waited a long time. Finally the door opened as far as the chain lock allowed it. A few words were exchanged between the half face inside and my father which I didn't hear, then the door closed on us and reopened right away just enough for me to squeeze through. My father bent to kiss me through the narrow opening and whispered into my ear, "Be good, now. I'll be back at four."

Inside I was greeted by an unfamiliar, offensive odor, a suffocated grumbling of children (*l'ebrea*, the Jewess, seemed to be the only intelligible word that reached my ears), and half a dozen nuns.

"You are late!" said one nun.

"What's your name, dear?" asked the first nun who knew perfectly well who I was.

I didn't understand her playing such a game and I was too terrified anyway to be able to open my mouth. She then talked to me as if I were an imbecile. "We don't have a tongue, huh? Well, we'll talk later to the mother superior," she said with a nasal voice that was supposed to imitate a child's talk. Then, changing her tone of voice to a stern one, the nun added, "Now you'd better put your smock on and get yourself in line!"

I had never been addressed in such a harsh manner and didn't comprehend the meaning of her words. What mother superior was she talking about, as opposed to mother inferior? Besides, why did she think I had insisted on wearing the beautiful dress hand knitted by my aunt? To cover it with a smock?

I soon found out that I didn't have to cover my dress with anything. The nun hastily pulled it off me in front of everybody, and on went the smock over my white cotton petticoat.

The dress vanished. I felt chilly.

The same nun took me by my hand and pulled me to the head of a long line of quarrelsome brats. The line was formed according to height and I was the shortest of all. Still holding my hand, the nun began to walk past the other nuns who lined the wall, and ordered the children to follow in silence. The other nuns flanked the long line in echelons and made sure—with a rap on a head, a slap on a hand, a pull on an ear—that the children kept quiet.

We entered the chapel. We were led to our places at benches with kneeling stools. The nun who held my hand released her clutch and left me at the center seat in the front row. The children took their places on both sides and in back of me. Then all the nuns lined one of the chapel walls. A bespectacled nun, older and taller than the others, stood directly in front of me under a haggard wooden crucifix all painted in gloomy faded greens, ochre and browns with bright red drops spilling all over its gruesome body. The bespectacled nun's face was no less fearsome.

The room was suddenly filled with an ominous silence. The older nun—who, I later found out, *was* the mother superior—brought her fingertips, with knuckles touching, to the middle of her chest and ordered everyone to make the sign of the cross with her. She began, bringing her right hand to her forehead, then moving it down to her chest, to the left shoulder, to the right shoulder, "In the name of the Father, of the Son and of the Holy Ghost..." And then joining both hands palm to palm, "and let it be so."

I had been inside churches many times before, but somehow this chapel, though not so dark as a church nave, appeared more sinister to me. I didn't move from my standing position. I was stiff with shyness and fear, my arms hanging alongside, my eyes shifting from the wooden figure to the mother superior's face, with occasional glances at the girl immediately to my left, whose face was covered with large, crusty pocks.

Suddenly, with an extremely swift motion of her hand, the girl at my left bestowed upon my face a very painful scratch. Without hesitation I returned the favor, and realized with consternation that some of her pocks were bleeding and that my finger-nails had retained some crust and blood. I kept on wiping my nails on my smock, dismayed by my reaction to her since this was the first (and only) time I would ever use physical violence even in self-defense. The girl didn't cry, nor did she make any fuss about her bleeding. I felt the burning pain on my face and imagined how much more painful hers must be and wanted to say something nice to her; but in the end I didn't, not only because my timidity and cowardice always stood in the way of my intentions, but also because I was angry that she had started the action in the first place, and my acute sense of fairness prevented me from saying that I was sorry. The mother superior ignored what she had undoubtedly noticed and the prayers and the chants went on uninterrupted.

I tuned myself off, vaguely aware of the children sitting, kneeling, standing again, while I remained frozen in my standing position, prey to a prolonged bout of panic. I wanted to cry, I wanted to run away, but couldn't do either. What was I doing in this alien place with all these strangers? I was in a state of shock. I am not sure of how long this torture lasted, but I am sure that torture it was.

The rest of the day—after a *long talk* with the mother superior, whose cunning and mellifluousness were aimed at molding me into someone I was not—was spent playing (I had the feeling of being pushed around a lot) in the *gravel*-covered yard, getting scraped knees and palms ("woe to you if your pluck took notice of your wounds... "), watching the children eat (I didn't touch the food that Mamma had made and packed into the elegant lunch box for me, and never again could I eat that same food). I felt like—and indeed was—an outsider. What was going on among the children also frightened me.

At one point one of the bullies took a smaller boy and held him belly-down on his lap. He pulled the lad's pants down and invited anyone who wanted to do so to stick a finger inside the child's anal sphincter, giving a clue himself. (Where were all those nuns, now?) I was not accustomed to this kind of behavior, I had never been exposed to so much violence and sex play. My brothers by comparison wore halos above their heads.

Four o'clock never came. When it finally was signalled by the ringing of a bell, I was dressed again in my knitted red dress (which by now had lost all its magic power to evoke wonderful memories), my untouched lunch box and my dirty white smock clutched in my hand. My father arrived and he, too, had a *long talk* with the mother superior while I was standing at a distance, watching all the other children go, not without throwing dirty looks in my direction.

On the way home, Father didn't ask any questions, not even about the red scratches on my face, and I didn't volunteer any accounts of what I had gone through that long, unforgettable day. At home he and Mamma had a *long talk* with each other, then they reassured me that I didn't have to go to nursery school anymore.

La Piazza

Back in the streets, I slowly began to approach the urchins at play, some of whom I had seen at the nursery school. At first, as I stood at a distance observing their rapid gestures and listening to their shouting in a dialect that was alien to me, with a mixture of wonderment and fear, they either ignored me or looked at me with suspicion. But gradually, conquering my timidity, I got closer to them, and they, still recognizing my being different from them and not expecting me to behave like them, ultimately accepted me almost as one of their own. What fascinated me about them was their total lack of inhibitions. My upbringing was interlaced with all sorts of restrictions and codicils; theirs seemed to have none.

Among the boys the one who stood out in the crowd was a tall fellow with a bony structure, dark complexion and black straight hair, nicknamed Topino, little mouse. (Almost everyone in Pitigliano had a nickname, and people were known more by the latter than by their real names.) Topino was regarded by most street urchins as their incontestable leader. He commanded the attention of all the kids and of the passers-by when, imitating Mickey Mouse's gait, he would mark his steps back and forth and sideways with a rhythmic waving of his hands and stretched-out arms, and with a loud smacking of his tongue. In no time I became the best imitator of Mickey Mouse's imitator, which included that peculiar smacking of the tongue.

I also learned how to whistle like the most expert of the street children (which made my mother furious because whistling was not lady-like), and even to use their dirty language—although I was incapable of grasping the meaning of it and used it just as a parrot would.

The children mostly played in the main piazza.

The main piazza in Pitigliano, the focal point of every public event and of almost every social gathering during the summer months, was flanked on its east and west by two open spaces overlooking the gorges excavated by small rivers over the course of millennia. At dusk, at that melancholy hour between the end of the workday and supper time, many small landowners, back from farming their plots several kilometers from the village, would lean side by side on the parapets of these large open windows facing the rural landscape. These men, unused to human interaction after a long day of solitary farming, sparingly addressed one another, and then mainly to counsel each other on what the weather might be like the next day. One would ask, "Do you think it will rain tomorrow?" and another would invariably answer, "Ehhh..." They never looked at one another, their eyes fixed straight ahead to catch the first sight of the blue buses, returning from their daily trips to Rome and to the distant railroad stations, as they appeared from behind the large bends and began winding their way up to the center of town.

The arrival of the buses was the single most important daily event. They mainly brought back the few local people who had left at four o'clock in the morning to tend to their businesses elsewhere, but they also might bring a relative from one of the large cities, or, on occasion, a foreigner, a total stranger, the harbinger of excitement, and everyone wondered what had brought the alien among them, how long would he stay, what kind of life he led in the part of the world he came from.

A few steps from the eastern parapet, the corner bar was crowded with civil employees relaxing with a beer before going home to their dinners. Outside the pharmacy—the gathering place for the village intelligentsia—the usual group of professional men discussed Tazio Nuvolari's victory in the latest car race of the *Targa Florio,* or the merits of a recent performance of an itinerant company's staging of *Nabucco* in our small theater. The two monumental fountains were not only used by the farmers to water their sweaty donkeys that had transported them to and from the farming areas, but by their wives as well, who came to fetch water in large copper jugs to start preparing supper, and to partake of the gossip and the crepuscular animation.

The arrival of the buses was anxiously awaited by the street children, too. The competition to jump on the back ladder to hitch a dangerous ride, from the entrance to the square and around a loop to the final stop, was fierce. I was never able to run ahead of those daring urchins, but was contented with being enveloped by the cloud of dust and the exhaust fumes emanating in full strength from the rear of the buses.

I would rarely associate with the female urchins. They were truly vicious. Their favorite pastime was to make the life of young people in love utterly miserable. They achieved their wicked purpose by stealthily following the unaware couples on their romantic walks outside the village. At the signal of their leader, these diabolic girls would pop up and engage in obscene enactments of the basest sort in front of the bewildered couples, who would lose their romantic momentum and try to get away. The outrageous mob would not leave the embarrassed couples alone. They followed their victims to the village yelling and jeering, and from that moment on the reputation of the ill-fated couples (especially that of the girls!) would be seriously compromised.

There were two such gangs in Pitigliano, and they were feared by everybody. They operated in such numbers as to protect themselves from any direct reprisal. Furthermore, they seemed to know every little intrigue involving adults, and perhaps these would rather close an eye to their despicable behavior than risk being exposed.

Of course, not all the female urchins were so wild, and in fact some had talent. With these few I did once in a while engage in creative activities. We made our own toys. With wax drippings we made miniature furniture; with straw we made roller blinds or wove small baskets; with yarn we made puppets and crocheted for them little dresses and hats. In spring we took long walks into the woods and competed with one another as to who would be able to pick the largest number of wild cyclamens. They knew the fields better than I, and always gathered big bunches from amidst the moist underbrush, whereas I only succeeded in picking a few. However, they would always offer to share their flowers with me. Generally, though, I preferred the company of the boys, who displayed a far greater imagination then the girls in the games they played and the toys they made. The boys made three different types of wooden tops; they made *marbles* with clay gathered near the river and fired in the hearths of their kitchens; penny whistles; rattles with empty wooden thread spools, disks of cowhide, horse hair and a wooden handle that could imitate the sound made by cicadas or tree frogs or toads according to the thickness of the horse hair; and many other toys. I would admire their creativity, and confess to a thrill when through their ripped pants I could get a glimpse of their juvenile genitalia.

At home I behaved impeccably, and in fact I was very reserved. Only once, out of sheer desperation, provoked by one of his tricks, did I call Gino *puttano*, an epithet only used in its feminine gender—which I had picked up either from the street children or from the common women who threw it at each other during their colorful fights from facing windows or in the streets. But Mamma quickly shoved a pinch of ground black pepper into my mouth, threatening me with similar treatment should I ever use that kind of language again.

Mauro's Death

The globe acacias in the main piazza had shed all their fragrant, snow-like flowers, and their green, ball-shaped mane had thickened. The heat was upon us, schools were closed for the summer recess, and Father took Lello and Gino to the "Baths of the Jews" to teach them how to swim. Most of the other children learned to swim in the nude from each other at one of the icy-cold creeks, but my brothers, after a few trials, stopped going because their peers played foul with them, ganging up on them and making fun of their *lopped tails*, their circumcised penises.

The twins—different not only in gender but in appearance and personality as well—were surrounded by a great deal of affection. The male twin, Mauro, was a contented baby with a lovely disposition, healthy and strong. Mamma, not without some reticence, let Santina the maid take care of him so that she could give herself entirely to the baby girl, Marcella, who was tiny, frail, and more demanding.

49

One day, when the babies were five months old, Santina asked permission to take Mauro with her. She was going to the country to meet with Felice, her fiance. Mamma did not want to let her baby go, but Father was in favor.

"Santina is a mature girl," he said, "and the baby will benefit from some fresh air."

Mamma tried to dissuade Father from interfering. But in the end she consented.

When Santina and the baby came back several hours later, Mauro was crying in a new and frightening way. One side of his face, and the arm and the leg on the same side, were crimson-red.

Santina seemed to be in another world. With her head in the clouds, she answered Mamma's questions ambiguously.

"I don't know what's wrong with the baby," she said. "He nicely finished his formula and then he slept peacefully all afternoon."

Father ran to call the doctor and the diagnosis was just what he and Mamma had suspected and feared: severe burns from prolonged exposure to direct sunlight. The next day Mauro developed gastro-intestinal complications, and after a couple of days he died. Santina was fired on the spot, but this measure did not alleviate the pain and the tremendous guilt both my parents carried with themselves to the last of their days.

I had confused ideas about death, and when people came to pay my parents a condolence visit, I sang and danced. I learned the meaning of death shortly after, from one of the succession of maids Mamma tried out to replace Santina. This girl told me, with a wealth of graphic details, about the nether world as she knew of it. She made sure to let me know that Satan, the devil in person, would eventually break loose and take people *like me* straight to hell; and then it would be the end of the world!

But for the moment what I felt about Mauro's death was a vague sense of guilt for not having held him in my arms as much as I did Marcella, who was much lighter and easier for me to handle.

There was no formal funeral for the child. The little coffin was wrapped in a black cloth, and my father's uncle, Great Uncle Raffaello, carried it under his arm to the cemetery where my father and another dozen men met for the *Hashkavah*.

Both my parents were inconsolable, but Mamma carried on for a long time. Eventually she became seriously ill with what was then termed *poliarthritis,* and was bedridden for several months. During Mamma's long and life-threatening illness, the entire family seemed to fall apart. Lello contracted pneumonia which, at a time when penicillin had not yet been discovered, kept him between life and death for weeks on end; Gino began to associate with bad company; I came down with a dreadful case of lice; Marcella, the surviving twin who was not quite three, went on a hunger strike.

Our father was at a loss.

Eventually Mamma recovered, but not without a long convalescence. When she finally returned to normal, she discovered that she was pregnant again. She wasn't too happy about it. She felt that she had spent the best years of her life going from "a big belly to a big breast," and was determined to get rid of this pregnancy. Without telling her husband, she ran to her former obstetrician in Rome begging him to grant her an abortion on the ground that she was too old (approaching forty) and too weak to have another child.

"If you were old you wouldn't have conceived," the doctor said, "and although you went through a lot with your long illness, you seem to be healthy and strong, now."

"Cheer up," he added as he walked her to the door. "This child will be the pillar of your old age."

Mario's Birth

When on a beautiful April afternoon the future pillar of Mamma's old age was born, the four of us were sent to a neighbor's house to prevent the bustle we had provoked when the twins were born. Toward evening, when all was quiet again in our house, we were allowed to go and see the new baby boy. Lello noticed that his face was all covered with soft hair and commented on it. Mamma—never in want of witty remarks—teased him, "We'll have to send for the barber!"

Lello feigned horror. "He might hurt him! Nobody's *ever* going to hurt this baby, I'll make sure of it!"

Gino, a poet at heart but also a very practical child, aware of the fact that schools in Pitigliano ended at the eighth grade and that only wealthy people could afford to send their children to larger towns for higher education, pledged on the spot to go to work very soon (he was only ten) and save enough money to send his little brother, when the time would come, to get the education he knew he himself would be denied—a pledge he later honored.

I, at eight, had not yet overcome the fear of death that had been planted in my head by one of our maids a few years earlier. The first thought that crossed my mind in seeing this beautiful and helpless tiny human, was that he, too, would die one day. I was overcome by anguish. For what seemed a long moment, I was in a whirlpool of dizziness, ablaze with a rush of blood to my head. All my faculties were semi-paralyzed, my throat felt dry and coarse. When I came to, I was quite shaken. I finally kissed the baby on one cheek, and, like my older brothers, I felt very protective of him. As a female eight years his senior, I considered myself to be his little mommy, experiencing all the joys and anxieties generally reserved only to the real parents. Marcella, who was only four years old, was the sole exception. She couldn't help but feel jealous of her rival for Mamma's attention, and she dealt with her jealousy in a very direct and healthy way: she pulled what had been her little pillow from under his head, she climbed in bed and tried to lie down between him and Mamma, and the like.

The arrival of the new baby, and Mamma's diminished attention, helped Marcella grow up in a hurry. In fact, the gap between Marcella and me grew narrower and narrower each day, and in spite of my being four years older than she, we blossomed almost at the same time. She handled the appearance of her first menstrual cycle smoothly and even joyously, whereas for me the whole process was an ordeal, a true trauma. With me nothing was ever casual. I had intense feelings about all that touched me or even just brushed me lightly. My psyche was like photographic paper where the impressions, perceived in stark, contrasting colors, were forever fixed.

At a very early stage in her life, Marcella taught herself how to read so she could turn to the written word for enjoyment and solace, and inevitably this practice widened her horizon and nourished her imagination. Although we were born in the same house and brought up in the same environment, we reacted to our surroundings in widely different ways.

Ours was one of the few Jewish families still living in the ghetto, where most of the old Jewish homes were now occupied by the poorest and lowest classes of Christians. Thieves and prostitutes were not a rarity in our neighborhood, and fighting and name-calling broke out among them almost daily. I was distraught by this state of affairs, and fancied to live in the outskirts of the village, in a modern home, as our wealthier and *less Jewish* relatives had moved to. But Marcella's inner world was so rich that the surroundings hardly made a difference to her.

"Just imagine," she would respond to my lamentations. "Just imagine that we live in the underworld of Paris, or in the Moroccan Casbah. Don't you think that our lives are more interesting than those of our cousins who live in the *case nuove*? What difference does it make where we happen to live, anyway? Don't you see that what we value means nothing to our relatives and vice versa? They might live in better homes but they don't own the most important and updated encyclopedia; their records are childish whereas our collection includes many educational and classical discs; we own the most furbished book collection and have free access to the public library which is practically in our home. Besides," she would conclude, "it is the world that we carry inside ourselves that counts."

It was not too long before she ceased to be jealous of her new sibling to become, like the others, protective of him. The new baby, whom my parents called Mario, was a remarkable boy from the very start, lovable and the beloved of everyone.

As he put it later on, all the attention made him feel as if he had six parents instead of just two. With three fathers and three mothers, each one with a different—and not infrequently selfish—approach to his or her task, there was an awful lot of pulling in all directions. Six people older than he were constantly telling him what to do or not do, and he had no recourse. As a consequence he developed a quiet personality, listening to everybody but hardly talking at all.

To an indiscriminating observer, Mario might have seemed quite unremarkable. But to those of us who knew him, his extraordinary brilliance showed up in many different ways, including a keen sense of humor. As soon as he was able to stand, Mario began to play with the phonograph that Father had bought me when the twins were born. He first learned to turn the crank, then to change the records and the disposable needles, and played those discs over and over again for years to come, discovering each time new and more interesting meanings in the words of Aesop's and La Fontaine's fables, and getting ever greater pleasure out of the operatic arias and classical music that constituted the bulk of my collection. He became a fine musician and pianist, without ever taking a music lesson.

From his early years, Mario's favorite pastimes were to solve intricate mathematical problems and to fix things around the house. He was so capable that from the time he was seven or eight, Mamma never had to call any professionals for repairs, because Mario could do any electrical, plumbing or other repair jobs better than any of them. Right after World War II—he was barely ten—he fixed with patience and skill my sewing machine that had been rescued, all warped and dirty, from under the rubble of the bombing of a house where—when stolen during our absence—it had been brought. It was so badly damaged that it had been declared unrepairable by the two top sewing-machine repairmen in Pitigliano.

In school he distinguished himself with the highest marks in all subjects and by tutoring children in classes above his level in Mathematics, Italian, Latin and Greek. When he took his last Liceo examinations, *La Maturità,* and did poorly in History and had to take a make-up exam in October, we all screamed with joy that the *"monster"* was also human!

Chapter Two

My Parents

Both my parent's lineage as Jews in Italy traces back to at least the arrival of Titus with his contingent of the Jewish captives he spared when the Temple in Jerusalem was destroyed—70 C.E.. According to the historian Cecil Roth, whom I met in New York in 1958, their ancestry in Italy might well go even further to biblical times.

Father

Without having had formal education beyond the sixth grade, Father was an encyclopædic man. The son of two scholars, he was versed in a number of subjects, some of which he mastered far better that many people who had formal training in them. An innate teacher himself, Father was forever didactic in all his interaction with us.

As a child he distinguished himself both in the Yeshiva learnings and in secular studies. He had read his first *Haftara* when he was barely five and had had to stand on a chair to reach the lectern at Temple. By the time he was in third grade, he was considered by his teachers and the school principal a mathematical genius.

In his youth he had been a successful journalist at *Il Secolo* and at *Il Corriere della Sera*, both of Milan. However, having been chosen by his father to be the one to hand down to posterity the glories of Jewish Pitigliano, Father abandoned the pursuit of secular professions to become the head of our Jewish community. In this role, he conducted the services and delivered the sermons at Temple, which at that time was open and functioning every day; prepared children for their B'nei Mitzva, performed marriages, counseled people in their troubles, assisted the dying, and ritually slaughtered the animals to provide his congregation with kosher meats. His calligraphic Hebrew was so beautiful that he was sought after from many parts of Italy to write *ketubot* (artistic marriage contracts), mural inscriptions, tombstone epitaphs, book illuminations, etc. Only when a male child was born, a *mohel*, a physician who was also a ritual circumciser, would come from a city to perform the little operation, and, periodically, an ordained rabbi would be sent to Pitigliano to relieve Father of his many duties (the three rabbis I remember were: Ugo Massiach—the father of five; Angelo Orvieto—a very young man who was deported and perished in the Nazi camps; and Abramo Disegni—who instructed me for my Bat Mizvah), but even so his responsibilities were very many.

Settimio Sorani, secretary of the Jewish Community of Rome, and a Resistance fighter who saved the lives of many Jews during World War II, in a manuscript he left, remembers my father with these words:

> The last guardian of the Temple, of Pitigliano Judaism and its glories was Azeglio Servi, who for nearly 40 years led his community and, diligently devoted to its traditions, took care on Yom Kippur to contact all the Jewish natives of Pitigliano now dispersed throughout Italy to come and recite, for as long as has been possible, the prayers according to the Italki rite with the melodies that were peculiar to the Pitiglianesi.

In addition to performing all his duties as a religious man (and being the secretary of the *Giuseppe e Affortunata Consiglio*, a foundation that provided the dowry for poor Jewish girls of marriageable age), Father had to hold other jobs to round out his small honorarium. He represented a few important firms, one of which was Singer Sewing Machines. When the sales fell below the expected level, in order to remain an agent for the company, he would buy a few pieces in our names, so we always had the latest models in our home. He was also the accountant for the farmers in the area. Most of the latter used him not only to keep their books, but also as a mediator in their disputes with the landlords, and as a counselor in their family troubles. In most cases the farmers didn't have any money to pay for his services, and compensated him by presenting him with a little of what they produced: a wheel of cheese, a basket of ricotta, a chicken, a few fresh eggs, and so on.

Father was a friendly, patient, and loving man. Looking at him, one would say that God's hand was constantly stretched towards him to drop *b'rachot* on his head. In any situation, joyous or sorrowful, he saw the signs of the Divine Presence, and was grateful for all that was good and accepted with unflinching resignation what was not so good. He had his share of trouble, to be sure, but seldom, if ever, was he heard complaining about the difficulties with which all humans are afflicted. His irremovable faith made him see even his own sufferings as part of the human experience for which he had to be thankful.

Father had only one bad habit: card playing. Because of this passion for what he considered to be a bad vice, he managed to bring us up hating cards and any form of gambling.

He who had married many young couples was not yet married in his mid-thirties. Father considered himself a modern man who didn't believe in making matches for others, much less to make use of the services of a matchmaker for himself. He didn't have to: his God would provide him with a clue when the moment to meet his mate would come about. In the meantime he lived his life as fully as possible. In addition to the traveling he did for his business, and whenever his community duties allowed it, he would take time off and go to a beautiful resort for a few days, or to visit one of his many relatives who lived in different parts of Italy.

One early summer morning, as he was boarding a bus for one of his pleasure trips, an old peasant man approached him.

"Where are you going, Signor Azeglio?" asked the stranger.

"To visit my cousin in Porto Santo Stefano," answered Father, not without wonderment at the man's inquiry on a personal matter.

"Perhaps," began the old man, who knew that my father often traveled without any precise destination, "would it be too inconvenient for you to slightly change your plans and go to Livorno instead?"

Father was puzzled.

"You see," the other continued, "my daughter is leaving for America from the port of Livorno and needs some assistance with the American Consulate there."

Good-hearted Father did not hesitate a minute about changing his destination.

In Livorno he escorted the young lady through the red-tape ordeal and saw her off at the pier. Then he went to visit a distant relative living in that city.

When he rang the doorbell, he was met by an astonishing beauty, who introduced herself as the sister of his distant relative's wife, visiting from Rome. God's clue, as far as he was concerned, was right there. He even saw the change in his itinerary as a portentous sign of his destiny.

The young lady, at first, did not recognize the visitor as the man of her life. But fate helped. During a rowboat excursion they took with another young couple, the Roman girl fell overboard. She went straight to the bottom. When Father realized that she could not swim, he quickly dove in and rescued the almost lifeless girl who had already recited the *Shema'* before losing her senses. When she regained consciousness, she sweetly smiled at the man who had saved her life with a bit more than just gratitude.

The following April the two were married.

Mother

Mamma was a very attractive, sagacious, quick-witted, and generous woman. She dressed elegantly at all times (even if with hand-me-downs from her rich sister in Livorno), and when Father brought her home, she immediately conquered the hearts and the respect of her in-laws and everyone else in the village.

She was gregarious and reserved at the same time. When in company, she was an extrovert, the true life of the party, but seldom did she seek to be with people. She spent most of her time taking care of the house and the children, and in meticulously preparing the most delectable dishes for our everyday meals.

On Shabbat days Mamma spent the mornings at Temple, and in the afternoons she dressed her children up again and took us to visit and pay respect to the elderly and the home-bound.

As if she didn't have enough children of her own (there were five of us), Mamma often picked some destitute ones from the street and brought them home. She would wash them, dress them with things we had outgrown, and feed them.

When she set down to read to us, all our cousins would gather around to hear her stories, because she had such fecund imagination—she added, made changes, used various tones of voice and facial expressions—that the same story became many different ones, new and more exciting with each reading.

She also had what she called her regular "customers," the village beggars, who would knock at her door every Thursday for scraps from the table and a few cents.

Mamma didn't care for pets, but she did at one point keep a little chick Father had received in payment from one of the peasants he helped with the bookkeeping. She kept the bird in a large hen coop outside on the terrace that led to our house and fed it every day, possibly with the intent of making a Shabbat dinner when it became nice and fat.

But one Friday morning, as she went to feed her chicken, Mamma found the cage empty. She had an inkling which beggar might have stolen her chicken, and in fact the next Thursday the suspect didn't show up, and sent one of her little children to our door in her stead.

Mamma gave the child the usual small change and food, then asked,

"Do you happen to know where is the chicken that was in that cage?"

"My mother took it," said the child without hesitation. "We all went to have a picnic at the baths of the Jews."

Mikva

Some five kilometers northeast of Pitigliano, off the post road that connects the two main Roman roadways, Via Appia and Via Aurelia, there used to be, until very recently, thermal baths which the Christians called, "The Baths of the Jews."

Only years later, after the Jewish community of Pitigliano had been destroyed and dispersed, and the baths, now the property of the village along with all the other properties of the defunct Jewish community, had been transformed into a public swimming pool, did I discover that this name—given to it by the Christians after our Hebrew *mikva*—had its roots deeply embedded in the history of all Jews.

In antiquity the *mikva*—total immersion in a body of running water for hygienic and ritual bathing—was mainly used by women after each menstrual period and before and after copulation. Without this immersion a woman was considered impure and therefore not fit to be an active member of the community. To today's people, a religious law which prescribes bathing at least a few times a month might seem superfluous and a bit ridiculous. But at the time when this law was first added to the body of Jewish Law, plumbing was centuries away from being in existence and millennia from being so widely spread as it is today.

The origins of the *mikva* can be traced back to biblical times and even today a conversion to Judaism cannot be completed without this immersion, and it is still very much part of the ritual for modern Orthodox Jews.

During my childhood we occasionally went to these baths for picnics, all jammed with all the foods and drinks in the horse-pulled carriage that our father had hired for the occasion, along with its driver. Those were exciting times! The picnics at the baths have a special place in my memory. When the carriage reached the muddy and bumpy path that led down to the springs, we jumped out and hopped down on foot, stopping on the way to gather blackberries among the thorny bushes that lined both sides of the path, and always arrived before the scrawny horse with our parents and the food did.

We raced each other to the site of the *mikva* through a tall archway. Upon entering the archway, immediately to the right, was what looked like a farmhouse. Inside were many little doors along a corridor. The doors opened into many tiny rooms, each with an in-ground cement tub through which ran naturally hot water. To the back of the building were two large walled outdoor pools, one for the women and one for the men, where Father taught the boys how to swim. In the front lawn stood the long picnic tables and benches for the singing and eating that went on following the bathing.

We loved these trips to the *mikva*. It was there that the boys had learned how to swim (we girls did not learn until when we were adults in America!); it was at the *mikva* that we took our first photographs with the little box camera Father bought us when Mario was born; it was at the *mikva* that we went with other Jewish families to lift our spirits when, after mimicking and assimilating with the Christian world, we were forced to look again at the richness of our own heritage.

Part 2

Assimilation
and
Anti-Semitism

King Carlo Alberto of Savoy, who emancipated the Jews from the Ghetto in 1848 and granted them full civil and political rights..

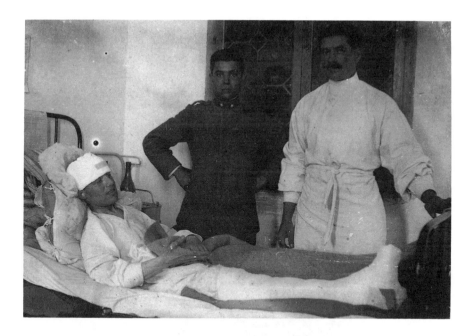

Uncle Angelo lying in a hospital bed after being wounded at the battle of Caporetto.

Flanked by Mario and Marcella. In background cousin Lida, dressmaker Rosina and Gino.

My Bat Mitzva

Uncle Guido with Primo Carnera.

With Uncle Guido and the boatman, Omero, in Porto Santo Stefano.

Chapter Three

Before the Racial Laws

T he world is plagued with anti-Semitism—a disease for which no
cure has been discovered so far. Pitigliano was no exception. In spite of
the mostly peaceful cohabitation between Christians and Jews for many
centuries, and in spite of a high occurrence of intermarriages, it was not
immune to it.

Breathing Anti-Semitism

I don't know precisely at what age I first became aware of the anti-
Jewish sentiments that most of our Christian peers harbored against us.
Anti-Jewish remarks on their part were so diffuse and frequent that most
of the time we did not pay attention to them. They were like the atmos-
pheric fine dust one breathes with the air all the time without becoming
aware of it until it is brought into focus by an intense beam of light. My
being Jewish was as much a part of me as was my being a girl. As I found

myself envying the boys for the privileges that were theirs because of their gender, so I might at times have longed to be a Christian and be part of all the pageants and festivities from which I was excluded. But for the most part I was happy with my lot. There was a passage in a prayer book that went, "Blessed be the Lord, our God, for not having made me a woman" which Father had changed to "...for having made me a man." Obviously this prayer was for the boys. Our Father, however, expected also the girls to recite the same prayer by saying, "Blessed be the Lord, our God, for having made me according to His will." But I changed it to "...for having made me a woman." And just as I pitied men who had to go to war and could not bear children, I also pitied the masses who were so shamelessly ignorant (I once shocked one of our maids out of her wits by revealing to her that her God had been born a Jew like me) and didn't experience the great pride and privilege of being born and educated into the magnificent world of Judaism.

Thus armored, I shouldn't have been easily touched by the malevolent feelings of those Christian children. Nevertheless—those feelings being there and often enough explicitly expressed—I was indeed chagrined by the continuous unprovoked stings. It was nothing like the pogroms and the bloodshed that had been going on for centuries in other parts of Europe against the people of my faith. By comparison, I was only experiencing a mild form of anti-Semitism. But I didn't know of those atrocities, and aside from comparison, *any* form of anti-Semitism was intolerable to me and a sign of barbarism on the part of the perpetrators. I remember that often, during our Sabbath services and sometimes during the High Holidays, groups of urchins would come to our temple and sit on the last benches inside the sanctuary. We dreaded their arrival, since we knew how it all would end up, but Father wouldn't prevent them from entering. "The Temple is a place of prayer and togetherness," he would reply to whoever suggested to keep the doors closed during the services, "and it is open to anyone who is respectful of the House of God." And in fact in the beginning those children would come and sit almost *respectfully* for a while.

Eventually, though, they would become so rowdy that the *shamash*, the temple beadle, *had* to intervene by chasing them away and closing the sanctuary's door to allow the service to continue.

In the streets matters were not better. Once a group of five or six urchins overpowered my brother Gino and held him supine on the ground. They extracted his penis, tied it inside a slip-knot, and tightened the knot while yelling obscenities, that included the word *ebreo* in all its disparaging connotations. I began to scream, and only then did they release their prey. Gino was more overcome, I am sure, by my having witnessed his humiliation than by his pain and anger.

In general we held our own. After a good fist fight, my older brothers went back to play with their peers as if nothing had happened. Unlike the boys, however, I was not good at fights that involved bodily contact. My only weapon to respond to these unprovoked bashes was the use of my tongue. Either I would stick it out as a token of my contempt, or I would respond with an insult similar to the one received. But these mild reprisals could not make up for the constant attacks I was subjected to. I never did anything to them. Yet, the hoodlums terrorized me on a daily basis, and the adults in their lives—whether parents, teachers or religious leaders— did nothing to stop them, and in many cases they were the ones who instigated such behavior.

The first clear memory I have of manifest anti-Semitism on the part of an adult, goes back to when I was about three. I was standing in front of the pharmacy waiting for my father to come out. Marino, the town tax collector, was a tall man in his early thirties with straight black hair greasily combed back from his narrow forehead, teeth and fingers blackened by nicotine, and a strange, thick, dark nail a couple of inches long on one of his little fingers with which he constantly shook the ashes off his cigarette. In his spare time—and he seemed to have plenty of it—he would come out of his office and stand on the doorstep of the fabric store, between the pharmacy and the town office, to chat with the owner, his Jewish friend. When his friend was busy with a customer, Marino would just stand there, twirling one of the lead-ball-weighted curtain ropes around his forefinger back and forth, a cigarette stub hanging from his lower lip. I was but two steps away from him when a quick word skirmish between a boy and me took place.

"*Abbreaccia!,*" the stranger boy hurled at me.

I quickly responded, "*Cristianaccio!*".

Marino halted his idle movement and, pointing his ugly fingernail at me, scolded, "Hey, you! Why did you call that kid dirty Christian?"

"Because he called me dirty Jew."

69

"Is that so?!" said Marino with a stern voice, rendered more opaque by his chain smoking, his frightful fingernail waving closer to my face. "Two wrongs don't make a right."

I hated Marino and his untimely intervention. Why did he scold only me? It was the first time that I felt an adult had openly perpetrated an injustice against me for the sole fact that I was Jewish; but it was certainly not the last.

Government Edicts Concerning Jews in Italy

From King Carlo Alberto's Statute of Emancipation of 1848 (the Statuto Albertino, which included the symbolic destruction of the ghettos' doors and the gradual restoration for all Jews of their Italian citizenship with full civil rights) until the second half of the 1930s, being Jewish in Italy had been only a question of heritage and religious persuasion. The Jews, having had uninterrupted residence on the Italian peninsula since biblical times, were as Italian as anyone else there. The false accusations, persecutions, forced conversions, and murders, which had plagued them at intermittent periods since antiquity and had intensified with the advent of Christianity, were aberrations of the past and had finally given way to an era of enlightenment and of peaceful cohabitation between Jews and Christians. This era of freedom and equality, now in its fourth quarter of a century, had created an atmosphere of enthusiasm for secular scholarship among the Jews who, even in the humiliating confinement of ghetto life, had been able to maintain a high level of literacy by dedicating themselves to the study of the Hebrew language, the Torah, and other Jewish learning.

This intellectual enthusiasm resulted in a short period of time in a disproportionate number of Jews who became accomplished in jurisprudence, medicine, mathematics, the sciences, and the arts and letters, [1] contributing beyond compare to the cultural and economic development of Italy. Jews were also active in the political arena and played a prominent role in the Risorgimento that led to the unification of Italy in the

70

latter part of the 19th century. Whenever their country called upon them, they proved to be valorous soldiers and unsurpassed patriots. During World War I—just to cite one example—five of the six brothers in my father's family were in the forefront of the combat; two of them were seriously wounded at the battle of Caporetto and a third, my father, was awarded two medals for military valor—a bronze one given to him on the field, and a gold one received by my mother fifty years later, just after his death. The sixth and youngest brother, only twelve, was given the task of running the tax collector's office of our town for the duration of the war.

As the economic and political situation of post-war Italy deteriorated, and with the takeover of Fascism in the early 1920s, the position of the Jews began imperceptibly to decline once again.

Benito Mussolini—who had seized power by force but with the connivance of the monarchy—professed pro-Jewish sentiments on the surface. He favored Zionism (undoubtedly to set a foot in the door of the Middle East). After the suggestion of his Jewish mistress of the early thirties, Margherita Sarfatti, he passed a law that recognized Jewish marriages performed by a rabbi to be legally valid. However, he was a true anti-Semite at heart. It was he who, in February of 1929, stipulated the concordat between the Catholic Church and the State, automatically making the Jews slightly second-rate citizens. And a decade later, when he went to ask King Vittorio Emanuele III of Savoy—the great-grandson of the originator of the Statuto Albertino—to sign one of the first racial laws that would prohibit Christian help from serving in Jewish homes, the king was hesitant. He reminded Mussolini of many prominent Jewish patriots, citing eighty-year-old General Pugliese, "loaded with medals and scars," who would have to do without house help, and expressed an "infinite compassion for the Jews." Mussolini responded that in Italy there were "20,000 people with a weak backbone" and he, the king, was one of them.[2] His association with Hitler was no coincidence. The German leader did not, it appears, impose upon him a policy of anti-Semitism as a condition for the Axis Pact. Rather, his involvement with the Nazi regime helped bolster his already strong, ancient, Church-inspired hatred

1. H. Stuart Hughes in his *Prisoners of Hope,* Harvard University Press, Cambridge, MA, starts right off by saying that "an inordinately high percentage of Italy's leading contemporary writers [...] were [...] Jewish."

of the Jews, and on his own, mimicking the Nuremberg Laws, he carried out his own brand of anti-Semitism.

During his first decade as a dictator, Mussolini was able to attract in his cadres quite a few Jews. These either believed in his ability to resolve the nation's economic problems and offset the crippling labor unrest, or felt that their partnership in the new regime would strengthen their own position as citizens. When the moment was ripe to slash at the Jewish community, however, the services of his Jewish loyalists were repaid by Mussolini with short-lived favoritism. The first Racial Laws were paralleled by mock laws that "discriminated" (exempted) the Fascist Jews from some of the measures taken against all others. Many were lured into accepting this partiality, not realizing that it was only temporary and that they would eventually share the fate of all other Jews.[3]

Although quite a number of Jews (such as the brothers Carlo and Nello Rosselli, who were murdered by hired assassins while in France) did become very active in the fight against the regime, the majority—even though they disapproved of fascism—remained outwardly neutral. For instance my father, the quintessential anti-fascist by temperament and training, was a close friend of a parliamentary deputy, Paride Magini. The latter successfully nominated him for *"discrimination."* My father declined the offer, saying to him, "I have never been incriminated in any crime, and need not be discriminated."

The changing of the political climate vis-a-vis the Jews of Italy didn't happen overnight.

At a popular level, and especially among the children of the lower classes, anti-Jewish sentiments were always present and we couldn't help being aware of them. However, on an official level as well as on all other levels of life (at least on the surface) there had been no difference between the Jews and non-Jews. And in fact if prejudice there was, it was in favor of the Jews, who were considered by most Christians as being "better" than anyone else. As late as 1936, there were still Jews in key positions in the Army and in the Government. A few even volunteered to fight in

2. Monumento al Fascismo - A Cura dell'Associazione Volontari della Liberta` - Sezione di Grosseto

3. For an especially tragic example, see Alexander Stille, *Benevolence and Betrayal,* (Simon & Schuster, New York, 1991), Ch. 1 passim.

Spain on Franco's side. Since the advent of Fascism, periods of tranquillity and signs that things might become precarious for the Jews succeeded one another; but very few people—Jews and non-Jews—were ready to acknowledge the seriousness of the latter.

By 1937, the snowball of official anti-Semitism began to roll, and in spite of the ostrich policy adopted by most Jews, it was only a question of time that it would swell into an avalanche.

At first it was a subtle campaign of slander that Mussolini himself launched with several anonymous newspaper articles. But quickly other newspeople began to write in the same vein. The campaign gained momentum, and, with the publication of *Il Manifesto della Razza*, in mid July, 1938, became outright anti-Semitic propaganda that poisoned the ears and the hearts of many who had until then professed themselves as our friends, and culminated with the passing of the *Leggi Razziali* against the Jews in the fall of 1938.

During the 1937 campaign, it was no longer the occasional invective hurled at us by some of the street children that hurt us, but also the defamation and the abusive behavior of some of the adults who took advantage of the fact that they would remain unpunished, or would even be encouraged by those in power, to attack us. Hundreds of times, in the course of my formative years, I was subjected to some form of psychological violence. Instead of getting used to it, however, I became more and more sensitive to its effects, more vulnerable to each new insult, angrier at its perpetrators.

Child of the Ghetto

I was about eleven years old when my long-cherished dream of becoming a piano player seemed close at hand. It had been Mamma who had first recognized that I had a knack for music, and on Purim of 1929, around my third birthday, she had presented me with an almost true-to-life toy piano. Sitting in front of that lovely instrument, I pounded on the keyboard, and to the tune of that cacophonic accompaniment, I sang in perfect tune the songs I had learned from our maid Santina who would constantly sing while tending to her domestic chores.

Now, eight years later, the opportunity of taking real piano lessons came my way. When I made the suggestion to Mamma, however, she replied in sullen tones that we didn't own a piano and above all we didn't have money for such frivolous ambitions.

It must have hurt Mamma a lot to be compelled to frustrate me this way since she knew I had potential.

"I know, Mamma," I said understandingly. "I didn't mean to go to a regular teacher; but I have a friend who's willing to give me lessons for nothing and to let me stay at her home after each lesson to practice for a few hours."

"For nothing? Which friend?!"

"Liliana," I said brightening up with hope. "She's older than I, but she likes me and often, on our way home from school, she walks with me to talk about music."

I was lying a little. Liliana, a very pretty girl of sixteen, tall and shapely, with big, green eyes and a cascade of long chestnut locks, was in love with my fifteen-year-old brother Lello and took every opportunity to be with me to talk about him.

"Liliana..." echoed Mamma. She seemed to want to add something. But hesitated, repeated the name, and finally said nothing.

I knew exactly what went through Mamma's mind. In that late spring of 1937, the anti-Semitic campaign was beginning to be voiced by the press daily in a louder and louder tone. More and more people took heart from this semi-official propaganda to begin to surface their own atavistic anti-Semitism. Liliana was a Christian, and with all this anti-Jewish atmosphere our relationships with Christians had, against our will, much deteriorated of late. Besides, her family had only recently moved to Pitigliano, and we did not know how they felt about us.

There was no need for paranoia; it was all a big noise on the part of the press, picked up only by a few fascist extremists...

Reluctantly, Mamma acquiesced.

I became so close to Liliana and her family that I was almost part of the family myself. I was making enormous progress at the piano and Liliana, beside rejoicing at talking with me about my brother, derived genuine pleasure in teaching me. I came to regard the time I spent in her house as a sort of prize, a reward, a delightful counterpoint to the humiliations I constantly had to endure from other children, and always looked forward to my music lessons with great anticipation.

A few weeks into my newly-found pleasure something came up that transformed my dream into a nightmare.

One hot afternoon, a few days before school closed for the summer recess, Liliana's mother, back from having had a confrontation with the school principal regarding some disciplinary action he had taken against her younger son, stormed into the house right in the middle of my piano lesson. Heedless of my presence, the wiry little woman began to pace the room in big strides, and to throw and scatter everything that came her way as she related to her daughter the heated discussion she had had with the principal.

I kept to myself, silent, not knowing where to cast my eyes, waiting for the storm to be over, and trying very hard not to listen. But in spite of my efforts, I heard every word that was yelled, and one sentence particularly struck me.

"He had no right to talk to me like that," she sputtered, beating her chest vigorously like a madwoman. "I am a respectable person, I am not a child of the ghetto!"

There were several boroughs in our village—Capisotto, La Fratta, Le Fabbrerie, Il Piano—which derived their names either from the kind of activities that were carried on in them or from their particular location, and one of them was called Il Ghetto. At age eleven I, who was born and lived and played in the heart of the ghetto, did not know what the word *ghetto* meant. My parents, in their eagerness to protect us, had carefully avoided any reference to the shameful conditions in which the Jews had been compelled to live in the past. All I knew was that Il Ghetto was the poorest section of the village and that we were one of the very last two middle-class families still living there.

But I was born in the ghetto. I *was* the child which that "respectable person" was so proud not to be, and even though only scantily did I perceive what she meant, I was deeply hurt by her words.

As always when terror took possession of me, a rush of blood rose to my head blurring my vision and dulling my senses. As always when I was faced with injustice, I turned inward. I sneaked out of that house in tears, and ran home. Mamma reacted to my account of what had happened with anger at how prejudice had spread among all classes, and above all at how some people didn't hesitate to vent their hatred for the Jews even in front of innocent children.

"She didn't mention the Jews," I sobbed. "She said that she was not a child of the ghetto. We and the Paggis are the only Jews who live in the ghetto!"

But even as I said so, I knew deep inside me that there was more to it than I had been willing to admit. The Temple, the Yeshiva, the Hebrew library, the Hebrew school, the Jewish archives, the Matza oven, were indeed all in the Ghetto. I beseeched my protective and loving parents to make clear to me the implications of that angry woman's words. It was only then that I learned that the ghetto (the word is derived from *getto*, the casting of metal, because in 1516 the Venetian Jews were forcibly concentrated in one of the foundry areas of Venice) was the site where Jews had been enclosed at various times in the history of their Diaspora to live in crowded, insanitary conditions, compelled to obey hateful laws, separated from their Christian neighbors, lest they be stoned on sight or worse.

As I listened with fascination to the details of the miserable kind of life my ancestors (my grandparents!) had to endure in that walled section of the village where I, too, was born and lived, the terror that had gripped me earlier began to give way to a collected serenity, an inner contentment. I now envisioned my ancestors not as the static, faded, worm-eaten photographs hanging on the walls, or the decomposed dead bodies en-trapped inside those marble sarcophagi besprinkled with weather blotches and inscribed in poetic Italian and incomprehensible Hebrew, but as the young, vigorous living people they had once been, with good qualities, with faults, with desires and aspirations. As I began to imagine how much more stifling their environment must have been as compared to mine, all the more I admired them for keeping their sanity and their high level of literacy; for maintaining their healthy dietary laws against very large odds; for living in poverty, yet always finding ways of helping those in greater need; for keeping and handing down a high standard of ethics and morality.

These new thoughts were exciting. I not only had just learned the meaning of the word *ghetto,* but also how much I was part of it and how much it was part of me. I felt a burgeoning awareness of my heritage and of my own attachment to it that was worth any suffering. Liliana's mother, who had turned from friend to foe in an instant and had at first frightened me so, had in fact done me a great service: she had opened my eyes. Yes, I was a child of the ghetto and I had every reason to be proud of it. I would have not wanted to be anything else but the Jewish girl I was, born in the ghetto of the *Little Jerusalem,*—as our village was nicknamed because of its rich Jewish life—of beautiful, honest, hard-working people who were dedicated to the learning of the Torah, the Law, and to performing *mitzvot,* good deeds, not only among their coreligionists, but among the Christians as well.

All this elation was suddenly toned down by the thought, the fear again, of losing Liliana's friendship and with it my cherished music hours.

My fear was well grounded. Indeed, that day marked the end of my piano lessons, and at the moment it appeared that it had marked as well the end of my assimilation—my more or less conscious desire to conform and be like everybody else. But of this I could not be sure. Assimilation— the blending of a minority group into the larger society in which it dwells, assuming the mores, the habits, and even the thoughts of the dominant group —was a natural, easy and inexorable process. It was the acceptance of being different that required courage, conviction and self-respect.

Did I have enough of these?

The ugly episode during my last piano lesson at Liliana's home had forced me to look into the richness of my heritage. Soon, however, my Jewishness would find its expression in something beautiful and positive.

My Bat-Mitzva

The scented clusters of the acacia blossoms had come and had gone; the little oval leaves had yellowed and twirled to the ground; and now an icy wind whistled through the thorny naked branches and lifted small clouds of dust from the unpaved piazza, the main square; it made my bare legs turn purple as I walked to school and back. For more than half a year now, Liliana had ceased to seek my company, and I walked home from school all by myself. Sometimes, on passing Liliana's home, I was reminded of her mother's sickening scene. But at home that episode was never mentioned again and eventually I stopped thinking about it. I was turning twelve, and my Bat Mitzva occupied my mind.

The practice of including girls in the religious coming-of-age ritual dates back, in Italy, to just after World War I. Rather than a manifestation of religiosity, this practice must be now seen as part of the general trend to become integrated with the society at large—a trend which had been in progress since the emancipation from the ghetto towards the middle of the 19th century. Our orthodox codes prescribed that only boys were to be prepared to become participants in the religious rites. But by allowing girls to go through their Bat Mitzva, the Jewish community approached more nearly the customs of its Christian neighbors. The Jewish girls, on the day of their Bat Mitzva, dressed up like little brides—with long white gowns, head garlands, and tulle veils—just as the Catholic girls did for the sacrament of their Confirmation. In Pitigliano, after the ceremony had taken place at temple or in church, the celebrants gadded about the village in their festive attire, and who could distinguish between a Jewish and a Christian girl? It was wonderful! We Jews practiced our beliefs and rites which were quite different in significance from those of the Christians, but on the surface we were all alike—no striking differences.

By the time I turned twelve, the age in which girls celebrate their Bat Mitzva in Italy, assimilation was no longer working for us. No matter how much we disguised as Christians—or how much we felt like them—we were regarded by a good many of them as despicable beings to be kept at a distance, regardless of our behavior or dress.

At first my family thought of having a quiet, private ceremony. But then this was regarded as letting the forces of evil get us down, and it was decided, instead, that I would have a more sumptuous ceremony than any of my cousins and friends had had before all this anti-Jewish campaign had started. An aunt in Rome sent the tulle for the veil and the taffetas for the dress, both in pure silk, and a Christian neighbor and good friend made the outfit. I studied diligently under the guidance of Rabbi Disegni, and by the time the acacia trees were again white with clusters of flowers that filled the air with their strong and sweet scent, I was excited and ready for the ceremony in which I was to take the entire role of the rabbi.

When the beautiful day drew near, Mamma prepared the cakes and Father bought the sweet vermouth. They hired the ice-cream man—who sold little ice-cream cones and boats and sandwiches in the middle of the main square from his pushcart on Sundays—to take a break from his outdoor business and come to distribute his fresh wares in our house.

On the festival of Shavuot 5698, June 5, 1938 in the secular calendar, the Temple was adorned with beautifully displayed bunches of roses, and rose petals were carpeting the floor. The sanctuary was filled with relatives and friends—in fact the entire Jewish community of Pitigliano—with men and women together on the ground floor. Under normal circumstances the women would be relegated to the *matroneo*, an upstairs balcony with a baroque gilded grate through which they could see the men but could not be seen by them, but by this time the Italian Jews had ceased to follow many of the more restrictive rules. My father escorted me to the Echal in front of the Ark with the scrolls, while the children's chorus sang *Baruch Habba*, blessed be you who enter (welcome!), the song reserved for the most joyous occasions. I had thoroughly entered the spirit of my role. With a clear voice I read, I declaimed, I sang. Everything went beautifully; everybody was moved to tears.

At the end of the ceremony, the rich and aristocratic ladies of our congregation congratulated me and complimented my mother.

"She has a beautiful voice," they all said. "Please make any sacrifice necessary to have her study bel canto."

Mamma knew that there was no more room for sacrifice, and I would never study voice or piano, but all this praise made her proud of me nevertheless.

However, in the perfect harmony of the moment, there was a strident note. Aside from the young lady who had made my pretty dress, no Christians were present. None of my teachers, not one of my peers. Tension between us and them had reached a point that no kind of socializing was any longer possible: in order to avoid any painful refusals, we had not invited anybody who wasn't Jewish.

After the refreshments, I went out of the house with a couple of cousins —as it had been customary in the past—hoping to meet some of my schoolmates and to be seen by them in my ceremonial outfit; but no sooner was I out of the ghetto, my elegant dress became a cause of great pain for me. It was a Sunday, a glorious spring day, and people were coming out of the Duomo all dressed up in their best festive clothes. Some looked at me as one looks at an oddity, and their glances made me feel naked. What was I doing wearing a confirmation dress in the midst of those hostile people? Didn't the Catholic girls dress up like brides on the day of their Confirmation because they received Christ? Why did the Jews have to imitate them?

I ran home and changed into something that was less "Christian" and more consonant with my personality. I didn't have to be like anybody else. All I had to be was me. And *me* was not a conformist.

Once again, the embarrassment I had felt in the streets when I had gone to look for approval and had found shame instead, turned into a feeling of well-being, of serene joy, of richness and contentment that nobody and no circumstance could ever take from me. This time I had really shed any vestiges of *assimilation* I could possibly still harbor. I had learned my lesson, the beautiful lesson that only animals of some lower species must use mimicry in order to survive. Human beings must preserve their character and fight for their principles if they are to survive as such.

The Rabbi's Daughter

Fascism—as any dictatorship must—relied heavily on propaganda and rhetoric to confuse and control the minds of the masses. In order to keep people from using their own judgment and reason, passionate and inflammatory speeches were frequently delivered by Il Duce, and were broadcast nationwide. Another way of lulling the disgruntled was to have great displays of parades—both of the military and of school-age children in their fascist uniforms. Those long corteges of chanting and marching humans in which nearly every family had someone involved, played on the emotional strings of everyone, and nobody thought of how restrictive and calamitous living under the fascist regime was. National holidays, religious holidays, funerals of prominent people, and many other lesser occasions were all good excuses to organize a parade.

Every year, at school's end, one such parade marched from the school grounds to the main square where all the children, neatly arranged in rows, performed some simple gymnastics in unison. *Il Prefetto della Provincia* and his entourage would come from Grosseto, the province capital, to review the parade, and for the occasion a special platform was built from which the fascist authorities could watch the children's performance.

By the end of my sixth grade, a few weeks after my Bat Mitzva, I was the one chosen to stand out in front of the huge mass of children as an exemplar, my being Jewish notwithstanding. The movements of the arms, the legs and the body, rehearsed during the school year, were prompted only by the voice of our coach who would count in a staccato fashion into a megaphone, "One - two - three - four. One - two - three - four..."

The coach had chosen me—a Jew—because he knew he could rely on me not to make any mistake. The local fascists who had known me since birth did not mind it: all they cared for was the success of the show so that they would shine in front of their foreign superiors; and as far as the outside fascist authorities were concerned, both the coach and the local fascists had counted on the fact that they didn't know who I was.

The function was a striking success. The authorities genuinely enjoyed the performance and applauded frantically, as did the crowds that included parents and relatives and friends of the children. The prefect—as I learned afterwards—asked to meet the girl who had guided the children with such sureness, and proposed on the spot to award her a medal for light athletics. But at the end of the meet, as instructed by the coach beforehand, I vanished into the crowd and ran home.

Our temple was considered one of the historical landmarks in the region. Whenever notables visited our village for any reason, there was always a formal visit to the temple complex.

As expected, that afternoon the fascists from out of town came for the customary visit. As usual, I joined my parents as they went to open the Sanctuary, the Yeshivot and the libraries to give those people a guided tour. Suddenly the prefect took notice of me and stretching an arm with his forefinger pointed toward me exclaimed in total excitement, "Here she is, here she is, it's *she*!"

I was startled and so were my parents. But the man continued with a broad grin and without making any attempt at controlling his enthusiasm,

"I recognize you! You *are* the girl in the forefront of the parade." And turning to one of his escorts he insisted: "Don't forget to give this girl the medal she so deserves!"

My parents and I smiled faintly.

The local fascist who had been called upon, got closer to the prefect and sheepishly murmured, "But Sir! She is the Rabbi's daughter!"

The Temple tour was hastened through.

Of course, I was never awarded the medal *Il Prefetto* had proposed for me. In fact, getting or not getting a medal for light athletics was irrelevant. What really mattered was that this was the first time in our lives that all the Jewish children of Pitigliano were promoted to the next grade without the usual year-end awards that we knew we had earned with our academic performance.

We didn't know it then, but this parade not only marked the end of our attending public schools altogether, but also the beginning of *the* end for a good many of us.

Chapter Four

Early Effects of the Racial Laws

The status of Jews in Italy suddenly worsened in 1938. Although the shock opened our eyes somewhat, we could not envision the ultimate consequences of the Racial Laws.

No More School, No Christian Help

By the end of that summer of 1938, the first laws against the Jews were promulgated and almost immediately enforced: Jewish children were banned from public schools; Christian help could no longer serve in Jewish homes (our maid of four years—who had come to us as a peasant child and was now a refined young woman—had to pack and go); Jewish teachers could no longer teach in public schools.

In Pitigliano schools went only up to the fifth grade with an additional three years of introduction to farming or blue-collar training; those who desired and could afford to further their education had to leave the village and go to study in one of the large cities. We had the desire and the ability but not the means. Lello, who was considered by all his teachers—but especially so by his 5th grade teacher, Maestro Brogi—an absolute genius and should have been sent to the city to study, had been already working as a bank teller since he was eleven and the only affordable means of furthering his education was to study by correspondence; Gino had just finished his eighth year; Mario was only four and had not yet started school. The law prohibiting Jewish children from attending public schools affected only Marcella and me, who had just finished second and sixth grade.

We received the news one early October morning, a few days before the reopening of the schools after the summer recess, when Mamma came back from food shopping with the newspaper in her hand and a sad, long face. We were still loafing in bed when Mamma entered our bedroom.

"It's incredible," she said. "We, the Jews, were the ones who established Pitigliano's first school, and now *our* children are forbidden from going to school!"

"What!? What?!" exclaimed the two of us who could hardly repress our delight at the news.

"You are not allowed to go to school anymore, that's what!," said Mamma, and proceeded to read the ordinance aloud.

Marcella and I jumped on our beds and danced and screamed with joy. School was a bore, its environment hostile, its regimentation unbearable. We felt sorry for Mamma who seemed to be so grieved, but as far as we were concerned, not having to go to school was the best thing that could ever happen to us. This was especially the case for me, since one of my teachers was a fanatical fascist who made my life miserable.

Our joy and excitement did not last. When we began to see all the other children walking to school while we were left behind, our humiliation increased as the days passed by.

Immediately a private school was organized in the premises of our old Hebrew school, and two teachers instructed children from first to fifth grades. Those like Gino and me who were beyond the fifth grade, were left to their own devices.

Mamma, in her wisdom, realized that something had to be done in a hurry to find some structured occupation for the two of us who had no school to keep us busy. A living repository of proverbs, sayings, and (sometimes) platitudes, she said; "Idleness breeds vice," and petitioned Uncle Guido, who had a wholesale dry-goods store, to employ Gino in his concern, and asked Cousin Lida, a refined dressmaker twenty years my senior, to take me as an apprentice.

Lida quickly found herself surrounded by a swarm of chatty girls (all the Jewish girls in Pitigliano who were beyond their fifth grade) who were willing to help, but customers—Jewish and Christian alike—were hard to come by, and the only way we could learn the trade was by altering and recycling our own wardrobe. But at least we kept busy and out of mischief.

I didn't fully realize how much I missed school until one day when we had practically no sewing to do, and we began to daydream of suddenly becoming very rich—perhaps an unknown distant relative loaded with money in a faraway land would die leaving his fortune to us. Lida, who was thirty-two but sometimes acted like a child herself, joined our game. She asked each one of us what would we do with that much money. The answers were varied but all in the same vein—except for mine. One girl said that she would use the money to buy a fabulous house; another dreamed of jewelry and fur coats; another yet had a desire to travel to exotic places, and so on. My dream was to hire five private tutors to teach me the five basics: Mathematics, Sciences, Languages, Visual Arts, and Music.

La Dama di Compagnia Becomes a Housekeeper

One of the mock "discriminating" laws, devised to make the harsh racial laws which were gradually depriving the Jews of all their civil and human rights appear more palatable, provided that the elderly and the sick could continue to avail themselves of their Christian help.

In Pitigliano there was only one Jewish lady who qualified for such "discrimination," having reached the venerable age of ninety-three years. Signora Elisa was a tall, stern lady, whose garb had not changed since she had been a bride in the 1860s. Her husband had died prematurely a few years after their marriage, leaving her a very young and wealthy widow. Like Queen Victoria, whom she admired and emulated, she bemoaned the loss of her husband for the rest of her life without ever considering the possibility of remarrying. The only diverting concession to her otherwise drab life was to have a few relatives stay at the house—preferably her late husband's—who would occasionally come to visit from out of town. Even though she had been left quite well off, she lived the Spartan life of a recluse, writing letters, reading and embroidering, going to temple on the High Holy Days, and receiving a few local visitors who came to pay their respects on the Sabbath afternoons.

As the lady that she was, she had never had to perform any of the household chores. She had always had a housekeeper and a cleaning lady—both Christian—who came in every day from early in the morning until late at night. For companionship, to share her meals at her dinner table and to sleep in her awesome house, she would only trust a Jewish person.

For three quarters of a century there had been a few generations of Jewish young ladies who succeeded one another at spending a few years under the roof of Signora Elisa. It was considered an honor to be chosen for this mitzva, since Signora Elisa had high ethical standards and a young woman could only benefit from this contact.

Shortly after my thirteenth birthday, I was the youngest person to be chosen for the mission. My mother—no doubt—felt honored and happy to be given the opportunity of vicariously performing this mitzva; but for me the idea of going to live with the almost centenarian lady was appalling. The gap between our ages was insurmountable. Signora Elisa was a contemporary—and indeed the twin soul—of the most puritanical and phlegmatic of queens; I was a dynamic, lively adolescent with extraordinary vitality.

Sitting at every meal with that mostly taciturn lady who was sparingly teaching me good table manners was, to say the least, tedious; and sleeping in the bed next to hers in that huge, dark bedroom with fifteen-foot-high ceilings and two Doric columns between the beds and the windows was scary enough. But having to move from one room to the other at night was absolutely terrifying. The table lights were dim under the silk, bead-fringed shades, and projected long, dreadful shadows on the ceilings and on the walls. In almost every room, I was greeted by a dark dresser surmounted by a distorting, yellowish mirror which was flanked by a pair of huge, darkly painted, shiny ox horns. It was stretching the notion of mitzva a little too far. But as the good, obedient girl I was, I hadn't dared to pose any objection to the plan. With deadly feelings in my soul, I had become the *dama di compagnia* of Signora Elisa.

A few months after they had been devised, all the discriminatory laws were abrogated, and all Jews were treated alike, regardless of their age, health condition, previous rank in the army or in the Fascist Party. All the Christian help was peremptorily ordered out of Jewish homes, and I found myself—at thirteen—as the sole individual responsible for Signora Elisa's household.

Mamma, who had not anticipated this turn of events, began to feel sorry for me and tried to help, especially with shopping and cooking, but she had her own home and husband and the other four children to take care of, and little time or energy was left in her to come to my succor. To make matters worse, Marcella, at nine, had a nervous breakdown. Mamma took her to the top psychiatrist in Rome, Professor Panegrossi, who suggested that the child needed the quiet atmosphere of the country-side, away from all the problems, and all talk about the problems, that afflicted the Jews. Mamma found a farm several kilometers from the village, and leaving Father behind to take care of the two older boys, moved there with Marcella and Mario, who was then five.

My days at Signora Elisa's were crowded with household chores, from early in the morning, when I had to start the fire in the kitchen hearth for all the needs of the day, until late at night, at which time I would drop on my bed exhausted from fatigue. I had not been trained for this kind of physical work, having been brought up with household help myself, and no matter how much I trotted all day from one chore to the next, I never seemed to be able to catch up with all I had to do. There were beds to be made, floor and carpet cleaning to be done (no vacuum cleaner), shopping for food every day (no refrigerator), preparing for three meals a day on the embers of the hearth (no electric or gas stove, or even a charcoal range!), setting the table three times a day, dish washing, copper and silver polishing, and so on; and there was always massive ironing to be done. The linens—which a Christian woman would surreptitiously come at night to take to her home and return after they were laundered and dry—were forever piling up in the cloakroom.

By the time I entered her household, Signora Elisa could no longer embroider, but she could still read, and after I had brought her breakfast in bed and helped her get washed and dressed, I walked her to the drawing room near one of the large windows heavily framed by velveteen drapes. Here she would sit on her rocker, with a book in her hands, for the better part of the day. In the afternoon, while the lady took a nap and after I had cleaned the kitchen, I had a little time for myself.

"Time is not to be wasted," she would admonish me on her way to her bed. "Here, this is a precious book of poetry, or pick up a classic from the shelf and read while you rest."

"Yes, Madam."

My favorite spot was a chair on the stoop near one of the windows that looked into the main piazza. But after a few lines, Leopardi or Kolorenko faded away, I began to daydream and to look out of the window, watching with envy all the children at play, free and careless. Once I even dropped a dried flower at a passing boy I secretly had a crush on.

When Signora Elisa had guests from out of town, my life was some-what enlivened. Even though it meant more work, it provided me with diversion and a little excitement. But overall, this was no life for a pubescent girl and I often found myself crying, overwhelmed by the burden of the household and by the need to be near my mother. Once or twice, during the period that Mamma spent at the farm with Marcella and Mario, I got up when it was still dark, sneaked out of the house, and rode my bicycle to the farm just for the sake of seeing Mamma for a few moments. But upon my return I was heavily scolded by the old lady, who had been pulling incessantly at the heavy ribbon that activated the bell on top of her bed.

"Where were you? You scared me to death when you didn't answer!"

Again my sense of duty prevailed over my needs, and I didn't run to see Mamma anymore.

When Italy entered World War II on June 10, 1940, I was still working at Signora Elisa's. Eventually a more mature person, the unmarried sister of a rabbi, came from another city to take my place. For a while Franca and I both lived with the old lady while I was passing on my knowledge of the household, and we became close friends even though she was double my age.

One day Franca, out of the blue, asked me, "Have you ever kissed any boys?"

I was shocked beyond telling at the question.

"Of course not!" I answered with sternness. "If someone wants to marry me," I added as a way of explaining my firm answer, "I am too young; if he wants to play... Oh no! I am not that type!"

Franca was amused at my being so naive at age fourteen.

"People can love each other without having to be married," she said laughing. "And they can be married without loving each other!"

"Perhaps," I said just to say something. And when Franca, a chain smoker, asked me to try a cigarette, I braved it for fear of what she would think of me if I refused. I was beginning to like Franca, but I was helplessly embarrassed by her kind of talk and by the fact that she washed herself naked in front of me in the kitchen. (There was no sink nor bathtub in the toilet.)

I was happy to be finally released from that unpleasant situation and to go back to my cutting and sewing.

Uncle Guido

Uncle Guido was one of the five brothers in my father's family who had fought for their country during World War I. He had served in the Bersaglieri—an elite corps of the most valorous men in the Italian Army—and bore with pride the large scars that mapped his whole back. At the end of the war, a few days after his twenty-first birthday, he left Pitigliano to join an important textile manufacturing company in the north of Italy, rising with diligence and talent to a high rank. After nearly twenty years with this company, Uncle Guido went back to Pitigliano where he established his own wholesale dry-goods store. His company quickly expanded and became well-known in all of Tuscany and beyond, counting even a few customers outside of Italy—Zagreb, Yugoslavia and Tirana, Albania. At the beginning, Uncle Guido was able to carry on his business almost entirely by himself—his only help being old Great Uncle Raffaello, a retired businessman, who was in charge of the warehouse.

Two years later, when the first of the racial laws banned Jewish children from public schools, Gino, not quite fifteen, joined Uncle Guido's enterprise, mostly helping in the warehouse. After Great Uncle Raffaello passed away, Gino, besides taking on more responsibilities at the store, began to travel as a salesman. The business bloomed rapidly, and after a while Uncle Guido had to hire another employee. At fourteen—just freed from the yoke of housekeeping at Signora Elisa's and barely back at Lida's atelier—I was chosen to fill that need. The modest salary I would bring home would certainly help the family. Mamma, however, encouraged me to keep that money for myself. With my first paycheck, I bought shoes, stockings, and a few lengths of material. Then I regularly deposited my salary in a bank in the nearby village of Manciano.

Before leaving Lida's dressmaking shop, I made myself my first brand-new winter coat and, to go to work, a black satin smock with floating pockets and a white pique collar—a delightful but proper dress for a secretary at the time.

Christian boys admired me in my new outfit and began to flock around. I didn't encourage them, since it was against the law for the two "races" to mingle, but I didn't discourage them either, especially since all we exchanged was an occasional furtive glance, or at most a few words. This innocent game, however, which had passed unnoticed even by the fascist authorities, didn't escape the attention of Uncle Guido. He kept a sharp eye on me and spent long hours teaching me how to keep the books in perfect order, in a neat calligraphic handwriting.

I liked my new job. It gave me the opportunity to interact with adults —customers, manufacturers' representatives, the local bank's "big shots"—and to acquire a number of new skills. On the other hand, although I admired my uncle for his ethics, vast erudition, and aristocratic manners and always behaved with deference toward him, deep inside I hated working for this strong disciplinarian almost as much as I had hated working for old Signora Elisa. Again, I longed to be a girl my own age, going to school, playing with other children. But again, the good girl inside me didn't let me voice my feelings, and in spite of my reservations, I remained at this job for nearly three years.

Occasionally Uncle Guido, who often traveled to Milan on business, would take me along. We would be guests of his older brother in the villa where I had once stayed with my parents as a child, and while he attended his business, I would have a grand time with my cousins. These introduced me to their vast music collection, and I became especially enthralled by the second movement of Beethoven's Seventh Symphony; but I got to appreciate many other classical and chamber pieces as well. Once, during the opera season at La Scala, Uncle Guido took me there to see Boito's *Mefistofele*. It was by far the most magnificent production of this opera I was ever to see. I still can hear the sweet, melodic voice of Ferruccio Tagliavini as Faust; I remember Pia Tassinari as Helen/Marguerite, Tancredi Pasero as a powerful and convincing Mefisto; Composer Gian Franco Malipiero as conductor. The theater itself, the staging and scenery were most impressive. I had seen *La Traviata* in Pitigliano when I was 12 and I had liked it immensely, but it was *Mefistofele* at La Scala that truly transported me into the magical world of music and visual splendor that an opera can be.

Mainly Uncle Guido traveled alone.

During one of his business trips up north, he was hospitalized for surgery and didn't come back until a month later. With Gino on the road all the time, I found myself, at fifteen, as the sole person responsible for the operation of the business.

This responsibility would have been too much for anyone my age even under normal circumstances. By late 1941, with the war in its second year, it was even more taxing. Bookkeeping was a very complicated matter. All merchandise was rationed, and every item or meter of goods was given a value in points. The merchants who bought from us had to pay for their wares with the points they had collected from their own customers. We, in turn, had to use these points to buy from manufacturers. With this triple control of what was bought and sold, nobody could hoard anything. Of course, this was true only in theory. In reality, all these restrictions created a flourishing black market that made unscrupulous people rich almost overnight. Members of the families that at one time had been my mother's "customers" for alms were now wealthy and powerful. However, Uncle Guido was a law-abiding man, our business was immaculately clean, and I kept updated books and an accurate inventory of the merchandise and of the points.

During my uncle's prolonged absence, two men from the *Finanza,* paid the business a surprise visit. After hours of fastidious research they found nothing wrong. Frustrated, they stormed toward the door. However, considering my age, they then stopped and turned to thank me for my time and even complimented me saying that never had they seen books kept with such diligence.

Bookkeeping with points troubled many merchants who found it difficult to understand the complexities of the law. Uncle Guido offered his customers help to set up their books and to keep them updated. I happily traveled with my uncle to all the nearby villages and didn't mind the hard work. In exchange the merchants—Christians, many of them also landowners—invited us to share with them their meals (the abundance and the taste of which we had not known in years), and often presented us with some of their fresh and preserved produce to take home.

"Passing"

But a few lavish meals—attractive as they were in those times of penury—were not the only reason why I was always looking forward to these trips. For me they also meant the excitement of meeting new people, especially young people, who didn't know that I was Jewish and with whom I could behave without inhibitions or fears.

In Nazi-occupied Eastern Europe, the Jews had been compelled to wear a yellow star that identified them as such, and by now—May 1942— were already being systematically slaughtered. We in Italy had no knowledge of all this. We wore no signs to distinguish us, and as soon as we were away from the place where we were known, nobody suspected our true identity and we easily passed for Christians. Changing environment had become a vital necessity, a breath of fresh air away from the suffocating atmosphere of Pitigliano.

So we traveled around.

As the main ally of Nazi Germany, Italy was host to thousands upon thousands of German soldiers—though the battle fronts were far away, in the Pacific, in North Africa, and in Russia. It was during one of these business trips that I met Engelbert, the German soldier.

We had gone to Porto Santo Stefano to help a few customers there. Coming from Pitigliano, where the only soldiers we ever saw were the occasional boys on leave, we were struck by the number of uniformed men—mostly Germans—we encountered everywhere. In all of Italy's seacoast, the sea was the bluest in Porto Santo Stefano: it was heaven for the Germans stationed there.

After a day of heavy and uninspired work, Uncle Guido hired Omero the boatman to take us for a boat ride before supper, while the sun was still high and the sea was as smooth and as tranquil as a mountain lake. I had no desire to go but, reluctantly, I went.

The port at the close of the day was somewhat somnolent. A white civilian ship had dropped anchor and was being refueled, spot-painted, supplied with fresh foods, and made ready to sail the next day. Next to its elegance the ugly gray German warships docked on either side looked even gloomier than usual.

On the other side of the wharf, nothing, not even a solitary sailboat, was in sight. The horizon was a perfect, uninterrupted line.

From a porthole of the civilian vessel, a young officer took a few snapshots of us as our rowboat passed close to his ship. I made sure to flaunt my most beautiful smile. But Uncle Guido, who at first had showed annoyance, got close to me to be also in the pictures, and my smile waned. Then Uncle Guido decided to move on.

"Let's go down the coast to the Grotta Azzurra," he ordered the boatman. And to me, "You'll see something incredibly beautiful; at this time of the day the grotto shimmers with light and colors."

But I couldn't care less. It was certainly not with my uncle that I wished to see the famous Grotta Azzurra. I became sulky.

While old Omero was lazily rowing toward the end of the wharf and while my uncle was beginning to doze off, to curb my annoyance I sang a new hit—a zesty song which told of sirens and enchanted sailors. When my song was over, to my surprise—and my uncle's fury—a loud cheer came from the rafts and the shore swarming with German soldiers. My surprise increased when, as if in appreciation for my performance, all the

Germans began to sing *Lili Marlene*.

We immediately returned to shore.

At supper time, while the adults talked business, I chatted with Luigina, the daughter of the shopkeeper who had invited us, and after supper we were ordered to bed. But as soon as we were out of sight, we left the house and ran to the wharf where we met with several other local girls.

The entire village was talking of what had happened that afternoon. Because of that, the local girls stood in awe of me. One of them—a pretty girl herself—recited for me an old flattering doggerel about the combination of my eyes and hair color:

> *Occhio verde, capello nero*
> *La più bella del mondo intero.*
> Green eyes, black hair
> The most beautiful everywhere.

Even though I was not what one might call a stunning beauty, I had developed into quite an attractive girl. I had always kept my hair cut *à la garcon* with a single tuft falling over my spacious forehead which, together with my broad shoulders and the frank manners I had learned from my brothers and the street urchins, gave me the aspect of a tomboy. Of late, however, I had let my hair grow long over my shoulders, and I often posed in front of the mirror delighting at the sight of my firm, conic breasts—which I hardly touched even when I bathed for fear that they might get spoiled.

The young officer who had taken the pictures approached our group and introducing himself as Capitano Ragusa, asked me for my address so he could send me the photos when they would be ready. I readily complied and the officer, after suggesting that we should not be out in the streets so late, politely said good night and left us.

The German Soldier

Clara, one of the older girls, dared me to go to the German headquarters and ask for the lyrics of *Lili Marlene.*

Before the others became aware of Clara's challenge, I had left and started running up the ramp that led to the German headquarters.

I found myself in front of a little gray door, panting, unable to think. Automatically, I knocked.

The German sentry on duty was armed to the teeth. I told myself that my heart was pumping furiously from the effort of having climbed the ramp in a run.

"Was wollen Sie?" shouted the sentry in a loud, scratchy voice.

I didn't know German, but understood the question and began to mumble something in Italian, my knees shaking. What was I doing here? What had made me come to this scary place at this dark hour? The sentry kept on looking at me with his stern, frightening expression.

Another soldier who was sitting at a desk behind a partition came to my rescue. He dismissed the sentry with a wave of his hand and looked at me questioningly. I raised my eyes on him still panting and saw a man in his early twenties. Tall, blond and curly-headed, he reminded me of movie actor Leslie Howard. Visibly amused, the young man calmly introduced himself in perfect Italian.

"My name is Engelbert Berner," he said. "I am the interpreter for my company. I heard you sing this afternoon. Is there anything I can do for you?"

I quickly stated the purpose of my visit.

"I know that's an excuse," said Berner arrogantly. "You came here to see me. My raft was the closest to your rowboat; you must have heard me translating your song to my companions; you must have noticed that I was devouring you with my eyes."

No, I hadn't heard or noticed anything. Actually, it had been a chubby, childlike soldier who had caught my fancy. I recalled thinking that he must have been not older than I was—sixteen.

I scowled and didn't say anything.

The young soldier sensed that I was hurt and changed his tone.

"Come back tomorrow night and I will have the words of *Lili Marlene* for you."

"I won't be here tomorrow night. My uncle and I will leave tomorrow at noon. Thank you anyway."

I turned and ran all the way back to the wharf with a feeling of conquest—and confusion.

The Tan Letters

The shuttle that connected Porto Santo Stefano with Orbetello, the village where we would take the bus for Pitigliano, was an open-car train that reminded one of the little riding trains in children's amusement parks. Uncle Guido and I—hardly on talking terms now—had to run to the station to catch it in time. As we sat down, the locomotive moved. Feeling flushed and restless, I got up and walked a few cars away from my uncle. I leaned out to drink in the beauty of the dark promontory plunging into the multicolored sea as it passed in front of my eyes, and to let the breeze run through my hair and cool my face and neck.

Someone else seemed to have the same idea and came to stand near me.

I had just begun to go over in my mind all that had happened the previous day and night, and this presence so close to me was a disturbing one. I stretched up to move to another car and found myself staring at the German soldier. A mischievous, amused smile, crooked on one side because of a fever sore in one corner of his mouth, lightened his face. From a thin briefcase he extracted a tan sheet of paper on which he had written, in beautiful calligraphy, the lyrics of *Lili Marlene*—and his address. He asked me for mine and pointed out that he still didn't know my name. I was hesitant, but the soldier kept importuning me.

"Is it because of this," he teased pointing at the fever sore, "that you don't want to tell me your name?"

I was determined not to tell him, or else to give him a fake name, but just as the short shuttle ride was coming to an end, and just as I spotted my uncle making his way through the car toward us, I hurriedly whispered: "Edda Servi, Pitigliano (Grosseto)."

Afterwards, back in my parents' home in Pitigliano, I began to worry. Leaving our address with an Italian officer was all right, but I should never have left it with a German. Although nobody in Italy had yet heard of the concentration camps, we were aware that the Germans' hatred for the Jews made the anti-Semitism of the Italians pale by comparison, and I knew that what I had done was not right.

My worries were somewhat assuaged a few days later when I received the first of a long series of letters and poems which Nino—as the German soldier called himself outside the army—would send me almost every day. In each he assured me, with his perfect calligraphy, that after having met me, even though for so brief a time, he couldn't conceive of loving anyone else. I was sixteen and longing for romance: it didn't take much to convince me of his sincerity. Nevertheless, though courteous in my letters (one to five or six of his), I would not allow myself to fall in love with any Christian, much less with a German!

Mamma became very angry each time that one of these letters arrived, and I promised her to make them stop. But how? Nino didn't seem the type who would be easily discouraged. Short of telling him the whole truth, nothing was likely to work. But how could I tell him the *whole* truth? I wrote to Nino that I could feel no love for him, hoping to discourage him this way; but he replied that he felt confident that he would, in time, win me over.

I did not love Nino, but I did love to receive those tan-colored envelopes with their symmetrical addresses, filled with gallant declarations. At the same time I was aware that, in the forbidden game we played, I was cheating because I knew what the German soldier didn't know: that the lovely little girl of his dreams was a *Jüde*. If he knew this, I felt sure, he would finally stop writing. The thought that the German soldier might turn against me and my family didn't even cross my mind at this point. What did occur to me, was that the censors might realize that a German was corresponding with a Jew. The conflict tore me apart.

It was seeing Mamma so unhappy that made me quickly come to a decision one day. Defying the military and fascist censorship, I wrote my suitor that his dream could never come true, not only because I didn't love him, but also and above all because I was a Jew.

For the next several weeks I held my breath. The letters had stopped coming, but now I had tangible reasons to worry that I had put myself and my family in jeopardy. Also, after three or four months of correspondence, I missed Nino's elegant love letters.

Eventually a tan-colored envelope arrived, but right away I could see that something was wrong: my address was typewritten. The letter inside was also typed and had no salutation nor signature. Although Nino's letter was carefully worded so that he would not reveal what he now knew, I was able to interpret his message to mean, "I love you just the same; this madness will soon be over and I will marry you."

It was the last letter I received from him.

The Name-Plate

Laws against the Jews continued to be fabricated at a very fast pace. First, Jews were banned from employment in public institutions, then in private ones, such as banks; eventually they were not allowed to work for any Christians at all. Making a living was becoming more and more difficult by the day, and more and more we depended for our subsistence on the ever-shrinking number of Christian friends who had more than we had and were willing to share with us.

Most of the racial laws were inhumane, but some were utterly ludicrous, such as the one that obliged every Christian owner of a store to display a sign, well in view in the window, that read: THIS IS AN ARYAN-RACE STORE. The implications were clear, and the owners who unquestioningly abided by this law were proud not to do business with us.

Since in Italy we were not forced to wear any external sign such as a yellow star, the only way we could be identified as Jews was through our ID cards which had the words *RAZZA EBRAICA* stamped across them in bold letters. Moreover we were obliged, like everyone else living in the country, to carry ID cards with us at all times.

In a small village like Pitigliano, however, where everybody knew the life, death, and miracles of everybody else, so to speak, the lack of external identification didn't help at all. Even those few shopkeepers who had not adhered to the law and had not displayed the ridiculous sign felt uncomfortable when we entered their stores, and this, in turn, made us feel uncomfortable and rejected.

The majority of people seemed to be indifferent to our plight; some were sympathetic and remained somewhat friendly with us, but some would behave with gratuitous nastiness. With them, it was impossible for us to know how to behave. If when meeting in the street we didn't properly greet them, we were likely to be harshly reprimanded or even threatened. If we acted friendly, it might also prove dangerous, as had happened once to Uncle Guido. He had met, in the middle of the Piazza del Duomo, an old acquaintance, Gino Poli, who had moved to another town and had just come back for a visit. Uncle Guido, like the majority of the Jews, had not grasped the entirety of the enormous changes that were taking place in our society. He greeted the man with a big grin while extending his arm towards him to shake hands, but his friendly gesture was not appreciated. Six-foot-five Poli responded with a sonorous slap on my uncle's face. Uncle Guido—a slender 110-pounder—had no choice but to swallow the affront and walk away.

Our business, which had been an example of integrity and ethical conduct, was beginning to decline. All the good customers whom we had helped when in need now feared to come to us, and with them the great bulk of those who owed us money simply disappeared. Gino, during his sales trips, experienced rejection wherever he went, unless he visited the few businesses owned by Jews, who were still trying to carry on. They would hardly buy anything, but were eager to share their apprehensions and sadness with a fellow Jew.

One morning Uncle Guido and Gino went early to open the store and found that in front of it there was a pile of rubble. At first they thought it was a practical joke staged by some of the village hoodlums. But then they raised their heads and saw that the name-plate which had read for so many years, GUIDO SERVI - MANIFATTURE, and the street number, both engraved in black on white marble, had been chiseled off, together with part of the cement wall, and smashed into a million pieces.

The powerlessness in the face of this kind of vandalism was terribly frustrating. There was no use going to report it to the authorities, who were conniving, if not downright accomplices, with the perpetrators.

We were highly disturbed by this significant incident, but continued to go to the store as if nothing had changed. Some time after the smashing of the name-plate, however, we went to work only to find that the door to the store had been sealed shut. This time Uncle Guido did go to the police to explain that inside there was a whole new shipment of pure linen sheets (the only ones available, since cotton—which Italy had to import—was a rare commodity in wartime) and wool blankets which he wanted to donate to the local hospital. Uncle Guido was known for his generosity. However, now, there was more to his gesture than mere philanthropic sentiments: there was also his unwillingness to let the beastly fascists enjoy the fruit of our hard and honest work. At the same time he wished to retrieve some of our personal belongings—his briefcase, Gino's address book, my attractive black satin smock—which had been locked inside with the merchandise.

"Whatever is behind that door," was the sarcastic, horrifying answer, "is no longer yours. You may not dispose of it as you please."

Uncle Guido pleaded, insisted, bribed. But he was laughed out of the police quarters.

We felt raped.

Shortly after, Uncle Guido disappeared from Pitigliano. No one knew where he had gone. Gino and I were suddenly unemployed and once again catapulted from a structured life into uncertainty.

Our First Long Hike

The acacia trees in the main square had shed most of their manes and the roast-chestnut and salt-pumpkin-seed vendors were stationed at strategic points to catch the attention of the children walking to school. School had not been part of my life for over four years, now, and in the past few weeks I had not even had to go to work. I didn't really have any incentive for getting up early in the morning.

One morning, however, I woke up at about five o'clock with a feeling of urgency, as of having forgotten something important I had to do. As the mental fog that usually followed my sudden waking began to clear, the thought occurred to me that the savings I had earned with years of hard work and had duly deposited in a bank in Manciano might be confiscated by the Fascists at any moment: I had better go and collect it before it was too late. But if I asked my parents permission to go to Manciano to retrieve my money, I was almost certain that they would object. So I decided not to tell them. I got dressed in the dark and went to wake up eight-year-old Mario, who was sleeping in our parents' bedroom.

"Marcella and I are going for a long hike," I whispered in his ear.

Mario opened his eyes and started to say something, but I quickly pressed the palm of my hand over his mouth and said, "Warn Mamma of our disappearance as soon as she wakes up, before she and Father begin to worry. We'll be back soon."

Marcella didn't know that I had plans for her, and in fact she was still soundly asleep when I returned to our bedroom. I began to shake her vigorously while telling her about my plan, but she did not want to wake up. Finally she half-opened her eyes and reluctantly listened to what I had to say.

"Nothing doing!" mumbled twelve-year-old Marcella. "Leave me be. I am sleepy and I want no part in your scheme."

I insisted, "How can you be so selfish and think of your comfort when the future of the family is at stake?"

My savings would hardly make a dent in our situation, but to me they represented a treasure.

"The money is not only mine," I explained. "It may be used for any emergency." I told her that it was her duty to come along with me.

She didn't seem to be impressed.

I persisted, convinced that I was absolutely in the right.

It was not easy, but I finally succeeded in getting her out of bed, and, whimpering and cursing me, Marcella got dressed. We tiptoed to the kitchen and washed our faces with the cold water of the kitchen sink.

By the time the bell-tower clock struck six, we were at last out of the house and on our way. The daily bus that passed through Manciano on its way to Orbetello, had left our village two hours earlier and, as I had already explained to Marcella when I first disclosed my plan, we had to cover the twenty-kilometer distance on foot.

We didn't know any short cuts as yet and we began to walk the long way taken by buses and trucks and the occasional automobile. It was still dark out and quite chilly: we had to move fast or else we would freeze. Marcella was still groggy and recalcitrant, so I made up a parody to a tune of a fascist march to make her keep her pace. She liked the game; she added a few lyrics of her own, and we both sang and laughed and marched on without ever looking at the dark mass of the village on our right.

The tall wild trees were the only fence that separated one side of the uphill road from the bluff dropping to the deep valley below. We walked on the opposite side, near the upward boundary slope which we believed to be the edge limit of the legendary Lamone forest. We had heard fantastic stories about the near-impenetrability of this forest which only a score of years back had been the abode of some of the most infamous brigands.

We wondered how we would feel if one of these fierce men would suddenly appear in our presence as it had happened to our grandmother Debora some two decades ago. The story we had heard as children filled us with terror.

"Do you think that Nonna Debora was really alone in the kitchen?" inquired Marcella.

Yes, Grandmother was alone one night that her husband was away and all her children were asleep, when someone knocked at the door. She went to open, and there stood a man, his face covered by stubs of a rusty beard, who asked for something to eat. Although the man looked fearsome, good Grandmother let him in.

The door opened directly into the vast kitchen and the man unceremoniously took a seat at the kitchen table. Only then, in the pale glimmer of one candle, could Grandmother Debora see that from his filthy clothing were hanging guns and knives as accessories, and a few rounds of ammunition crisscrossed his chest. Without losing her composure, she hastily prepared some food which the stranger ate ravenously and in complete silence. At the end of the meal he asked for a pencil and a piece of paper and scribbled something. Then he left the note under his plate, got up, and fled through the door without so much as a thank you. When Grandma Debora recovered from the shock of the unexpected visit and made herself look at the piece of paper, she read: "The man you just fed was the bandit Fioravanti."

We shivered.

Domenico Tiburzi and his violent lieutenant, Luciano Fioravanti, were two well-known brigands who lived in the heart of the forest we now believed was on our left, and would periodically come out to assault the post coach on the very road we were now walking. Grandma Debora and the brigands were all dead now, but for the two of us the fear of the latter was very much alive. We held hands and walked in silence.

A sudden breeze pushed the front panels of our coats open over our bare knees, lifted the dead leaves from the ground, and forced dust into our eyes, ears and nostrils. We stopped and looked around, our bodies stiffening with terror; then, our heads half buried inside the collars and lapels of our dress coats ("casual" clothes as we know them today didn't exist at that time, and only rich people who went to ski resorts owned ski outfits), walked against the breeze without singing or talking.

The cloudless sky was turning gray above us, and the tops of the tall forest trees were gently swaying against it. The grayness of the sky gave way to a pale blue—which to our left, the east, glowed with yellow, purple, pink and green as well—and was becoming bluer by the moment. As suddenly as it had appeared, the cold breeze subsided, and the first golden rays of the day, filtered through the thorny branches of the half-naked trees, gently kissed us.

We resumed our song, our laughter and our chats.

The first six or seven kilometers went just like a breeze. At each milestone we counted one kilometer down with a sense of accomplishment. After another six or seven kilometers, we were beginning to feel the fatigue. We had taken no food or drink and our stomachs were grumbling. But we kept on and on, not singing or talking anymore, to save our breath for the last stretch, which seemed infinitely longer than the first two legs of our hike combined.

Finally, in the distance, we sighted the outskirts of Manciano—a few sparse houses over a hilly expanse. We were tired. The village, instead of getting closer, seemed to recede in front of our eyes. These last few hundred meters were the hardest.

We entered the village a few minutes after eleven. We washed our flushed and dirty faces and cupped our hands to drink from a public fountain, then we sat on a stone wall to rest a while and to summon some courage before heading toward the bank.

The bank was almost empty of customers. I handed my passbook to the teller and told him that I wanted to close my account. I was asked to show my ID card—which I had recently renewed since everybody had to carry one updated. By an inadvertence of the town clerk in Pitigliano it did not display *RAZZA EBRAICA* stamped across it. This stroke of luck helped expedite the operation. I pocketed my money and as soon as we were out in the open again, my sister and I hugged each other and jumped with joy. We wished we had wings to fly home, now, but we only had aching bodies and numb legs, and decided to stop at a friend's house to eat and wait for the evening bus to take us back.

At home we were greeted with mixed reactions. Our parents were happy to see that we were all right, after our disappearance of over 12 hours during which they did not know where and why we had gone. But they were also very angry, especially with me who had engineered the whole plan.

But I was proud of myself. I had passed a test of determination and physical endurance. After explaining where we had gone and why I had not told them of my plan, I handed part of the money to my father and kept the rest for myself. Soon the whole matter was forgotten.

The thought of Uncle Guido's disappearance, though, still haunted us, especially me and Gino, who had been closely associated with him for such a long time.

Part 3

AMBIGUOUS WARNINGS

Marshall Badoglio at Fiuggi. Father is to his right and in the next row above him.

Chapter Five

The Doldrums

There were new faces in Pitigliano and we were hoping that this would change our lives for the better. When people live in a small community, new blood makes for excitement.

The Refugees

With the intensification of the American bombing of large cities, an exodus of refugees began flowing towards smaller centers seeking relative safety away from the potential targets. Pitigliano, having no military base or industry, gave shelter to hundreds of people. Some of them had means, while others were so poor and unskilled that they took up any kind of odd job, even enlisting in the *squadracce*, a corps of mercenaries at the service of the most extremist factions of the Fascist Party.

Among the many who flocked to Pitigliano in that period I recall with particular fondness a young dentist—a welcome addition to Pitigliano's medical profession. Before the arrival of this gentle, reserved and skilled young man, few people in Pitigliano took care of their teeth altogether, and those like us, who did, had to travel to larger centers. Lately, with all the restrictions and hardships imposed on us, it had become difficult for us to travel for any reason, and we were thrilled to have such a good professional man so close at hand. Our family was among the first to use his services, and the young dentist did not conceal a special and immediate liking of us. Instead of being unpleasant experiences, our visits to the dentist were entertaining diversion, since—so we presumed—he did not yet know that we were Jewish and for the moment, inside his office, we could behave without much inhibition or fear. We actually looked forward to our check-ups!

Also of interest to us was a lovely family that had moved into the apartment above ours—the same apartment where I, the twins, and Mario were born. At first we kept our distance, since we had learned to be suspicious of strangers. However they, just like the young dentist, behaved very cordially toward us.

The man of the family, an army colonel, was said to be listed as missing in action (although nobody in the family seemed to be overly upset about it). Signora Maddalena—a beautiful, tall woman in her mid thirties—lived with their three lovely daughters, with Bassano, the orderly the government afforded her as the wife of an officer, and Pess, the huge German shepherd that right away made friends with our little kitten Mustafino. Signora Maddalena's oval face was illuminated by a pair of vivid, green eyes that reminded one of certain small Alpine lakes, and by an almost constant, irresistible smile. She kept her thick brown hair in large, neat curls on the summit of her head. Her carriage was regal. Her northern accent (or was it a foreign one?) added to her natural charm.

The three girls were friendly, although sometimes they behaved strangely, as if they had a big secret they couldn't share. We wished they were Jewish.

"Do you think they might be Jewish?" Marcella wondered.

"How can they be Jewish if their father is in the army?!"

"I didn't mean *Jewish* Jewish," said Marcella. "But perhaps they could be Marranos!"

"What do you mean by *marranos*?"

I had only heard the word *marrano*—literally, swine, in Spanish—uttered by the Christians in its disparaging connotation. But Marcella, who at thirteen was widely read, explained to me that those Jews of fifteenth century Spain and Portugal, who after being forcibly converted to Catholicism continued to practice their Jewish faith in secret, were called disparagingly *marranos*, and then became known as Marranos.

Marcella had a fecund imagination, but that these people might be Marranos was a bit far fetched.

A few weeks later, a Jewish family did come to Pitigliano in order to escape the bombings of Livorno, their city. The arrival of the Cavas was a blessing for us, especially since the children were a girl Marcella's age and a boy a little younger than Mario. Marcella and Franca became instant friends, as did Mario and Enzo.

"What are the air raids like?" inquired Mario one day.

"First you hear that scary and mournful whistle of the sirens," explained Franca. "Then you run to the shelter—I mean run, without even getting dressed, if the alarm sounds at night. Often, on your way there, you hear the droning of the bombers advancing in formation, and suddenly the frightful roar of the explosions. The whole earth shakes and sometimes you see a hail of fire and rubble falling all over."

"Were you scared?"

"Overcome by fear!" said Franca thoughtfully. Then she continued, "When the sirens blast again, you know the danger is over and you feel relieved, but if the bombing was nearby, as you climb out of the shelter you still breathe an air full of dust, you see utter destruction around, and you hear the wailing of the wounded still alive under the rubble."

"Do you like to read?" Marcella asked Franca, to change subjects.

Yes, Franca liked to read almost as much as Marcella did, but her mother was very strict and selective about what she read and she felt stifled by her protectiveness. Our mother was just as protective and stifling, but Marcella had discovered a secret place to escape each time she had an urge to read undisturbed. The old Jewish library and archives had been in disuse for many decades now, but some of the precious books were still in their worm-eaten shelves. These underground rooms were now used by our family for storage. We kept charcoal and wood in one room, our bicycles in another, and lately we even kept a live chicken in a room with a large, floor-to-ceiling window. Marcella had to do a lot of dusting and remove a lot of chicken droppings before she could sit on the brick floor and immerse herself in her reading.

"You can come to my *private* library," said Marcella playfully to Franca. "But I warn you, it's not the cleanest place in the world."

"I won't mind it. I will bring an old smock."

Franca was a soft-spoken, kind girl who never used a bad word in her life. She had shiny, black, wavy hair, and dark, big, dreamy eyes. She always dressed neatly and elegantly—even though those white organdie pinafores looked a little ridiculous on that very tall thirteen-year-old girl. Marcella, accustomed as she was to all our squabbling and laughter, was fascinated by the gentleness of this city girl. Marcella played with the colonel's children only in the privacy of our terrace, away from the glances of strangers. But with her Jewish friend Franca she was free to associate in broad daylight wherever she wished to.

Our picnics at the baths of the Jews became more frequent. Once we would go with one family, once with another, and although we continued to be close with our Jewish fellow Pitiglianesi, we somehow preferred the company of the foreign ones, especially the lovely Cava family. The parents, just like their two children, were an incredibly sweet couple, and it would have been difficult not to love them. Aldo was a native of Livorno, but Elda was born in Pitigliano and was a distant relative of ours. I don't remember Elda before she got married and moved to Livorno, but I do remember her father, Abramo Moscati. He was a respected shopkeeper and refined tailor, who, besides being a prominent member of our Jewish Community, was a municipal trustee and the president of the *Società Agricola Operaia*. This was a foundation established by another Jew, the late husband of my Signora Elisa, Geremia Sadun, to educate and help the farmers of Pitigliano (all of them Catholic). Moscati was a first cousin of our grandmother Debora as well as of her cousin, the scholar Dante Lattes.

The Swastika

A Jewish child came running to our home, late one morning, to warn us that a man wearing a swastika on his arm had been seen circulating in the village and going in and out of a few Jewish homes.

"He pretends to be a photographer," the child said, "but my father said that he is a spy for the Nazis and that he has come to gather all the names of the Jews."

There was very little we could do. We waited with some trepidation for the man to come to our home, prepared to be cautious and determined not to give out any information, hoping in our hearts that he would never show up.

In the early hours of the afternoon, though, the stranger did come to our door. He was tall and slim. A frown on his face gave him a stern look; his battered but dignified charcoal suit and hat and everything about him would have suggested that he was a harmless individual, perhaps a university professor, but for the white band with a black swastika on one of his arms that classified him as a Nazi collaborator.

As soon as he was inside, the man asked to talk to our father in private. We dreaded this demand, partly because we were anxious for our father's safety and felt that the presence of the six of us would discourage the stranger from playing any tricks, but mainly because we were all extremely curious since nothing of the sort had ever occurred in Pitigliano. When Father let the man inside the dining room and closed the door behind them, we remained outside with our ears at the door, ready to break in if we heard anything suspicious.

But the two men spoke so softly that not one word reached us. The conversation went on for what seemed a very long time, and we became impatient and fearful. We had just decided to go inside with an excuse, when our father opened the door.

"Sara," he asked Mamma, "go and fetch the studio pictures of the two of us, the ones that were taken in Rome the day of our official engagement."

It took Mamma a long time to dig the photos up from inside the carton where most of the old family pictures were kept. But she finally came back with them, and we saw with dismay that our father gave them to the stranger, who, we noticed, had for the occasion put a sweet expression on his face. Was our father out of his mind? These photographs were very precious to us; what was the idea of giving them away? And what hidden purpose might this man have in asking for them? Father closed the door on our noses again, and again the two men talked softly for a while.

Finally Father escorted the visitor, whose frown had returned to his face, to the door. With the door wide open, the stranger thrust his right arm with the swastika on one side and yelled, "Heil Hitler!"

We were appalled at this sound and, as soon as the door latch clicked behind the man, began to interrogate our father.

At first he was reluctant to talk; he had promised the man, he said, the most tight secrecy, but we made pests of ourselves and promised that whatever he had to say would remain a secret in our family. Father knew that he could count on us, and finally gave in.

"The gentleman is a German Jew who has been able to flee his country with false documents and is now living in Italy pretending to be a Nazi collaborator..."

"And you believed him?" we interrupted.

"Let me tell you the whole story!"

We kept quiet because we wanted to know more, but we were already angry at our father for his naivete.

As the story went, the man had been indeed a university professor, but now he was making a living by enlarging people's photographs.

"When he first told me that he was a Jew, and recited for me the *Sh'mah*, I also didn't believe him—anyone can memorize a Hebrew prayer—and was determined not to give him any information he might request."

"Of course not!"

"But then, when all he asked was a picture or two to enlarge so that he could keep on eating and surviving, I had a sudden inspiration and decided to believe him."

"What inspiration? He is an impostor, don't you see?" We took turns in yelling at Father.

"I thought of it as a possibility. But if he were an impostor all I would lose would be the two photographs and the money..."

"What money...?" We interrupted again. "You also gave him money?"

"Of course, I did. He had to be paid in advance, he could not send me a bill!"

"Oh, Father," I almost cried, "couldn't you have given him just money and not the pictures? We have very little money now, but one day we might have more. But the pictures? Those can never be replaced!"

Our father, who rarely lost his patience with us, began to show annoyance. But, philosopher that he was, he went on to explain to us that giving the man only the money would have offended his dignity. He was aware of the risk involved. If the man was indeed an impostor, he admittedly would have lost both the money and the pictures. But what if the man was telling the truth? Wasn't it his precise duty to help a fellow Jew in need?

Father had a point, and we stopped harassing him. But we all remained convinced that he had been swindled by the man. We honestly didn't mind as much the money as the photographs of our parents on the day of their engagement. They were postcard-size portraits, brown, as studio pictures were at the time, and both of them looked so young and attractive, we had cherished these photographs so much. We had thought of having copies and enlargements made of them, but we were waiting for better times. Now they were lost forever.

We felt our father was an incorrigible dupe.

Learning English

Lida's atelier was the answer to the query of all the out-of-school and unemployed Jewish girls seeking to keep busy. Marcella had joined the group after she finished fifth grade in the private school that had been organized when the Jewish children were banned from public school. Now that Uncle Guido's business had been destroyed by the fascists, I was also free, and I joined my cousin's group for the third time. There was not much work to be done and we were so many to do it; but we were a bunch of young girls together, and for all our deprivations and sadness, we found within ourselves sufficient *joie de vivre* to spend most of the time singing and laughing and finding faults with everyone that passed under our windows.

One of our frequent targets was a young Jewish lady who had come to Italy from Poland a couple of years earlier to visit her sister, who was married and lived in Genoa. The war had caught her still in Italy, and she had not been able to go back to her family. Now the Fascist government—as part of its policy to keep "suspected subversives" and foreign Jews in small villages to maintain better control over their whereabouts—had forced her, together with her sister's family, to leave Genoa and to go in confinement to Pitigliano. There were three adults and two little children in the family; the three adults were to report to the police station every day. First went the two parents while the young woman watched the two boys, and then she would go.

We had not yet met any of the Polish refugees. The reason why we found any fault with the young lady was that she wore funny clothes, very elegant and obviously expensive, but unquestionably out of fashion. To us, who were constantly remodeling and updating our wardrobe according to the tyrannical dictates of Italian fashion, she looked as if she had come out of a fashion magazine of the early Thirties. Aside from her appearance, we really knew very little about her and the rest of the family.

However our father, as the head of the Jewish Community, soon went to pay the new family a visit to offer them help. I went with him, and for the first time I met the young lady, who called herself Bruna, from her Yiddish name B'rucha. I was pleasantly surprised to find her so agreeable. She spoke Italian with a heavy accent, but her grammar was impeccable. She seemed to be insatiably curious and began to ask me thousands of questions about me, my family, the other Jews of Pitigliano and our way of life, while examining me with her piercing eyes. I asked a few questions of my own. As it turned out, she was a very learned person who spoke—beside Polish and Italian—Yiddish, German, French, Russian, and English, and knew Latin and Greek as well. The two of us became good friends and through me she got to know all the other Jewish girls. We, at Lida's, stopped making fun of her, and realized that if things were difficult for us, for her they were even worse. Neither she nor anyone else knew it then, but the visit she paid to her sister at the time she did was what saved her life, since of the numerous family she had left in Poland, not one single member would survive the Holocaust.

The other girls found her a little stuffy, but I really liked her, and I asked her if she would teach me English.

"English is a forbidden language," said Bruna looking intently at me. "If we get caught we will both be in trouble."

"I'll be very careful," I said.

"Why do you want to study English, anyway? The Germans are here, and you should be able to speak German."

"They will not be here for long, I hope. Please, teach me English?"

I stealthily bought myself a notebook and began to go to Bruna's every day. The only English word I had known before starting the lessons was *yes*. But after a couple of weeks, I was able to carry on a simple conversation. Marcella began to go to Bruna to learn German, but even without one single English lesson, she picked up from me whatever I learned, and after a couple of months the two of us knew very little German but spoke good English. Bruna got such a pleasure out of teaching us that she charged us a fraction of what was the going price for private lessons. We were so pleased with Bruna's way of teaching that we recommended her to the other girls. Eventually she became the private tutor for Latin, Greek, Mathematics, French, German, and English for all the Jewish children in Pitigliano.

Marcella and I didn't have a real job; but as girls belonging to the middle class, we were not expected to work for strangers, and in spite of the great necessity for income, staying at home was the "natural" thing to do. Besides, between the house chores, the sewing atelier and the foreign-language lessons, we were certainly very busy all the time.

For Gino, being suddenly without his occupation, there was not such an easy solution. He spent some time writing poetry and essays, and he also began to study French with Bruna, but the need for a paid job was still great. Lello, after losing his position at the bank, had moved to Rome where he was working as an accountant for a Jewish-owned concern. Gino decided to follow his older brother's example and left the family to go to Rome, too.

Lello and Gino Go to Rome

Lello and Gino—by a willful decision of Mamma—were both born in Rome. Even though they had been brought back to Pitigliano when they were only weeks old, they were proud and a little snobbish about their birthplace, and—surely influenced by Mamma—had developed an irresistible attraction for their native city. As soon as they were old enough to travel by themselves, they went to *La Capitale* as often as they could, and during their numerous visits there, they formed many solid and durable friendships. The only aspect of the city they couldn't digest was that Rome, being the seat of the Vatican State, had more than its share of churches, priests, nuns and pilgrims—a disturbing sight for Jewish children who were constantly subjected to smarting, if often subtle, religious persecutions on the part of their Catholic peers. Great Uncle Settimio, a Hebrew scholar, took them to see all the churches that had some Hebrew phrases on their facades—a testimony of past Jewish grandeur, he would tell them. However, although some of those buildings had indeed been Jewish synagogues originally, on some the Hebrew writings had been added by the Church authorities to warn the Jews against trying to make conversions of Christians to the Jewish faith.

Now, as the capital of the first country that had allied itself with Nazi Germany, Rome was the place where all the hideous laws were being engineered. In that beautiful baroque city everyone—but more so the Jews—breathed an atmosphere of terror. Harassments, harsh martial laws, and all sorts of punitive actions on the part of the militant fascists were the order of the day. Rome had lost any trace of its original attraction for them.

Lello and Gino had chosen to go there because Rome, with the largest concentration of Jews in Italy, offered more opportunities for a job within the Jewish community. Moreover, Mamma's relatives and close friends all lived in Rome and would offer economic and moral support to the two youths far away from home. Finally, since Rome had been declared an open city, the likelihood of air raids and bombings was virtually nil. Therefore, in spite of all its drawbacks, Rome seemed to be the best choice for Lello and Gino to go and hunt for a job.

The risks of moving from one place to another were many. It was forbidden to everybody to move even temporarily without a permit, and—Jews having no status—Lello and Gino couldn't even apply for any kind of permit. They had both reached draft age and the police might stop them in the street at any time to ask for proof of their age. In this case they were prepared to make up a plausible story, but they still might be recognized as Jews with all the likely horrible consequences. Nevertheless, these were risks they had no choice but to take.

As expected, Gino found a position in a Jewish-owned firm and for a while things went not too badly for the two of them. Our relatives took turns inviting them for dinner at least once a week, and even though they lived in separate pensions in order not to attract notice, they kept in touch with each other every night.

The whole winter went by uneventfully. It didn't take too long for them to became accustomed to the negative aspects of the city, and in spring Rome—with her thousand fountains and bird songs—was a true delight.

But spring also seemed to have unnested the hawks, and one day, as he walked toward his work place, Gino was stopped by the police and asked for documents. He was not going to show them his ID card with JEWISH RACE boldly stamped across it, so he "confessed" that he was on leave from the army, was from Grosseto and had come to the capital to have a good time; he had just arrived, he told his interrogators, and he had been robbed of his wallet at the station. (He and Lello had rehearsed many times a few such stories they would give the fascists in case they were caught.)

Blond and blue-eyed Gino could easily be taken for an *Aryan*. In fact—he could not believe his good fortune—the policemen actually believed him, and instead of taking him into custody for further verifications, escorted him to the station and put him on the first train back to his supposed hometown, Grosseto, with a *way-bill*.

When Lello didn't see Gino at the usual place of their encounters that night, he began to worry. He made the round of all the hospitals, the morgues and the jails in town, and when he could not trace him anywhere, he figured that Gino must have gone back home. And in fact a few days later he received a card signed GINO from Pitigliano.

Pitigliano was also beautiful at this time of the year with its globe acacias drooping with clusters of white, heavily scented blossoms. The screeching of hundreds of swallows rushing back and forth past our windows announced that summer, indifferent to human vicissitudes, was keeping its rendezvous with the flowering fruit trees. Soon there would be plenty of cherries and we wondered whether some of our old Christian friends who owned orchards would invite us to pick as many as we could eat, as had been the case in the past.

But nobody approached us.

Between the rampant inflation and the lack of income, our savings were thinning out frightfully. If it hadn't been for Father, who was still called by some farmers to keep their books and paid him with their produce, we would have been near starvation. Cousin Lida had no more work to do, and Marcella and I didn't bring home even the few pennies Lida shared with us at the end of the week, in the rare occasion that she had been lucky to have a paid job.

The lack of income, however, was not Gino's major problem. Marcella and I kept busy helping Mamma with the household chores and using our inventiveness to make food stretch almost indefinitely. We mended and darned and knitted (using yarn that had been retrieved by ripping old, torn sweaters and underwear). For relaxation Marcella read and I drew. Mario was attending the makeshift school for Jewish children and was busy with schoolwork. For Gino there was not much to do. Had Lello been around, the two of them would have kept each other busy and challenged. But without Lello he was at a loss, and being idle at his age was neither desirable nor pleasant. Gino—just as Marcella did—liked to read, but there was a limit to how much reading a vigorous and active youth could do day in and day out.

Even though the season was marching towards the warmest days of the year, Gino finally resorted, as an occupation, to going into the forest to cut wood for the coming winter. He borrowed a hatchet from a friend, and every morning, after eating a piece of dark, heavy bread (we often wondered whether they made it with sand), off he went on his bicycle to cut and bring home some wood. He was not able to do more than a couple of pieces at the time because his palms had become sore with blisters. Gino, a poet and philosopher, was not cut out for this kind of work. But he had plenty of time. The blisters soon gave way to calluses, and cutting wood was better than staying home all day long doing almost nothing. In fact what he liked to do at home, he could do better in the open. He always took with him a book or two to read, and his inseparable notebook where he entered his thoughts and feelings. He even wrote novellas, filled with philosophical insights and poetic depictions of the sylvan landscape.

Mamma was happy to see him around. One child away from home in these terrible times was enough worry for her.

Chapter Six

Menacing Clouds Gather

E ven though by now we had become aware of the approaching storm, we still trusted our fellow humans. However, important events were soon to take place which would have dire consequences for us.

Full Moon

Franca's vivid accounts of the bombings had made such an impression on us that we could envision the destruction as if we had actually seen it. Marcella and I were terrified by what we had heard and never talked about it, but one night an unusual thing happened: we did express our concern and fear.

"Where will they go tonight?"

We uttered these words in perfect unison. Ordinarily, whenever it happened that we said the same thing at the same time, we would burst out laughing hysterically while trying to beat each other to the next convulsive phrase. But this time we didn't laugh.

"I didn't know you were awake," I whispered toward Marcella's bed. "We said good night over an hour ago."

"I knew you were not asleep," Marcella replied. "Who could sleep on a night like this?"

The night was crystal clear: a beautiful, warm, early summer night. The Meleta, the little stream rushing over its pebbly bed down the valley below, and the wild bamboo canes under our window aroused by the gentle night breeze, were vying with each other to send forth a refreshing murmur. From our beds we could see the full moon through the rectangle of the wide-open window. Just on such a night, exactly one year later, the heart of Pitigliano would be rent by bombs. But this June night in 1943, on the eve of Corpus Christi, we didn't have to worry about ourselves. We knew that the American bombers were only striking military targets in much larger cities. It was not until later in the war, in fact, that they began to bomb small villages as well, as the front advanced north.

Marcella and I couldn't sleep because we also knew that such a bright and clear sky made the buildings in the cities visible despite the black-out, and that on nights such as this the American bombers were spreading terror and death also among thousands of civilians somewhere. On the other hand, the thought of the Nazi-fascists winning the war was even more terrifying, so we regarded the air-raids with a secret feeling of hope, too. In our family the American bombers—whether they were Liberators, Flying Fortresses, or Constellations—were always called *the liberators.*

It was not easy at our age (I was seventeen and Marcella thirteen) to cope with fear and hope at the same time. Especially not in the middle of the night. To dispel our anxiety, we tried to associate the full moon with more romantic thoughts. We began to talk about boyfriends. Boyfriends! We didn't have any. Not that we weren't attractive; but there were no eligible Jewish boys in Pitigliano, and by now, five years after the official persecutions had started, the Christians weren't even talking with us, let alone making love! Besides, my sister was still too young and I didn't believe she had yet had any experience with boys. And as for me, though not so young, I was emotionally immature for my age. Brought up in a sheltered household by a progressive, naive father, and a puritanical mother whose main concern seemed to be what other people might think or say, I had the unrestrained coquetry of a very innocent girl. My association with the street children coupled with the wing-clipping experiences of working for Signora Elisa and Uncle Guido at a young age had greatly contributed to my being a living contradiction. At seventeen I had not so much as kissed a single boy—well, with the exception of that one time when I was kissed by my cousin Raffaele, a bachelor of nearly thirty to whom I was kind of betrothed.

Raffaele had been an only child, had never married, and, at thirty, still lived with his parents in a Tuscan villa on the beautiful coastline of the Tyrrhenian Sea. I had visited my aunt many times as a child, especially in summer, but Raffaele had never taken notice of me—not even the time when I was fourteen and I thought that I had fallen madly in love with him.

The previous fall, however, during a weekend trip my parents let me take by myself shortly after I had retrieved my money from Manciano, things had been different. Raffaele had taken me to see Puccini's romantic opera, *La Fanciulla del West.* On the way back from the theater, I let him kiss me on my mouth, and I quivered with a hitherto unknown sensation, as if my whole body was melting.

"What a kisser!" remarked Raffaele. "Who taught you to kiss like this?"

"Nobody!" I replied offended. "You are the first one who ever kissed me on my mouth!"

"Not even Engelbert, your German friend?"

A chill ran up and down my spine. How could he think, really, that I would let a German soldier kiss me?

"No, Raffaele," I said resigned to the fact that he seemed to have made up his mind and would not understand. "I have told you time and again that words, letters, are all I have exchanged with him, and now even this platonic relationship is over."

I don't know whether he believed me or not, but he seemed to be relieved by my reassurance, and after a while he told me that for quite

123

some time he had been thinking of me with love that wasn't precisely brotherly, and would I marry him?

He took me so much by surprise that I didn't know what to think and how to react.

I was wearing a white sweater with a little pink house topped by a red roof and surrounded by tall trees embroidered on its front. Raffaele passed a finger gently around the contours of the little house and said, "Wouldn't it be marvelous to have our own little home for you to be the happy lady of the household, and for me to find you there when I came back from the hospital at night?"

It didn't seem to me to be such a good idea. Even though Raffaele was remarkably young-looking for his age, I was still a baby next to him. And marriage, at sixteen, was the furthest thing from my mind. But being fondled and kissed by him—a doctor who had been educated in England and was constantly surrounded by flocks of beautiful, rich, and sophisticated young ladies—what flattery!

Without giving myself a chance to think it over, and without really meaning it, I responded affirmatively to his proposal. The next day he communicated the news to his parents, and they seemed enthusiastic about his decision. That same day I went back home (where my mother was much less enthusiastic about the idea of my getting married to a first cousin!) and we began to write to each other.

Seven months and many letters later (which by now had become less frequent and devoid of any enthusiasm or real meaning), the memory of those first kisses and of those promises had considerably faded away.

My sister and I had no *real* boyfriends to talk about, but had, on occasion, met non-Jews in nearby villages and fantasized about those Christian boys.

Suddenly, the thought of Engelbert, the German soldier whom I had met in Porto Santo Stefano, came vividly into focus. Thirteen months had now elapsed since I had met him for the first and only time; at least ten since I had received his last letter.

"I wonder what happened to Engelbert," I said.

Marcella pretended she hadn't heard me.

"Sometimes," I sighed, "I feel sure that his superiors found him out and..."

"Not at all," interrupted Marcella impatiently. "It's more likely that he found another girl."

I hoped so.

I tried to push the thought of Engelbert away, but it persistently came back to me. Since I wasn't able to sleep, I began to talk about him. As usual when I spoke about people Marcella didn't know, her interest waned and the conversation became a monologue. I became very loquacious and my sister very quiet. But I went on undaunted as if guided by a force beyond my control. With a wealth of minutiae, I went over every detail of the unusual circumstances under which Engelbert and I had met, until I had reached the point when I had received his last letter in which he had declared his unconditional love and his intention to marry me when this horrible war was over.

Even though I knew that I would never be able to marry a non-Jew, and much less a German, the idea that Engelbert might have died because of me, or even only made to suffer, didn't give me peace of mind.

"Do you really think he is still alive, Marcella?"

My sister was sound asleep.

It must have been close to four o'clock in the morning by now, since the metallic moonlight had given way to the softer and more diffuse light of pre-dawn, and I, too, fell into a deep, dreamless sleep.

Engelbert Returns

I was awakened a couple of hours later by Mamma—her hair disheveled and her morning bathrobe unfastened—trying to get me out of bed and explaining at the same time that my German friend—God help us—was at the door—so early in the morning—and wouldn't come in. Half-naked, I hurled myself at the door in disbelief, shocked at the sight of Engelbert. He stood there, his cap in his hands, his chin on his chest, almost unrecognizable all covered as he was with a thick layer of whitish dust. A dusty old bicycle was leaning on the parapet of the terrace.

"Won't you come in?" I almost screamed, and tried to pull him into the house. But Engelbert resisted and without raising his head he said, "I feel ashamed to enter a Jewish home wearing Hitler's uniform."

When Mamma and I finally got him inside, he refused to sit. He insisted that he must speak with my father.

Father was an early riser. All his life he had been going to temple every morning before sunrise to recite *Shacrit,* the morning prayer. Raimondo the *shamash,* a distant relative who helped him with his religious duties, would call him from under the windows when it was still dark: "Azeglio! Whenever you're ready!..."

The Temple, in the past few months, had been shut down by order of the fascists, but Father, after reciting the morning prayer at home, kept his habit of leaving the house early. Normally by this time he would be on his way to meet the farmers to buy a few fruits and vegetables cautiously and inconspicuously. But on Corpus Christi, the Catholic holiday when the statue of Christ the King was carried in a procession from the Duomo through the main streets of the village, the farmers wouldn't open their stalls. Moreover, it would have been embarrassing, if not dangerous, for a Jewish leader to be seen in circulation on such a day. When Engelbert arrived, Father was still in his room.

Marcella had been awakened by the commotion and came to meet the much-talked-about German soldier. The young soldier was standing between the huge dining table and the rickety upright piano Father had bought for me from a second-hand dealer, together with a pair of German army boots for Gino. On the wall directly behind him hung the two brightly colored reproductions of Moses and Aaron by an unknown early Dutch painter. From my angle I could see that Engelbert's frizzy and dusty blond hair was being touched by the slender fingers of the two Patriarchs. Marcella went to call Father, while Mamma and I began to ask Engelbert millions of questions; but she ran right back in order not to miss one word of what was said.

We learned that Engelbert was now stationed in Sardinia. On his first leave in more than two years, instead of going to see his mother in his village up north, he had decided to come and see me and my family. It hadn't been easy. He had reached the port of Civitavecchia with a military ferry-boat, hitch-hiked his way to Porto Santo Stefano, borrowed a bicycle from a friend there, and covered the more than sixty kilometers to Pitigliano by night, hoping not to be seen by anyone.

We were stunned by Engelbert's account. His behavior was not only unusual for someone who served in the German army—it was indeed unique!

Engelbert Berner was born in a village of the Alto Adige, an Italian area near the Austrian border where sectarianism and contradictions thrive side by side. Individuals have been forever divided into pro-Italian and pro-Austrian factions, and often families are torn by this geopolitical issue. It was not rare that one member of a family fought on the Austrian side and another on the Italian side when the two countries were enemies during World War I. Engelbert was certainly not a Nazi, but he had chosen to be an Austrian citizen. He had been drafted by the German army as an interpreter because he spoke both Italian and German equally well, had calligraphic handwriting, and could type. In his role as an interpreter, he learned about things that nearly nobody in Italy knew, and this knowledge had prompted him to come to see us.

When Father entered the dining room, Engelbert stood straight and almost at attention. After a brief introduction of himself, almost all in one breath he made a long speech about the atrocities that the Germans were committing against the Jews (he did not specify) and warned my father to leave.

"Please, don't let them get you," he concluded.

Father looked at him, half incredulous, half amused, and said, "Where am I going to go? With a wife, five children and no money?"

"Go somewhere," said Engelbert. "Change your name. Do something."

"No, young man," said Father. "I am sixty years old and blameless; here is where I was born and lived all my life respected by everyone. Nobody is going to do me or my family any harm."

Then with that sense of fatalism which people of irremovable faith possess, he added, "If God decrees that I should suffer or perish, let it be His will."

It was Engelbert's turn to be incredulous this time, and he started to insist, but there was a sudden and strong knock at the door that made everybody freeze. Someone had informed the Carabinieri that a German soldier had been seen entering a Jewish home and they had come to get him. There was no big scene or explanation. They simply asked the young German soldier to go with them. Engelbert moved toward the door ahead of the two carabinieri, without resisting and without uttering a word; but as he left, he gave me and my parents a long, imploring look.

I got dressed, prepared a small bag with some food and a tooth brush, and headed for the headquarters of the Carabinieri. On my way there I saw that the clergy, the fascist authorities (including the lieutenant of the *Real Carabinieri* in dress uniform), much of the population, and the municipal band were all gathered in the Piazza del Duomo ready to start the Corpus Christi procession. The coordinators, holding the banners, were running up and down along the forming cortege, shouting at the top of their lungs, trying to arrange the groupings and to get the pageant started. Everybody was dressed up, excited and cheerful.

Before the racial laws had forbidden Christian help from working in Jewish homes, Eda, who had been hired when Mario was born, had been part of the Corpus Christi procession. (Mamma had always encouraged all of our maids to practice their religion whichever way they saw fit.) In my mind I saw Eda barefooted, her long hair falling disheveled, all wrapped in a light blue, silky drape; holding an amphora with both hands on her left shoulder, she represented Mary Magdalene.

I ran as fast as I could to the Carabinieri headquarters and lied to the sentinel on duty who interrogated me.

"I have just met the lieutenant at the procession. Caught in the religious fervor of the moment, he gave me permission to visit the prisoner."

The young man probably did not believe me, but pretended he did and let me pass. Another carabiniere ushered me through a long corridor, opened the door where the prisoner was held, and left me there.

I entered the dark, narrow cell and closed the door behind me. Engelbert was standing near a small window, carved high near the ceiling, looking up toward the sky. He slowly turned his head when he heard the door being opened and shut again, and a smile lit up his face when he saw me.

"I brought you some food," I timidly began. Engelbert gently drew me to him and held me in his arms without saying anything.

It was the first time that we had such intimacy. It felt good; at the same time a feeling of uneasiness crept into my consciousness to be cuddling in the arms of a German soldier—even though Engelbert had never behaved like a German at all.

After a moment, Engelbert told me his mother's name and address in his native Italian village in the Dolomites near the Austrian border, and repeated it several times, making sure that I wouldn't forget it until I went home and wrote it down.

"My mother," he assured me, "would pretend that you and your family are relatives from another city and would let you stay with her until the war is over." He paused to think for a moment, then he added, "Your older brothers, of course, would have to stay in hiding."

One more tender hug, and then he insisted that I go. If the carabinieri released him without reporting him to the German authorities, he would have a chance. But if the lieutenant found *me* there, who knows what he might do.

I dashed out without looking back, repeating to myself the name and address of Engelbert's mother, and I matched it with the rhythm of my loud steps on the cobblestone-paved Ghetto streets I took in order to avoid the Corpus Christi procession.

At home nobody asked any questions; they were just relieved to see me back. I threw myself on my bed emotionally exhausted, a whirl of confused thoughts crowding my mind. Although what Engelbert had told my father seemed unreal, a vague presentiment of doom pervaded my whole being.

I lay there in that nebulous state for a long time, but all of a sudden the thought of Raffaele appeared clear in the midst of the confusion. I had to let him know what had happened that morning. I was still sort of engaged to him and would not keep any secrets from him. I got up and went to write a long letter with all the details of Engelbert's visit (leaving out, of course, that he had said about his fellow German's treatment of the Jews).

My "confession" caused the breaking of our engagement. He wrote back to me that he was appalled at *what I had done.* Even though his letter arrived badly censored, it was clear to me that he didn't want to have anything to do with me anymore. I felt terribly hurt. Raffaele had failed to see the goodness and the risks involved in Engelbert's action, besides having misconstrued *my* actions.

I was neither in love with my cousin nor with the German soldier, but now I felt that my little world of make-believe romance was crumbling too suddenly. The news of the breaking of my engagement to Raffaele was a great relief for my mother, but I was inconsolably lonely. I had no close friends, no one to talk to. Had I been a Christian, I thought, I could run to confession and talk matters over with my spiritual leader... Not a bad idea! Don Omero, our good friend Don Omero Martini *was* a priest; perhaps he would be able to help me. The next day I went in tears to talk out my desperation with... a Catholic priest!

When he heard my story and saw me so dramatically upset, Don Omero asked me, "Do you really love your cousin so much?"

"Why, yes! I can't live without his love."

"Would you be ready to give your life for him?"

"I don't know... No, I don't believe so."

"Then all you are feeling now is the anger and the frustration that come with rejection. You are very young, my child, and have not experienced true love as yet. You'll soon get over this pain, I promise you."

He escorted me to the door, saying, "You have a whole future ahead of you!"

Don Omero's words didn't make much sense, the future was an abstract concept I could not grasp; there was only now and me—my poor, desolate me with a huge void inside my chest.

But as I walked home still in tears, I had to admit to myself that I was feeling a lot better.

The Bombing of Rome

With Lello still in Rome and hardly any possibility of communicating with him, we worried. Did he have enough to eat, was he lonesome, had he been caught and not so lucky as Gino had been? The censorship had been tightened, and rather than risk making the authorities know of Lello's being in Rome, we didn't write at all. Only once in a while did we get in touch through postcards we exchanged with Nonna Fiorina or one of the other relatives, signing the message with a false name, just to see one another's handwriting. But even this minimal contact had to stop.

There was no use in writing anyway. No mail, including family letters, was allowed to be written in one's own idiosyncratic fashion. It was forbidden to begin a missive with the usual salutation, "Dear Grandmother," for example, or have a closing such as "Love" or "Affectionate-ly." Simply, "Grandmother!" was the government accepted standard form of addressing a member of one's family; and "*Vinceremo!*" literally, "We shall conquer!" was the only closing that was allowed—indeed compulso-ry—before the signature. And the body of the letter was closely scru-tinized to make sure that it did not contain anything that might sound even remotely critical of the regime. It took tremendous skill for anyone to be able to write even the most innocent of family letters which would be delivered untouched by the inexorable ink of the censors.

Uncle Aldo in Milan, a civil engineer well known in Italy for having designed and built, among other major works, the Acquedotto Pugliese, was an astute and convinced anti-fascist, and the only one among us who was able to write letters that confounded the fascist censors. They were written in the style that would please them, while expressing all his true feelings of antipathy toward the regime with allusions and metaphors which those blockheads were unable to decipher. With the exception of Uncle Aldo's letters, we largely depended for news of relatives who lived in other cities on the occasional friend who would visit Pitigliano. When a long time passed without hearing from any of our Roman relatives—and therefore from Lello—we became anxious.

Lately, we had let him know that Father had been suddenly hospita-lized for surgery, and the outcome of the operation was anybody's guess. We'd urged him to come home. But now—July 19, 1943—ten days had gone by since our note to Nonna Fiorina, Father had successfully under-gone a complicated operation and was back home, and we still hadn't heard from Lello. Father was puzzled that his older son, usually so sensitive and caring and responsible, had not yet shown up. We did our best to cheer our father up, but he hardly spoke and went to bed very early.

We also went to bed, as usual, as soon as it had become dark. With the imposed blackout, the best way to prevent artificial light from filtering out through the windows even when the shutters were tightly closed was, of course, to keep all the lights off. Besides, it was very hot: we had to keep the windows wide open to let the evening breeze in.

A few minutes after going to bed, while I was still in that twilight state of half wakefulness that precedes deep sleep, I jumped out of my bed screaming, prey of a terrible nightmare. What I had seen was a huge fire enveloping everything. I heard the howling of hundreds of dismayed human voices, then a fast knock at the door, and Lello's agitated voice: "Open, it's me; they have bombed Rome and I came home!"

Everybody was awakened by my screaming, and when I told them what I thought I had seen and heard, Gino went to open the door. He looked right and left and called out for Lello, but there was no Lello there, nor anyone else.

"Nobody's at the door," he said.

"It was only a bad dream," said Mamma, hugging me.

We went to report to Father who calmly commented, "Rome, having been declared an open city, will *never* be bombed."

"Right," said Marcella curtly. "Let's go to sleep."

I felt quite embarrassed, but no one made a big deal of it and we all went back to bed.

A few hours later, in the heart of the night, almost the same scene took place again. There was less screaming on my part, but when Gino went to open the door, Lello was indeed there. I was the first one to run and hug him, almost to make sure that I was not dreaming this time.

Lello was perturbed and in great need to talk. But rather than letting him, we assaulted him with question upon question.

"What happened? Didn't you receive our note? Why didn't you come sooner? Did you have an accident?"

"Rome was bombed shortly before dusk," said Lello excitedly, without paying any attention to our questions. "Quartiere San Lorenzo with its beautiful Basilica," he continued, "has been heavily damaged and many hundreds of people have died, and many more are wounded!" He was still under shock at having witnessed the terrifying event.

Instead of asking questions, now, everyone looked at me with wonderment. I too was flabbergasted. Was I seriously empowered with extra sensory perception? Many times before, since my early childhood, I had had experiences that could not be explained rationally. I was convinced that they fell under the category of *psychic phenomena,* but when I talked about them, neither Mamma nor anyone else took me seriously: they either said that what I reported was the fruit of my imagination, or called my premonitions sheer coincidence. I learned to keep my thoughts to myself. This time, however, there was no need to tell anybody that something peculiar had been going on. I didn't need to feel frustrated, because finally what happened to me had been witnessed by others. But the thought that I could actually see things that were happening far away from my sensory reach frightened me.

Lello went to change into his pajamas, then we all moved into our parents' bedroom, so that Father could rest while listening to Lello's story.

He recounted with vividness and a wealth of detail the bombing of Rome, and I didn't want to miss one word. But in spite of Lello's exciting descriptions, my mind kept wandering back to the events that had preceded his arrival. Once in a while I felt someone glancing at me as if to say, "How did *you* know?" I didn't know how I had known, but it was a fact that I had, and I acknowledged to myself that together with some trepidation my E.S.P. gave me also a measure of gratification.

Lello had received news of Father's illness only that morning and had wanted to leave immediately, but in order to settle a few practical matters, he had postponed his trip for a few hours. In fact, he was about to leave for the station when he heard the unbelievable news. The bombing had created general chaos throughout the capital. But before going to the station, Lello managed to reach Quartiere San Lorenzo. His curiosity and his humanitarianism were in conflict with his filial duty, but the former had prevailed. Instead of running home to see for himself what was what with Father, he remained for a few hours at the scene of the disaster to help remove the rubble so that the dead could be carried away and the trapped wounded could be assisted—and to be a witness to such an unexpected event.

The Fall of Mussolini

July 9, 1943—the day our father had undergone his surgery—coincided with an important historical event: the Allies' landing in Sicily.

When Father regained consciousness from the anesthesia, Mamma was at his bedside with the evening paper.

"Look, Azeglio," she said with the intent of cheering him up, happy herself to see him coming back to life. "The Allies are already in Italy, the war will soon be over!"

"Not so soon," predicted Father with a feeble voice. "But you might be right that things will begin to brighten up a little."

Now, ten days later, Rome had been bombed in spite of the open-city declaration, and we didn't know what to make of it. Who was to be blamed for all this destruction? Why had the Allies not respected the declaration? Were the Germans preparing something foul? Indeed, there was much that remained unanswered, although the latter hypothesis was likely to be closer to the truth. But we were happy to be together again with Father at home regaining his strength.

One night, just a few days after the bombing of Rome and Lello's return home, the news reached us that the twenty-year-old Fascist Government had been overthrown by a coup d'etat organized by a few members of its own old cabinet. This sudden turn of events provoked terrible confusion among the populace. But for Lello and Gino it only meant one thing: Rome had been freed from the dreadful yoke of fascism and nothing would be more exciting than to be there *now*. They couldn't resist the lure of going to see the city of their birth wearing its new hat, and early in the morning they took the first bus, eager to get there.

They arrived when many people had not yet heard the news or had not believed it. Fascists who were leaving their homes wearing *l'orbace*, the black uniform, were assaulted and beaten by anti-fascists. It was not in Lello and Gino's nature to participate in any violent actions, but they did join those who were smashing fascist murals and slogans, and got a great deal of pleasure in finally seeing some justice done.

A new *ad hoc* government was formed by a group of politicians headed by Marshal Badoglio. In order to prevent bloody confrontations among opposite factions, it was necessary to impose a strict curfew. Lello and Gino were enjoying themselves too much to pay any attention, however, and remained out after 9 p.m.—the time set for the curfew— believing that for them it would not be enforced. As they wandered through the almost deserted streets of Rome, they saw a long line of people marching in an orderly fashion. They became very curious and approached the group—only to find themselves forced to the end of the line by the police who were taking the curfew breakers into custody.

Lello and Gino protested, "We just arrived from out of town. How else are we supposed to go home?"

The guards—the same ones who had served in the Fascist Regime until a few hours earlier—did not bother to answer. They kept on arresting people who were still out in the streets, as they marched everybody to the nearest precinct to be interrogated.

By the time the law breakers reached the police station, there were so many of them that there was hardly any standing room inside. The air was so thick and stuffy, it was almost impossible to breathe. The officer in charge began immediately to question people to determine whether they had a legitimate reason for being out at that hour—in which case they would be released with a special pass—or were provocateurs. Although Lello and Gino had thrown away their bus ticket, Gino, who had been a salesman and still kept his annual train pass in his wallet, produced it as proof that he had just arrived by train from out of town, and he was given permission to go. Lello, however, who had nothing to show, had to spend the night in jail.

The next morning Gino brought Lello a sandwich and used all his salesman's charm and shrewdness to get him out of that miserable place, and finally succeeded.

With the country liberated from the tyranny of fascism, Lello and Gino felt sure that they would immediately regain full citizenship. However, the fascist anti-Semitic laws were not abrogated despite the change of government, even though a political amnesty was immediately enforced.

All this was very peculiar. Fascism was no longer in power, yet the war against the forces that fought fascism was still going on, with Italy still allied with Germany. If the Jews were to be given citizenship and enlisted in the army, the paradoxical situation would occur that they would have to fight on the side of the Germans.

So the Jews were left in a political limbo. At the same time, all the political activists who had been kept for years in confinement in the most backward parts of the *mezzogiorno*, where civilization with the capital "C" had not yet made its appearance, were freed and came back. Among them was our cousin Giorgio, Lida's twin brother, who couldn't make out why he had been banished from his home in the first place, having been a pious Jew never politically involved, and the Fano brothers, two Jewish prominent dissidents from Rome, who were indeed very involved, and came to join some Grossetani members of their family who had taken refuge from the bombing of their city in Pitigliano.

Lello and Gino, still in Rome, decided to stay for a while, and wait there for new developments. But no real changes were in sight for them, and they finally resolved that the time was ripe for them to go back home. Luckily for them. Had they remained in Rome long enough, their destiny might have concluded tragically. A few months later, when 33 Germans were killed by partisans on Via Rasella—a short, winding street in the center of Rome—the Germans blocked that street at both ends and took all the males they could find there. Then, to implement their punitive ten-to-one rule, they went to Rome's main jail and rounded up all the Jews who had escaped the first deportation and had been subsequently caught and imprisoned there (68 of them), and enough other prisoners to reach the number of 330—335 for good measure. The Jews were treated, as usual, with extreme brutality.[1] The Germans then took these men to the Fosse Ardeatine—a huge cave southeast of Rome—massacred them, and left the fallen bodies there.

In Pitigliano we were all in a state of uncertainty and weariness. The fall of Mussolini, as we began to realize, had only brought us an ephemeral relief.

The Armistice

Father was still convalescing from his complicated surgery and seemed to have lost his flamboyance. We all suggested that he spend a few weeks in Fiuggi, a resort famous for its mineral water, where he had enjoyed a few vacations in the past.

"We have to preserve our savings for a rainy day," he protested.

But it was pouring already, we knew that he needed a break from all the tension at home, and we all chipped in to encourage him to take his vacation. Toward the middle of August, he finally went.

At Fiuggi he met Marshal Badoglio, the statesman who had taken

1. Giuseppe Mayda - *Ebrei sotto Salò* - Feltrinelli, Milano, 1979, p. 236.

charge of the Italian government after the fall of fascism, and who was there for a short period of rest. The two men enjoyed a daily game of bocce. One day when Badoglio didn't show up for his game, Father knew that the statesman had been called back to the capital for some important decisions. With this in mind, he himself came back home.

A couple of weeks later, it was announced that Marshal Badoglio had signed an armistice with the Allies.

That day—September 8, 1943—was a sorrowful day for many Italians, but tragically so for Italian Jews. The Germans, who until now had been Italy's allies, were suddenly transformed into an army of occupation.

At first, the news of the armistice was received by most with euphoria. Throngs of people poured into the streets and played and sang and cried and embraced one another. "The war is over!" was the cry that stood out. But as it turned out, we had not yet seen the worst.

The Italian army immediately disbanded, and the days that followed offered the spectacle of a great number of men—first one at a time, then in a steady stream—who began to fill the main roads and the back paths, filing past villages and countrysides, going north, going south, or in any direction wherever their homes might be.

We girls were bewitched by the sight of all these men of all ages (but mostly young) and from all walks of life, in battered uniforms or in poor civilian clothes, armed with rifles, pistols and hand-grenades or just a water bottle. Our families were terrified for us and imposed a curfew. This made the sight of all those men even more attractive to us and we managed to be out on our own once and even got to talk with some of them.

"Is the war over?" I asked one soldier with a reddish mustache.

"I don't know," answered the young man. "But if fighting starts again, this time I will fight *against* the Germans!"

"Do you have any cigarettes?" asked his fellow traveler.

"No," giggled Marcella and Franca Cava, who were now inseparable. "We don't smoke!"

But I, since my old friend Franca from Signora Elisa's had initiated me to smoking when I was fourteen, was secretly smoking a few cigarettes a day, and offered the soldiers the two or three I had.

"Where did you get those gorgeous eyes?" asked the red-haired soldier looking intently at Franca.

Franca blushed to her ears and pulled my sleeve. We wished the boys good luck and bid them good-bye before one of our brothers caught us talking to them.

The Fano brothers—the two outspoken anti-fascists from Rome who had returned from confinement right after the fall of Mussolini—were able to sort out events in a more realistic fashion than any one of us could. They saw no point in our unwarranted optimism. They could foresee that the peace treaty with the Allies while the Germans were still among us would have tragic consequences for the nation. We Jews, especially, would pay the highest price for this tactical error. Vito and Salvatore Fano saw the situation for what it was and had no illusions about the outcome of future events. They advised us to go into hiding, and within a few days they themselves with their relatives vanished from Pitigliano. This was the second time in three months—first the German soldier and now the Fanos—that we had been warned to be wary of the Germans and to go and hide ourselves. But once again, having no inkling of what was really happening in the rest of Europe, we didn't listen.

After the march of the returnees ended, a seemingly calm atmosphere had enveloped Pitigliano, which everybody accepted as a welcome relief. But the Fanos' predictions proved right.

A new Fascist Government was formed to continue to fight the Allies. The new republic set up under German control in the northern town of Salò attracted the most ruthless of fascists, and nothing but catastrophe could come from the collaboration of these two evil forces. We, in Pitigliano, were under their rule.

After the excitement that followed the armistice, we fell into a greater depression, not knowing which way to turn. Our conversations revolved more and more around the uncertainty over what might happen to us, and this uncertainty was taking the joy out of our lives. Even the children's play took on a morbid character. Father was the only one who never lost his faith and by now he had regained his spirit. He knew who, among the peasants he had helped in the course of years, were trustworthy and decidedly on our side. He secretly kept a list of these people and was counting on their benevolence in case of an emergency.

BBC - Its Silence on the Fate of the Jews

Our communication with the rest of the world had been completely severed when the Fascists confiscated our radios in 1942. The only source of news was the government-controlled media, which was filled with propaganda and lies. We did manage, once in a while, to listen to the BBC, but only at tremendous risk both to ourselves and to the Christian friends who allowed us to listen.

One such friend was Don Omero Martini, the young priest I had gone to see when I met my first disappointment in love. Don Omero, who had remained somewhat sympathetic to us, was not a conventional priest of the time. The majority of the clergy, like the Pope himself, at best kept a conniving silence about the atrocities committed by the Fascist Government against the Jews. At worst—like the Parish priest of Latera—they preached from their pulpits ferocious and inflammatory accusations which convinced many that the Nazi-fascists were right in their treatment of the Jews, and scared many others into not helping us.

But Don Omero was not quite in the mainstream. He was ahead of his time—indeed a precursor of the rebelliousness that took place within the Catholic Church two decades later. He defied some of the Church's dicta with pleasure and would, once in a while, let us listen to his radio.

Don Omero, an accomplished pianist with a powerful tenor voice, let us visit under the pretext of making music and singing operatic arias together. Of course, the music we made was to cover our heated political discussions and our attempts at organizing ourselves for the underground world of the Resistance. When we went to visit Don Omero, we took various precautions: one of Lello's few non-Jewish friends who still talked to us—Sesto—would go ahead to make sure that Don Omero was alone and free to receive us. After a while, if Sesto didn't come back, we knew it was all right for us to go too. One at a time, we dashed across the street to the large doorway and sneaked inside the dark vault and staircase that led to the apartment.

"Welcome, welcome," Don Omero would shout, hoping to be heard by someone outside. "What shall we sing today?"

Inside his home, where he didn't wear the cassock and starched collar,

Don Omero looked like an ordinary man. Only his countenance revealed his spiritual training and his religious commitment.

He would begin singing *Il Lamento di Federico* from Cilea's *L'Arlesiana*. But as soon as the boys located the London radio station, Don Omero and I would sing over and over the duet from the final scene of *La Boheme*, while they listened to it. Our voices mingled with the four opening notes of Beethoven's Fifth Symphony ("V" for victory), which were followed by the coded messages in Italian, such as *Rosina's slippers are too tight..., the elephants eat the snow..., the horses paw the ground...,* et cetera, and by the war news reports. The boys could hardly hear anything between the deafening whistles and other interferences added by the censors and our loud singing. But it was better than the offensive lies of the official press and radio.

This way, little by little, we learned about what was going on at the various military fronts. As for the fate of the Jews in the rest of Nazi Europe, however, nothing was ever mentioned. We were kept in the most complete darkness.

In spite of our precautions, the ecclesiastical authorities came to know that Don Omero was involved in helping some Jewish and anti-fascist youths. He was severely admonished to keep away from politics and was warned that if he didn't stop mingling with rebels, he would be transferred to another village where they would keep close tabs on his activities. Don Omero begged us to stop our visits, and even that tenuous thread that linked us to the free world was broken.

Trust Versus Reality

Had we been less trusting, and somehow able to face the horrendous reality that engulfed us, we would have paid more attention to the bits of information we received here and there, no matter how vague and imponderable they seemed.

In addition to Engelbert's warning that the Germans were doing *bad* things to the Jews, and the Fano brothers' plea for us to go into hiding, a third warning came from our new dentist. We had no idea why he seemed to know so much, but as a matter of fact he too, like the others, cautioned our parents. He told them that he had known all along that we were Jewish, that he knew for a fact that the Germans were indeed doing *bad* things to the Jews, and insisted that we all go into hiding. But he said nothing that even remotely suggested the horrors of the extermination camps, either because he did not know the full extent of what the Germans were really doing, or for fear that nobody would believe him.

As it was, nobody believed him anyway. Yes, there were rumors among our non-Jewish acquaintances about the existence of "work camps" in Germany. But, again, not only were they just rumors, hearsay, but they spoke of *work* camps, not *death* camps. What could the Germans do to us? Make us work? If need be, we would go and work and become strong... And besides, who would tell the Germans that we were Jews? The dentist was a refugee from the bombing of a large city, probably Milan, judging from his accent, and he obviously was an anti-fascist. But what did he know about our village where we were born and lived all our lives? Nobody would hand us over to the Germans!

So, we kept up our dreary life at home, one day indistinguishable from another.

Part 4

STORM

Marcella and I, seated, with some of the farm girls we met at Il Castellaccio and Le Capannelle. Photo taken after liberation.

Chapter Seven

Illusions Shattered

I f until now we had lived with the illusion of being safe in our village, the time soon came when we had to face the horrendous reality—and it took a stranger to warn us of impending danger. Although many Pitiglianesi must have been aware of it, none of them alerted us.

16 October 1943

Autumn arrived without much fanfare. The end of September in Italy can be beautiful and warm—a true extension of summer. But our spirits felt as cold as the coldest of winters. It was said that the new republic's fascists would go relentlessly after young men who had not yet joined the army, and September 24, 1943, was the designated day for the search.

Lello and Gino—who not only were draft age, but Jewish to boot—got up in the middle of the night to run with a small group of young people to the farm of a friend. (On that day, I suffered my first, huge, most unbearable migraine.)

After a couple of days they came back.

Periodically, when the word got around that the *repubblichini*—as the Republic of Salò fascists were disparagingly called—were out to round up the draft evaders, Lello and Gino ran into the woods with those youths who had no intention of serving alongside the Germans. To their dismay, however, my brothers discovered that as Jews they were not welcome even among these anti-fascists who were only beginning to talk about partisan formations. This rejection from people with whom they shared a common intent was even more painful than the one that came from the declared enemies. They had to swallow insults and innuendos in order to keep abreast with what was going on about the emerging Resistance.

After a while, when nothing came of the rumors, they would all come back to Pitigliano to resume their normal activities, but Lello and Gino went on living on the alert, trying to be as inconspicuous as possible.

We were all trim and slim by now, but Gino, a very active adolescent with a hearty appetite, suffered from hunger more than any of us and often went to eat leftovers at Aunt Lidia's. Her husband, Uncle Tranquillo, was still allowed to work in the privately owned bus garage of the Desideri brothers and had more than we.

One Sunday evening, on his way home from one of his visits to Aunt Lidia's, Gino met Felice, the husband of our former maid Santina, who had moved to Rome with his family many years back to become a doorman.

"What are you doing here?!" asked Felice looking at Gino as if he were seeing a ghost.

"What do you mean what am I doing here?" said Gino feeling a sudden pang of anxiety. "I live here!"

"Haven't you heard what happened in Rome last week? The Germans rounded up thousands of Jews from their homes. There are rumors that they were taken to Germany."

"What are you saying?" asked Gino, who didn't want to believe what he had clearly heard. "You are not serious!"

"I have seen them with my own eyes. Many were taken from my

building. At first we thought that they were looking for able-bodied men to take them to work camps, so as soon as I saw a German truck all covered with a coarse black drape approaching my building, I sent Santina to warn the men to hide up in the attic. But then I saw those beasts drag down into the wet street and push into that awful truck all the women, the old, the children, the sick.... They didn't spare anybody. The hand-icapped, or those who put up any resistance were spurred with the butts of their guns, accompanying the blows with shouts of the most heinous insults. Many of the men who had been hiding came back to their apartments, afterwards, only to find them empty, and one or two came down in time to jump into the truck with their families. Some had blankets wrapped around them, but some were in just their pajamas, and it was drizzling and mighty cold! There was a lot of confusion, men asking questions, women screaming, children crying...."

"We couldn't do anything, Gino!" added Felice guessing the unspo-ken question.

Gino felt sick to his stomach. He wondered how he would break the news to Mamma, who was from Rome and had all her family there. He went straight to bed saying that he was not feeling well.

The next day, over lunch, Gino finally got around to telling what he had heard from Felice. It didn't even occur to us that among the many that were caught in that first round-up there might be some of our relatives, much less our beloved grandmother, Nonna Fiorina. The newspapers had not reported one word about the incident, and although this time we believed that it was true, we preferred to think that Felice had grossly exaggerated the figures.

It was not until the end of the war that we learned the full story about the Jews who were deported from Rome, a great number taken that morning, and many more at different times. Over three thousand Roman Jews [1] were made to suffer inhumanely and then gassed by the Germans. Among those who were first rounded-up the morning of October 16, were in fact our relatives—our grandmother Fiorina Baraffael; her daughter, Aunt Rita Di Capua, who had never married and considered us to be almost her own children; Great Uncle Giacomo Di Nepi, a stately gentle-

1. Liliana Picciotto Fargion—*L'Occupazione Tedesca e gli Ebrei di Roma* Carucci Editore Roma—1979, page 42

man who had been recently widowed and lived with his daughter; his daughter Celeste Pergola, her husband, an attorney, and their daughter Eleonora, a gorgeous girl of thirteen whom Gino liked immensely and had pledged to himself and to Mamma, half-jokingly and half-seriously, to marry when she would be a little older; and many other close relatives and friends. Uncle Marco Di Capua with his wife, Bice Piperno—a half-Jew, and their two children, and Uncle Giuseppe Di Capua with his non-Jewish wife Emilia and their three children, were also rounded up that morning. But because of their mixed marriages, they were released before the actual deportations.

That morning—according to eyewitnesses—Cousin Celeste had gone out early to stand in line to buy some food for her family. (Even though the Jews were officially denied the ration card, most of them in large cities retained one under a false name.) She returned home just in time to see her father, husband, and only daughter shoved by the Germans into the "death truck" (so called by the Romans because these trucks used to round-up the Jews, had been painted black and covered with black cloth) that was beginning to move. On the impulse of protecting her beloved ones, she dropped her purse and her shopping bag, and ran like a mad-woman towards the truck to share the destiny of her family.

This operation of dragging people down from their warm beds when most of them were still asleep was very efficiently staged and choreo-graphed by the Germans, who carried it out without the full participation of the Fascists, although "... a few fascist repubblichini were seen circulat-ing with an arrogant frown ... and a satisfied air as if it were a festival".[2] It started in the middle of the night with a frightful four-hour-long barrage of gun fire near the site of the Ghetto, intended to scare people into making no attempt to escape. In the very early morning hours, the round-ups began throughout the capital and lasted a few hours. The Germans would enter a building where it was known that Jews lived (they had accurate lists), force themselves into the homes, and give the terrified residents a small note with a few orders, which included, "Take all your money and jewelry" and "be ready to leave in 20 minutes."[3]

The Jews were taken away from their home in front of thousands of

2. Giacomo Debenedetti-16 Ottobre 1943—Einaudi, Milano, 1961/Sellerio, Palermo, 1993, p. 60.
3. Giacomo Debenedetti - Op. Cit., p. 51.

eyes. Nobody moved a finger to stop the Germans—from fear of reprisals, to be sure, but also from the indifference that comes upon people when calamity doesn't touch them directly.

The first place where the rounded-up people were taken was the Collegio Militare. Here, among the shouting of the orders given in German and repeated in Italian by an interpreter, and the general confusion caused by the sheer number of people who could not begin to understand what was going on, a few were able to escape. But over 1000 Jews were arrested in Rome that day and soon deported to the death camps in Poland. Many more were captured in later round-ups, bringing the number of Roman Jewish deportees who perished in the German camps to 3175. [4]

But at the time we were ignorant of all this. All we knew was what Felice had told Gino.

Jack and Jay

One bright autumn morning toward the end of that ill-famed October, when our dejection had taken the form of a chronic malady, the monotony of our existence was interrupted by a sudden crackling of machine-gun fire. Heedless of the danger, we dashed to open the window to see what was going on. We witnessed a scene that was so new and exciting that we wouldn't want to miss it no matter what: two small reconnaissance airplanes were engaged in what seemed, at first distant glance, a graceful dance. They got close, drifted apart, circled each other, got closer again, skirmished.

Signora Maddalena, the new refugee who occupied our old apartment right above our present one, rushed down in her morning robe, a pair of strong mountain binoculars in her hands. Even though she had always behaved cordially when we met on the terrace, it was a big surprise to see

4. Liliana Picciotto Fargion - Op. Cit. p. 42

her in our home at this early hour. Obviously the sudden appearance of the two little airplanes almost at our eye level in our rarely traversed skies, had prompted her to come down to share with us this singular experience. But why with us? It seemed peculiar.

Through her binoculars, we could now see that the two little planes — one American and one Italian—were engaged in a duel to the death. We watched with excitement, taking sides with the American plane, but trying not to show our feelings to our neighbor. After all, we still did not know Signora Maddalena well enough, and even though it was apparent that she was not an anti-Semite and not likely a fascist, we'd better be cautious.

Suddenly the machine guns stopped sputtering. One of the airplanes banked and disappeared in the distance while the other, the American one, began to tumble down like a wounded bird. We saw two balls being ejected from it and at first we thought that they were bombs. But as the plane crushed to the ground in flames, we realized that the two bundles falling from it—now with the parachutes open—were two human figures. We could hardly contain our joy and prayed in our hearts that they would not be shot from the ground. The two silhouettes soon disappeared behind the treetops on the other side of the valley.

Lello had been the last one to look through the binoculars when the two figures disappeared from our sight. He calculated exactly where they had fallen, and without uttering a word left the house in a hurry. He went to call his friend Spartaco, who put together some of his raggedy clothes, and the two rushed to the rescue. They had to move fast and arrive where the two Americans had fallen before the fascists. Spartaco, a hunter, was as familiar with the countryside as he was with the streets of Pitigliano. With him in the lead, they took short cuts down the valley, waded the stream, then climbed the other side and ran toward the column of smoke.

They arrived near the burning plane before anyone else, but there was no time to waste. Lello and Spartaco quickly searched around the aircraft, then they began to move in an easterly direction, farther away from the village.

Without knowing the language and the surroundings, the two Americans couldn't have gone far. They wouldn't dare to move by daylight; they had to be nearby, awaiting nightfall. It was not long, in fact, before the two searchers spotted the khaki uniforms of the two aviators, who were lying in a ditch. They found them shaken, frightened speechless, but miraculously unscathed. Still under shock from the recent experience, the two Americans, even though armed, readily gave themselves up to the two unarmed strangers. Lello who knew a couple of English words, extended his hand toward them in reassurance.

"Welcome!" he said. Then, pointing at his friend and at himself respectively, he added, "Spartaco, Lello—your friends."

The chubbier of the two Americans took a deep breath, and conquering his mistrust mumbled, "I am Jack... and this is Jay."

The young Americans must have thought that they were in some sort of a dream. They had been defeated in a battle with the enemy and were hiding in enemy territory; their plane was burning and so must have been their spirits at the frightening prospect of what the future might hold. And out of nowhere, two strangers appear to tell them not to worry, they are now with friends who are here to help. They had no time to recover from the shock, but the sudden presence of these two well-intentioned young men must have seemed some kind of miracle.

In the distance they saw some urchins advancing rapidly towards the burning aircraft. The four young men quickly made for the woods.

After walking for quite some time, they came upon an abandoned old farmhouse. Here Jack and Jay changed from their uniforms into Spartaco's old clothes, and for the first time since the battle had started, they looked at each other and smiled. Spartaco was a tall and skinny fellow and his clothes looked funny on them. The smile broke into a contagious laughter. They laughed and laughed, nervously, hysterically, happy to be alive.

At this point Lello left. It was agreed that Spartaco alone would take the young Americans to a farm a few kilometers away.

All the eligible men in the farm area were at war, and although some had come back after the armistice, a great number of them had lost their lives on the battlefields or were prisoners somewhere. The old patriarch, the women, and the children all worked hard to carry on the farm chores, but they could use a few more pairs of strong hands, and escaped prisoners of war—whether Russians, British, New Zealanders or whatever— were welcome. Jack and Jay, fresh from college and basic training in the American air force, became overnight... two Italian peasants.

Lello came back incredibly excited. Signora Maddalena had long left our apartment, so he talked freely of everything that had happened since he had left the house precipitously a few hours earlier. But he did not tell us where Spartaco had taken Jack and Jay. Some of us might inadvertently drop a word about it and jeopardize their safety and that of the farmers who sheltered them.

Those two Americans were the first Lello had ever seen in all his life. Even though they had been defeated and were in great danger of being discovered and imprisoned, or even shot, it seemed to him that by merely meeting them he had been touched by a breath of hope and security. They represented the world of freedom and democracy the five of us had never known.

"Think of it!" Lello kept repeating. "I met two authentic Americans!"

America, the mythical country of our childhood dreams, was so far away... And Lello had actually met two of her children! We were enthralled.

Signora Maddalena

If the first half of the autumn had been like summer, the latter part brought furious winds and very cold days. Nights were even worse. They foretold an unfriendly, frigid winter. We had very little food to put into our mouths, but thanks to Gino we had plenty of wood for our kitchen stove. There was no other source of heat in the house, and we spent most of the time in the kitchen, gathered near the stove, reading or knitting, waiting for something extraordinary to happen that would bring some bright changes into our dingy lives.

More than a month had passed since the first German raid in Rome that had cost the Roman Jewish community so many lives, and we still had no confirmation of what Felice had reported to Gino. Mamma had written several postcards to her relatives, and no one had written back to us, but this did not alarm us since the postal service was used almost exclusively for the soldiers at the fronts. So we kept up our optimism about the fate of Nonna Fiorina and all the other relatives and friends in

Rome from whom we hadn't heard.

In the meantime, we heard rumors (rumors, rumors again!) that the Jews of Pitigliano would have to report to the fascist police to be taken to an Italian concentration camp. This measure—still according to rumors—would appease the Germans and we would safely wait there for the end of the war. A few meetings were held by the heads of the Jewish families, but there was disagreement on what action to take and no firm decision came of them. Besides, there was no way to confirm or deny the veracity of these rumors. If the rumors reflected some truths, we expected the authorities to spell out our verdict, and since nothing was officially announced, we continued to endure our miserable existence at home, taking one day at a time, still waiting for something to happen.

On the night of November 27, 1943 *something* did happen. The seven of us were gathered around the kitchen table when a knock at the door startled us. We immediately interrupted our somber conversation and our meal and looked at each other with ill-concealed anxiety. Lello and Gino, who in the last couple of months had been going back and forth between the village and *la macchia* (literally, the woods, but now a name that symbolized any refuge from the clutch of the fascists and the Germans), happened to be home that night. They ran into the dark room adjacent to the old Hebrew school—as they lately did at the least unfamiliar sound—and from there, if necessary, they could descend to the piazzetta and dash toward the countryside hopefully without being seen.

Father, with his calm and serene countenance that instilled in all of us great courage, wiped his mouth and went to unlatch the door—which opened into the vast kitchen through a small entrance hall—the white napkin still in his hand.

Signora Maddalena slid inside, and bringing her forefinger to her lips, closed the door behind her. We almost didn't recognize her in her modest coat, her hair disheveled, her face half hidden in a dark kerchief knotted under her chin in the manner of the old peasants.

This was the second time that this mysterious and beautiful lady had come down to our apartment uninvited. What could she possibly want from us? Her visit at that unlikely hour didn't promise anything good.

Before Mamma had a chance to offer her a chair, she told us in a muffled but matter-of-fact voice, "Do not waste one minute. Gather the few things you can carry with you and run into the woods. At any moment the fascists may be here to get you and hand you to the Germans."

We were astounded. Who was she? Why should we listen to her? How did we know she was telling the truth?

Signora Maddalena read disbelief in our faces. But this was not the moment for explanations. She firmly repeated that we do what she had suggested without wasting precious time, and quickly vanished through the door.

As the door latch clicked behind her, the boys came back from their hideout. For the first time, after so many previous warnings we had disregarded, we *knew* that we no longer could keep our heads buried in the sand. Some implications of what Felice told Gino finally penetrated into our consciousness. We couldn't pretend that the evil that was engulfing us would disappear of its own accord; this was our last chance to take matters into our hands and fight for our survival.

We all now stood around the kitchen table, but nobody felt like eating any more. We looked down at our unfinished supper in a perturbed mood, without uttering a word.

The Flight

Father was the first to break our gloomy silence. His speech was brief but every word was deliberate as if he had been preparing himself for this moment for a long time.

"This is a shipwreck," he said recognizing that all of us would have to be responsible for our own survival from now on, *"si salvi chi può!"*

After a brief pause he added, "Mamma, Mario and I will remain here until I have had a chance to warn the rest of the Jews, then we will see. The four of you are old enough to decide for yourselves."

Again there was a deadly silence in the kitchen. Then Lello, the only one with a sharp vision of the situation, vividly expressed himself against Father's decision to remain behind.

"Why do you want to make it easy for the executioners? Why don't we all go into hiding?"

"I cannot relinquish my responsibilities," answered Father. "In fact," he added with his usual naivete, "if I let them take me, the Fascists will be happy with having arrested the head of the Jewish community and will not take too much pain to try to capture the others."

Lello insisted, but Father would not yield. Lello then tried to persuade him to allow Mario to decide for himself, but Father was resolute. Mario was still too young, and it was up to him to make the decision for the boy.

During the whole argument, the rest of us hadn't moved, nor had we taken sides.

Neither Mamma nor Mario had any say in Father's decision. Mario was still a child, true, but did he have an opinion and not dare to voice it? What went on in his mind? Nobody really knew and nobody asked him. In a matter of life and death, the decision was made for him.

Mamma, at times, didn't quite consider our father's wisdom infallible, but in this particular instance, if she had any ideas of her own she kept them to herself. *"The wife follows her husband"* had always been her motto. She was not going to break her pattern at such a critical moment.

"I'm taking to *la macchia*, " I heard Lello say.

"I am going too," Gino added immediately.

Almost automatically, I echoed Gino.

For Marcella the decision didn't come so easy. She was not ready to separate herself from our parents, but neither was she willing to relinquish her freedom. The three of us held our breaths while her eyes shifted despairingly between the side of the table where our parents and Mario stood and ours.

We were all aware of time running out. Every moment of delay might prove fatal. But we said nothing. Finally Marcella, although torn by uncertainty, chose to come with us.

Father went to write a few letters to those farmers he knew to be trustworthy, asking them—in the name of their old friendship and reciprocal esteem—to give us shelter and food until things would get better. Meanwhile, the four of us got busy selecting what we would take with us while Mamma put together for us the little food that had remained on the table. Then she put her heirloom jewelry inside a porcelain candy box, and wrapped a linen handkerchief around the box knotting the four corners together to keep the cover tightly closed. She gave the little bundle to me and told me to bring it to the family of Assunta the wet nurse. Should we all perish—God forbid—Mamma wanted these wonderful and generous people, proven anti-fascists and friends, to have these valuable objects. And if we came back, she trusted them to give our precious jewelry back to us.

When the time came to say good-bye, Mamma could no longer contain herself. Her sobs penetrated our hearts. Father gave us the letters he had written to his friends, and raised his hands over our heads to impart his *b'racha* on us. We bent toward him, our heads touching, as we did when Father blessed us at the Temple during the High Holy Days, holding his oversized woolen *tallit of the Chacham*, with black lateral stripes and corner fringes, over his head and ours. We then kissed his right hand, which used to hold the *tzitziot* bunched in it, and hugged him. He enjoined us to love and respect and always to be helpful to one another.

Mario, all the while, had been following now one and now another of us silently, holding his kitten Mustafino tightly to his chest as if searching in this soft and warm contact the answers to questions bigger than himself. We hugged and kissed him, and we hugged and kissed Mamma in order of age, the oldest first.

When it was Marcella's turn to hug Mamma, they fell into each other's arms and kept so tightly embraced that we almost had to tear them apart by force. Mario then in a generous impulse stretched his arms toward Marcella and handed her the kitten muttering, "Here, Marcella, take him with you, I don't need him." Marcella brought Mustafino to her wet cheeks and stumbled toward the door. Lello, Gino and I were following close when another knock at the door paralyzed our legs. The three of us turned without making a sound and hastily disappeared into the dark room. But Marcella, as if nothing mattered anymore, kept on walking and automatically, unthinkingly opened the door. A blond, muscular young man stood at the threshold who looked more like a German than an Italian fascist. For a moment our parents' hearts sank. But it was neither! It was only Bassano, the orderly of Signora Maddalena, who had come down to bring us some of the ricotta pudding he had made for his colonel's family, and to make sure that we wouldn't linger around too long. His presence helped us overcome the agony of the moment.

With Bassano still standing at the door, we left our home, our parents and our nine-year-old brother behind to plunge into the unknown.

Assunta the Wet Nurse

We made our first stop at the edge of the village, at the home of Assunta the wet nurse to leave our jewelry and say good-bye. She insisted that we spend the rest of the night at her home to have a chance to make some plans. We ate our leftover supper, but, unaccustomed to sweets, we decided to defer our pleasure and to leave the delicious smelling ricotta pudding for the next morning. We sat in front of the hearth trying to determine what we would do next.

For the moment the four of us would stick together, without particularly looking for the partisans, who were not yet organized anyway. We would seek shelter wherever we could find it, and leave the farmers on our father's list as a last resort.

Assunta—whom we called the wet nurse because she had in fact breast-fed one of Aunt Lidia's children—was a stout woman, generous, but not at all talkative. She and her whole family were friendly with all of us, even at this juncture, when most other people either ignored us or were openly hostile to us. She went to look for something to give us, but she didn't have much to spare and came back from her bedroom with a small pouch full of dark tobacco.

"Take it with you," she said. "It will come in handy, I am sure."

I slipped the little packet into one of my coat pockets, next to an envelope full of my most precious photographs.

It was around one o'clock when we finally lay down over a couple of mattresses on the floor and tried to get some sleep. After a few hours of restless dozing, while the countryside was still immersed in the deepest darkness, we got set to go.

Each one of us had looked forward to the moment of sharing Bassano's pudding—a little bit of sweetness in the midst of so much sadness. But the first disappointment of our adventure was awaiting us. The ricotta pudding—which we had left on top of the table together with our knapsacks —had vanished. What we found in its place was the empty paper with a few crumbs attached to it. And the thief, little Mustafino, had taken to his heels through the cat hole.

Marcella was inconsolable. She, too, had looked forward to a piece of something sweet and was disappointed, but what grieved her most was the disappearance of her beloved Mustafino, who represented home, and on whom she had counted to provide her with some comfort in the days and weeks to come.

Long before the first glimmers of dawn, we were on our way. The air was icy, our faces and hands and feet soon became numb with cold. Lello guided us through unfamiliar woods over uneven terrains, down the valley, through the little river, over the other side of the valley, until we reached a plateau. We walked and walked, four trembling shadows, panting and silent. The sky was overcast and even when the sun rose we didn't see or feel it.

Through the mist we perceived a farmhouse in the distance. Stopping at an unknown place meant taking a chance, but we were too cold and too hungry to pass it up and we decided to stop, if for no other reason than to get some information. We arrived when the family was about to sit at the table to eat their first meal of the day. The sight and the aroma that was released from that smoking-hot golden cake of polenta on the kitchen table, ready to be sliced and topped with shredded fresh pecorino cheese, made our mouths water. But we didn't dare ask for anything. We stood at the threshold, our eyes on the polenta and the heap of cheese, unable to talk or move.

Then the unexpected but much-hoped-for, happened: the man of the house—one of the few who had come back from the army—asked us if we had had breakfast. Our eyes lit at the prospect of a hot meal.

But Lello, mannerly and ceremonious, answered, "Thank you, we've just eaten."

The three of us looked at him with such ferocious eyes that the farmer understood that Lello was being polite. He asked us in, insisting that we share in their meal. We took our filled dishes, sat in front of the fireplace, and ate ravenously without uttering a word. The farmers all looked at us quite amused. The women and the children, from the kitchen table, asked us a lot of questions and we lied about our identity and our place of origin. We said we were refugees from the bombing of our city and were going to stay with some relatives who had a farm some distance away.

"Tell me about the bombings, the bombings, the bombings!" screeched a little boy all agog.

We were not sure whether his excitement meant that he was amused or scared or absolutely ignorant of the meaning of the word he kept repeating. But we complied nevertheless, mostly to corroborate our story. Marcella and I had heard of the bombings from Franca and Enzo, and Lello had actually witnessed the bombing of Rome, so it wasn't hard for us to relate with a profusion of details. Before they would discover who we really were, though, we thanked them and went out into the cold again. Fortunately, by nightfall we had found a farm where we were able to sleep.

The next day we were not so lucky. We found people who slammed their doors on our faces, and even someone who knew who we were and threatened to hand us over to the Germans. But eventually we slept indoors. On the third evening we chanced upon a farmhouse full of self-styled partisans, and from one of them we learned that our parents and Mario had been seen in a farm nearby. We became wild with joy: our father had finally opted for freedom! The next day was his 60th birthday, and we would go and surprise him and celebrate together. At night, over the heap of straw that was my bed, I dreamt of presenting my father with the pipe tobacco Assunta had given us. We got up before dawn and began to walk toward the place where the rest of our family had found refuge. I put my hands inside the coat pockets anticipating the pleasure we would give Father with our little gift. But my pockets were empty. Someone during the night had stolen the few little things I was carrying with me, including my precious pictures and the tobacco!

Father's Birthday

I got very upset. I had chosen, among my collection, the most beautiful photographs to carry with me and look at when I would feel lonesome or scared. Now they were in the hands of some stranger and I had lost them forever. Weren't the partisans supposed to be better, more responsible than the fascists?

After a while I calmed down. My two brothers were able to convince me that I had plenty to be thankful for that at least my coat itself had not been stolen, and I shouldn't make a fuss about my photos or the tobacco. After all what really mattered was not carrying some symbols or bringing a present to our father, but being all around him with our love on his birthday, and becoming a whole family again. I tried to push the thought of the stolen things away and looked forward to meeting with our beloved ones.

We walked without feeling the cold, the hunger or any hint of fatigue. Marcella was laughing excitedly as we marched on. We arrived at the farm in the early afternoon. We knocked at the door full of expectations and anticipation, our hearts dancing in our chests. The door was opened almost immediately by a middle-aged woman whom we had seen a few times in our home. She dropped her jaw agape at seeing us.

We didn't pay much attention to her and whistled our family whistle to alert our family of our presence. But we didn't hear our father's whistle in response.

"Where are they?" we almost sang in one voice.

The woman looked at us with a sad face without saying anything. "Where are our parents? We were told that they were here!"

"They left this morning."

"Where did they go?"

"They didn't say. But they were very unhappy here. Your mother was coughing all the time. It was impossible for her to squat in the cold for her bodily functions—pardon my expression. She cried a lot. I really think they went back home."

Mamma, being born and brought up in Rome, was not equipped to adapt to the backwardness of Pitigliano (which she had nicknamed "the village of the flies and of the donkeys"), much less to this even more primitive environment. But the main problem with her, was that she had chronic bronchitis and emphysema. We could see how difficult it would be for her to endure the rough life of the peasants, the life even we— Pitiglianesi, young and healthy—had a hard time getting used to. But going back home? That meant suicide. They couldn't have done that.

Father's sixtieth birthday had passed without our being able to hug him and give him our love and best wishes. However, we felt sure that it would be not too long before we could be reunited with him, Mamma and Mario.

160

"You can stay here for a couple of days, if you wish," the woman offered. She was feeling sorry for us. We also felt sorry for ourselves, but we mainly felt frustrated.

We thanked her, but we could not bear to be in a place where our parents and Mario had stayed, now that they had gone. Besides, we wouldn't give up. We didn't believe that they had gone back home. We had to try and find them.

As we went from place to place in our desperate search for the rest of our family, however, it became apparent that the four of us could not stay together: we were much too conspicuous. One day soon we would try to locate our father's friends, but for the moment all our efforts were directed toward trying to find our parents and Mario. We split—Lello with me and Gino with Marcella—and marched in two different directions. We had no idea of where we would be going, but we knew that we did not want to lose each other. Before separating, we agreed on where and when to meet again.

Arrest of the Jews in Pitigliano

After another two days of aimless searching—it was now the fifth day since we had left our home—yet sustained by the thought that we were still free and sooner or later would find our parents and Mario, Lello and I met a draft evader from Pitigliano. He was walking alone, toward the farm of some relatives of his. We stopped to ask him whether he knew if our parents had gone back to Pitigliano. Yes, they had, he told us, but he gave us the horrible news that our parents and Mario had been arrested.

"What do you mean *arrested*?" screamed Lello. "Where? When? Are you sure?"

"Everybody knows about it in town. Most of the Jews apparently were tipped off and left before the fascists came to get them, but a few families were taken."

"Which families? Can you tell?" I asked.

"The family of your uncle Tranquillo, of his brother Adelmo, and those foreigners with those two beautiful children, I can't recall their name."

"The Poles with those two boys?"

"No, those other people from Livorno."

The Cavas. Franca and Enzo Cava and their parents had also been taken.

"What else do you know, where are they taking them, when?" asked Lello frantically.

"The bus with the prisoners will leave tomorrow morning and make the round, on route 74, of all the places where Jews are known to live, and then it will head north. That's all I know."

We parted from the young man, who did express his regret for what was happening to us, and decided to go immediately toward route 74. We would wait near the bridge over the Fiora River.

Nightfall found us not even halfway toward our destination, and no farm was in sight. We spent part of the night in a cave almost freezing to death. I had gathered a few twigs and started a fire. At first it felt good for a change to have one side of our bodies almost burning, even as the other side was freezing. But then we realized that the smoke might attract the attention of the fascist squads, so Lello insisted that we extinguish the fire. We lay next to one another to keep our body heat from escaping, but the terrain was humid and icy cold. We were two pieces of ice ourselves, and felt sure that we would soon die.

There was no way that we could rest. We got up and began to jump up and down and to clap our hands on our arms to keep our blood flowing.

In the middle of the night, tired of all this exercise, we left. We walked a long distance to reach the main road, dreaming up ways to free our parents. We arrived at our hideout and waited full of hope.

Then we saw a bus coming down the road and as it got nearer and nearer, we realized that it was the one with the prisoners. We wanted to do something to stop the unthinkable from happening, but without help any move on our part would have proven suicidal.

Leaning against the slope down the side of the road, our toes and fingers swollen from incipient frostbite, trying not to be seen, we saw the bus that carried our parents, Mario, and the other Jews to the site the Fascists had set up as an interim concentration camp until the Germans would decide on the prisoners' final destination.

Our anguish was unimaginable. We hugged each other and wept.

We walked the long way back to the meeting place we had established with Gino and Marcella and found them waiting for us. It was good to be together, but we had to break the news. Their fresh pain renewed ours.

Searching for Food and Shelter

Together we took off in search of food and shelter. During the first couple of weeks of our peregrination, we became somewhat familiar with the area. We moved from farm to farm during the night and stayed in hiding during the day. We didn't have a compass, and didn't even own a watch between the four of us, but we learned to read the sky. We used the North Star and the rising and setting of the moon for our orientation, and learned to tell the time from the position of Ursa Major, our friendly Big Dipper. On cloudy or rainy nights, we could not move. But we did move on new-moon nights, when the darkness was so complete that we had to hold hands for fear of losing one another. Sometimes the crackling of the ice under our feet, which accentuated the vast silence of the winter nights, was the only sound we heard besides our own panting, the occasional howling of a stranded animal, or the barking of a suspicious farm dog.

At night we didn't fear the fascists. Our major enemies were cold and wild animals. Gino and I wore boots (I—selfishly—had taken my father's riding boots the night of our flight from home, and Gino had a pair of old German army boots which Father had bought from a second-hand dealer). But Lello and Marcella were walking with their dress shoes—the only ones they owned—which were beginning to wear out and to let water in. Their feet developed very painful frostbite.

Our strategy was never to remain at the same place more than a couple of days, not even when we found friendly farmers willing to give us shelter for longer periods. It was a harsh life, and the thought of Mario and our parents, always with us, rendered our wandering more intolerable.

Much as the thought of a new separation frightened us, we decided to split again. Four youths, delicate in appearance and behaving differently from the peasants, engendered suspicion; but mainly it was difficult for any one farm to put up and feed four extra persons. Besides, those farmers who were willing to help were already sheltering one or more outlaws: draft evaders, escaped POWs, Jews.

By the second half of December, however, we had located two of our father's friends, one of whom did not yet shelter anybody, and the other had only one *guest*. With these we felt secure and decided to stay for as long as they would have us. Marcella and I were left in these two separate farms, Il Castellaccio and Le Capannelle, close to one another, while Lello and Gino went on to make contacts with other men, promising to come back periodically to visit.

Around Christmas, Gino came to Le Capannelle to spend a few days there with me. Lello had remained in another place and Marcella was still at Castellaccio.

Chapter Eight

Adapting to a New Life

How different was the life of the farmers from anything I had known at home! Only a few kilometers separated us physically, but a whole world of cultural dissimilarities had for centuries been standing between us—and still was.

Life on the Farm

With most of the young men at war, the farmers were quite busy even in these slumbering winter months. Every able-bodied member of the family had to perform a number of different tasks. Since each farm was almost completely autonomous, there was spinning of flax and wool to be done; weaving and knitting, dressmaking and alterations; shoemaking and shoe repairing; wooden and iron tools to be carved and forged; roofs and floors and furniture to be maintained; animals to be fed and shod; straw and hay stacks scattered by the winds to be rearranged, and so on. I was assigned to some of the household chores, but was mainly entrusted with teaching the children to read and write. Gino was immediately put to work with heavier jobs such as carpentry and cutting firewood.

With no electricity and little else to illuminate the long December nights, everybody went to bed—most of the time—right after supper and evening prayer. All of us made our way to bed holding a long flax straw that had been lit by blowing on the graying embers of the hearth (matches were a rare commodity and the hearth was kept afire all the time). Several hours before sunrise, everybody got up to start the day. While most went to tend their morning chores (to the barn to feed the animals and change their beds by the light of an oil lamp or inside the house to tidy up), some attended to the preparation of the first of the two meals of the day: polenta.

It was only after the farmers had put in two or three hours of heavy work that they came into the kitchen for their first meal. Depending on how poor or well-off the family was, polenta would be served either with only a dish of boiled dried beans and wild dandelion, or with cheese, pork, lamb meat, baccalá. A piece of bread and a slice of salami or prosciutto would in any case finish the meal.

Supper, the other main daily meal served at dusk, also varied according to means, of course, but generally consisted of a hot minestrone soup, some sort of protein, and lots of unsalted sourdough bread. A quick grace was recited before the meal, and before retiring for the night everybody had to remain seated for the long rosary, which comprised three prayers of devotion—*Our Father, Hail Mary, Glory be to the Father*—repeated a fixed number of times, with the leader—generally the elder woman of the household—reciting a verse and the entire family responding in chorus. In most cases there was no church within a radius of several kilometers, and the farmers found spiritual and religious gratifications in these nightly prayers.

There was no plumbing on the farm. People washed superficially with well water and used the open space for their bodily needs. I remember the first night that the girls, before going to bed, asked me to go out with them. My siblings and I had already learned that we had to hide behind a bush or a tree whenever we had a need to go; but the *going out* at a fixed schedule was new to me. As I quickly learned, it was part of the farmers' code that a girl, no matter how imperative the need, should not go out by herself, but wait until a large group of girls was ready too. So I went with them. The girls squatted, forming a semicircle, and talked and giggled and exchanged gossip while liberating themselves of their body wastes.

"Did you have a boyfriend back home?" asked one of the girls.

"No," I answered, amazed that anyone could talk about boyfriends while engaged in such unromantic activities.

The only accepted form of entertainment available to the peasants was *la veglia*, a gathering at one of the neighboring farms, which took place after supper and went on until the wee hours, mainly on Saturday nights and on the eve of holidays, but also, on occasion, on Tuesday and Thursday nights. There was a rigid etiquette regarding *la veglia* (or any other social behavior). People would go visit their neighbors only after a formal verbal invitation had been extended to them. These gatherings gave the farmers a chance to get dressed up, to exchange forecasts on the upcoming weather, play a game of cards, and dance to the tune of an accordion or a guitar. When an instrument was not available, someone would whistle a tune, since dancing was a very important part of the entertainment. As *la veglia* progressed, the men engaged in the dance with their sweethearts would call out to one another in loud voices from various parts of the room.

"*Che la duri!* Let it last forever!"

"*Non si faccia mai giorno!* May dawn never come!"

For the young folks of both sexes, *la veglia* was the only means by which they got to know each other better and the place where they began wooing. A girl who would be seen even just talking with a boy on the fields without the preliminary official courtship and the consent of the families, was considered a flirt or much worse, and nobody would want to marry her.

During this crucial period of the war, every farm whose owners were anti-fascists, or at least not actively pro-regime, accommodated a number of transient people—partisans, escaped prisoners of war, Jews—who would help with the farming in exchange for food and shelter. Gino, like all the men who didn't belong to the household, slept in the barn next to the animals; I, like all the female guests (there were fewer of these), shared beds with the female farmers. This was most difficult for me to take. I had been used to bathing every night before going to sleep, and this had to be reduced to soaking my feet in a small earthen basin with water heated on the fireplace (a practice that made my brothers and everyone else poke fun at me, since we were running for our dear life) and I had to give up many other good habits altogether. But sharing a bed with someone else was something I hadn't done since I was four and had occasionally slept for a few hours at a time in the large bed with my parents. I had never slept with strangers, however, and now I thoroughly disliked it and could not come to terms with it.

The farm girls were more sexually conscious than girls living in urban areas. They were exposed all day long to the sexual activities of the farm animals, the watching provided arousal, and a lot of sex play took place among them at night in their shared beds. My bed companions didn't understand why I would resist and shun what came so natural to them—a behavior well-accepted and even encouraged by the adults, since it precluded the risk of pregnancy!

Once in a while there would be a girl who didn't abide by the rules and preferred to play with the boys in the fields. But she would become an outcast, and pay a high price for her unconventional behavior. Such was the case of twelve-year-old Wilma, who played with her brother-in-law and saw her belly grow before she ever saw her first menstruation!

First Love

When Gino spoke to me, I was only half-conscious of having heard his voice, wholly absorbed as I was in my own reveries. After our morning tasks, we had come out to the porch to relax in the sun for a while. Gino was reading a book by Martin Buber and I was knitting. I was making a sweater with the rough sheep's wool yarn I had spun with the rudimentary spindle Gino had carved for me. The farmers had given me some fleece, and I was able to put the skills I had acquired as a child into good use. Not only had I spun, doubled and twisted the yarn myself, but I had also washed it in the icy-cold water down at the creek and bleached it white by letting the fumes from burning sulfur go through it—a process the farmers must have used for centuries, and which I had recently learned from them.

I hadn't heard Gino, however, not because I was absorbed in the difficult pattern of my knitting, but because I was daydreaming my latest favorite dream: Arthur. I had met him a few days earlier and I was going over in my mind, time and again, that beautiful moment.

The setting was the present farm; the time, the early afternoon hours on the day before Christmas. Everybody on the farm was busy preparing for the big holiday. Gino had just brought into the kitchen a pile of firewood and was resting near the hearth. I was shining my boots on the window-sill of the staircase landing overlooking the dirt road, when I spotted in the distance a man approaching the farm. I interrupted my job and ran to inform my hosts.

"It's the foreman!" someone yelled.

Gino and I dashed to hide in the attic.

The foreman was a fascist who had tried to intimidate the family with threats, warning them against giving any help to rebels and Jews. Everybody feared his presence.

But it was a false alarm. It was not the foreman, but someone the family knew, and we all relaxed.

When the man reached the porch under the window of the staircase landing that separated our kitchen from that of our neighbors, he noticed with glee that I was someone he had not met before. As a way of introducing himself, he said to me in a broken Italian, "Hi, do you have anything to smoke?" (Tobacco, like matches, was a rarity, but cigarettes and cigarette wrappers were not available at all and inveterate smokers would smoke a pinch of stinking tobacco wrapped in anything from the husk of corn ears to newspaper.)

"No," I replied in English. "I don't."

"Do you speak English?" said the stranger in surprise.

"Just a little. Are you English?"

"No, I am South African. What's your name?"

I hesitated.

Except for the patriarch of the family—a trustworthy man of a few words our father had often helped to settle disputes with his landlord—

169

nobody in our farm or in the vicinity knew our true identity. We all had changed our names and were known by them. Lello had suggested for me Liliana—Lili for short—after my former piano teacher who had been his first love; I had accepted it, because of the song *Lili Marlene*—in honor of Engelbert Berner, the German soldier who had risked his life to come and try to save ours.

"What's your name?" repeated the stranger.

"Lili..."

"Beautiful name, beautiful girl."

"What's yours?"

"My name is Arthur. Arthur Osborne Moss."

Arthur was a young escapee from a POW camp near Latina in the south of Italy, and was well-known in our neighborhood for acting as the connecting link between the political outlaws and the farmers. He was, in short, our *real estate agent.* He was on his way to meet with two Americans and spend Christmas with them, but meeting me had made him change his mind and he decided instead to remain and spend at least Christmas Eve at our farm.

After the big meal, the prayers and the chants, everybody crowded near the fireplace to wait for midnight, the conventional time for the arrival of the baby Jesus.

Arthur and I spent the whole night speaking in English to each other, oblivious of the presence of anyone else. Once in a while someone would try to enter our conversation, but we didn't seem to hear or see anybody: we were too busy falling in love with each other.

"Can you dance?" asked Arthur?

"I love to dance."

"Come, I'll teach you a few steps."

Arthur was a true Fred Astaire. He taught me the fox-trot, the slow waltz, and the tango with figures, arabesques and deep bends. There was no music to go by, only his marking of the tempo. I was agile and quickly learned what Arthur taught me. The peasants stopped talking to watch us dancing.

"I don't believe it," I heard myself say while we were dancing. "I just met you and I feel as if I have known you forever."

"I love you too," said Arthur as if reading my mind.

Nobody could see my blushing in the huge, dark kitchen, illuminated only by the blazing fireplace. I felt as if Arthur's words were the vehicle by which all those bright flames were ignited inside my body, and I became ardent with a sudden overriding passion for this stranger.

"Who are you? What magic power do you possess? Why do I feel so dizzy?"

"All you have to know is that I love you."

"Seriously!"

Arthur began to tell me about his life and everything he said sounded like a fairy tale. At home he was a civil engineer, at war he was an officer in the air force, and now he headed partisan bands. A true leader. Every few words, he interpolated "I love you." And I repeated incessantly, "I love you, I love you."

Words were no longer capable to express our intense feelings. We sat down again and fell into a long, sweet, and dreamy silence.

The peasants finally ignored us and went on chatting and yawning, awaiting midnight to resume the prayers and the chants.

"Can you sing?" suddenly asked Arthur.

"Yes, I can."

"Do you have a perfect pitch?"

"Maybe not perfect, but it is fairly reliable."

"I want to teach you an old English song. It is a beautiful slow waltz, but my pitch is lousy and you will have to learn the tune through my jarring notes."

Arthur began to sing.

If anyone else had sung so badly, I would have left the room. Every molecule in my body was rejecting that dissonant collection of sounds. But I was so much in love that I stayed and forced myself to listen.

I let Arthur finish his horrible singing and said, "It's a nice song," even as I felt goose bumps bunched up all over my skin. And he sang the song a few more times, until I began to learn the lyrics and, with difficulty, to make sense of the tune. The song was really beautiful. The music was enchanting and the lyrics told of how sinful and deadly it can be to tell someone "I love you" without really meaning it. It was sufficient to convince me that the man who had immediately captured my heart had also truly fallen in love with me.

By the time we all went to bed, the farmers had learned the phrase *I love you* even though, for the moment, they didn't precisely know what it meant. Gino knew, but he didn't pay much attention to my instant passion. When he was seventeen, two years earlier, he had had similar flames, but they didn't last. He didn't expect mine to last either.

That night I didn't sleep one wink, transported as I was into the ecstatic world of intense love and passion.

Ivan

When I thought I heard Gino's voice, I rested my hands and the knitting on my lap and tried to push my fantasies to the back of my mind.

"Huh?"

"Tomorrow is hog-slaughtering day at Castellaccio," said Gino again. "Didn't you hear me? Everybody on our farm is going to be there."

"Are we going too?"

"Of course we are. Don't you want to see Marcella?"

Indeed, I was anxious to see my younger sister, from whom I had been separated almost two weeks. But the idea of the quasi-mystical ritual of the slaughtering of the hog was repulsive to me. When we lived at home, pork had never been part of our diet, much less of our lives.

For these peasants, however, life would be inconceivable without the pig. Other livestock were raised for a number of staple commodities. Sheep provided wool, milk and meat. Lamb offered meat and fur. The cow pulled the heavy plow and gave milk, meat, hide and horns. The ass, in addition to being a very convenient and often sole means of transportation, provided milk very similar to human milk to feed babies whose mothers had lost theirs because of hardships. When the ass died of old age, its hide was sold to the government for drums. The pig, however, was raised only for food.

Yet, it was the most important of all foods because it could be salted and dried and preserved to provide for the family needs throughout the year. Much of the farmers' lives revolved around it. The first job a child of four or five years of age was assigned was that of watching the pigs. From the moment the numerous litter was born, a child was in charge of making sure that the sow didn't smother any of the sucklings. Later on, when the little ones were weaned, it was a slightly older child who herded them to the fields to forage and scavenge, and then, at night, back to the sty. It was a child who put water into their trough and brought scraps from the kitchen into their mangers.

When the piglets weighed about fifty kilos, they were all brought to the market to be sold except for one. This one was fed until it more than doubled its weight, then it was slaughtered for prosciutti, salami, sausages, and the very versatile lard. The hog-slaughtering days assigned to each of the neighboring farms, were agreed upon ahead of time by the farmers, and when each date arrived, usually between Christmas and Epiphany, it was a big event. The butchering, salting, grinding the meat, and filling the casings required many hands. Besides, there were parts of the animal—the blood and the organs—which could not be preserved and had to be eaten right away. So, all the neighbors went in turn to the designated farm to help and eat.

Until the year before, the slaughtering of the hog had taken place at every farm as part of the holiday season festivities. But this winter the region was faced with a new problem: the most important ingredient for preserving the meat—salt—had become scarce. Very few farms had enough to salt their pork. The news that at Castellaccio they were able to slaughter the hog was received by some people with ill-concealed envy, but by most with simple joy at the idea of the big feast.

For us it was an opportunity to see our sister, so we went too.

Although Marcella looked fairly well, the few weeks away from home had transformed her into an emotional and physical wreck. She missed our mother more than the rest of us, and was suffering from frequent hemorrhages.

We hugged one another and cried. But by tacit consent Gino and I did not make any mention of our parents and Mario. Since Lello and I had seen the bus taking them to the concentration camp, we had no idea of their fate.

Seeing Marcella so unhappy made me very sad also. More than my parents, I longed for Mario. He was constantly on my mind and the thought that he was now in the hands of the assassins and I might not see him ever again was driving me to insanity. I was very close to Mario; I had always thought of myself as his little mommy. Every little boy I met made my pain and my longing more poignant.

My newly found passion for Arthur helped to ease my pain. I wanted to tell Marcella about it, but seeing her so miserable I had to contain myself. I had looked forward to sharing my happiness with her, but I was drawn into her misery, instead.

There was another refugee living at Castellaccio. Marcella took us to meet him. Ivan Boris, a Russian officer in his thirties, was a tall, well-built man with big strong hands, straight black hair parted on one side, dark large eyes, and a grave expression on his handsome face. When we arrived at his shed, he was intent on carving wooden clogs for the women of the household and mechanical funny toys for the children. We learned from Marcella that on Christmas day, while everybody was celebrating, Ivan took care of the animals and worked at his project. When the farmers told him that it was a sin to work on such a big holiday, he had answered with his beautiful basso voice, *"Se Ivano mangiare, Ivano lavorare!"*

Meeting Ivan was a genuine pleasure. Despite his broken Italian, we managed to talk about Russian literature and politics, and even though we often disagreed with his philosophy, there was much we could learn from this knowledgeable man whose cultural background was so different from ours.

After a while Ivan put his carving aside and we all went to offer our help. The farm had been transformed for the occasion into a big laboratory of sorts. Everybody was assigned a task. We stayed away from the site of real action, and helped as much as we could carrying water and wood, setting long tables and benches in the sun, and performing other such chores. The job lasted all morning and part of the afternoon, and finally the moment of resting and eating arrived. There was plenty of wine. Gino, Marcella and I hardly touched any food. We had already violated our dietary laws in order to survive, but the blood and the organs just extracted from the animal turned us off.

In the midst of all the bustle, we saw three men approaching the farm—one lanky, slouching figure flanked by two shorter, stockier ones.

Always on the lookout for strangers, Ivan ran to the farmhouse and climbed the ladder two steps at a time up to the attic. We swiftly followed suit. He kicked the ladder away from the trap entrance to the attic, ordered us to lie face down on the floor, and covered us with some straw he kept to sleep on. He cocked his pistol and remained on guard. The shouting outside ebbed. We kept so quiet we could hear the pounding of our hearts against our chests. A few minutes went by, then the shouting outside resumed with even more vigor; a youngster was sent to replace the ladder and to tell us that the newcomers were not fascists. We descended still shaking, but rejoiced at the sight of Spartaco. Marcella and I had not seen anyone we knew from Pitigliano since before our flight from home and were overcome with emotion. The other two, although dressed in tattered peasant clothes, betrayed their somewhat loftier origin.

Ivan didn't even try to conceal his annoyance at the arrival of these strangers, and remained on one side. Gino stayed with him for a while, then he came back to our group.

Spartaco seemed preoccupied with some thoughts of his own and forgot to introduce his friends to us. Marcella—outgoing and grega-rious—didn't need any formal introduction. She asked the two young men whether they lived nearby, and from their poor Italian and their heavy accent we realize that they were foreigners. Eager to show off our English, we asked, "Are you English?"

"We are Americans."

"Americans?!" exclaimed the two of us in one voice. "Americans?!"

"Yeah, we are. I am Jack Lyon and this is Jay..."

"You must be Lello's sisters," interrupted Jay. "He and Spartaco saved our lives, you know."

It didn't occur to us to tell them our names. Since our flight Lello had changed his name to Giorgio, and Gino had become Libero; I was Lili, and Marcella was Ina. But the two Americans, who had first known him as Lello, continued to call him by his real name, at least when no strangers were around.

"We have met your brother a couple of times since," said Jack. "Wonderful guy."

"He worries a lot about the two of you," intervened Jay. "But I don't blame him; this is no life for such beautiful girls."

Marcella and I were dumbfounded. They were the two young men whom we had seen drop from their burning aircraft a couple of months earlier, and they were *our* first Americans! We were anxious to find out about their lives and we asked a million questions about their country, the far-away dreamland of our childhood castle-building. We were especially interested in New York. We had developed, through literature and movies, a fascination with New York, where we dreamed we would live one day. Jack and Jay were no New Yorkers, and had very little to say about this city. Nevertheless they *were* Americans and New York *was* in America!

Spartaco interrupted our merry conversation. "Jack and Jay will stay here a couple of days," he said pensively. "But now I have to talk to the three of you."

As we said good-bye to the Americans, I lingered a little and asked Jay, "Do you know Arthur?"

"You must be Lili," he said.

I blushed and nodded.

"He cannot talk about anything else but you since the two of you met."

I ran to join Marcella, Gino and Spartaco, who had begun to walk away from the farm. In the distance I saw Ivan moving alone toward the shed where he carved and painted clogs and toys.

Uncle Tranquillo

Spartaco had come with news. He told us that our Uncle Tranquillo had been released from the concentration camp and had sent for us. Spartaco had arranged for us to meet with him that same night.

"I have already informed Lello," said Spartaco. "He is going to be at Pecorella's mill after nightfall."

Spartaco went to tell our hosts that we were leaving and taking Marcella with us for the evening, and left the two Americans in their charge, praising their character and their willingness to work hard.

On the way to the mill, Marcella burst into tears. She told us that she was having nightmares every night, she couldn't live without Mamma, and she wanted to join her at the concentration camp. We had a hard time calming her down.

The encounter with Lello, whom Marcella and I had not seen in a couple of weeks, caused another emotional upheaval. We were all very nervous about meeting with our uncle. Why had he been freed? What news did he have of our parents and Mario? Why was he late to arrive? To dampen our anxiety, we started to update one another on our different experiences, but we didn't pay much attention to each other's accounts, as we kept our ears wide open for the slightest sound.

At last we saw the limping silhouette of our uncle approaching the mill. Lello begged us not to assault him with questions and to let him talk first. We agreed, but as soon as Uncle Tranquillo was close enough to hear us, we all began to shout together, asking a thousand questions, without waiting for the answers. When we finally calmed down a little, we heard him say, "They are all right."

We remained silent for a while.

Spartaco and Pecorella discreetly left the mill.

Then we started the questions all over again: How were our parents? and Mario? and the other relatives? and our friends? But his answers were generic, vague, unsatisfying. We became more specific.

"How is their health?" Father had undergone his complicated and lengthy surgery not too long ago, Mamma had emphysema, and Mario was not a strong child.

"They are doing fine, considering."

"Do they have to work?"

"No, and this is part of the problem. There are over one hundred people living together with nothing to do. Enough for anyone to go crazy. We Italians have been in captivity only a month, but there are people from Austria, Germany, Poland, who have been prisoners for the past five years. While being moved from one concentration camp to another, they were able to escape and reach Italy. Only to be captured again here! They left families behind from whom they have not heard. And—what's worst to see—even though some have lived in Italy for many years and speak the language, they are treated by the guards even more harshly than the Italians."

After a brief pause, Uncle Tranquillo continued, "A few days ago, on Christmas Eve, some were able to obtain permission to stay up later. Dandolo Nunes from Grosseto seized the opportunity to organize a talent show to make everybody forget their troubles for a while. But can you imagine your father dressed up in your mother's clothes singing from *La Geisha*?"

"It was his favorite operetta," we smiled. "He saw it seventeen times!"

"We laughed," Uncle Tranquillo proceeded. "People do not forget how to laugh. But we cried a lot, too."

Uncle Tranquillo extracted a piece of paper from his pocket and even in the dark I recognized our father's handwriting. I snatched it from his hands and ran to a corner to light a match to read it first. My hands were shaking. Poor Babbo. How many worries about us! Not one word about his own suffering and hardships. Only concern about us, fear for *our* safety (even though we were free to move and they were held prisoners), and only words of advice and solace. The letter ended with his cherished *b'racha*. What would I have given to reassure him that we were hundreds of times better off than they were; we didn't lack the essentials, and our only real suffering was the knowledge that they were where they were!

I looked at Uncle Tranquillo and saw that in a few weeks he had aged enormously and that his bright eyes and peculiar smile on one side of his mouth were veiled with great sadness.

Finally, we asked him why he had been freed. He explained that the reason why he had been allowed to leave the camp was the shortage of salt. With all the young men either in the army or in hiding, there was practically nobody who was able to operate Uncle Tranquillo's gazogene truck that had been confiscated by the Fascists. The few who could, pretended that they didn't know how because anything moving on the roads was being machine-gunned from the air or assaulted by the partisans lying in ambush for anyone who collaborated with the Nazis. He had simply been ordered to undertake the unsafe task of transporting the much-needed supply of salt from Volterra to Grosseto. He had been warned, of course, that any action taken by him that was not in compliance with the order received would be paid for by his wife and children who were still in the concentration camp.

The concentration camp, we learned, was situated roughly halfway between Grosseto, the capital of the province, and the salt quarries of Volterra. The complex, on the outskirts of Roccatederighi, in the province of Siena, had been the summer residence of Grosseto's bishop and of the Catholic Theological Seminary of that town. When the Fascists had seized it to use it as a transshipment concentration camp for the Jews, the Bishop had been able to retain his apartment, where he had moved with his sister and butler in order to escape the Allies' bombing of Grosseto. Although his presence at the camp did nothing to prevent or alleviate the abuses that the guards perpetrated against the prisoners, this cohabitation eventually resulted in a friendship between him and our father, with whom he could engage in philosophical debates under the astonished eyes of the Italian warders.

Uncle Tranquillo, who had gone back to live in his home in Pitigliano, had been granted permission to go and visit his family at the concentration camp once in a while.

When Lello and Gino heard this incredible story, they begged Uncle Tranquillo to take them with him to see our parents and brother. But his answer was a big NO. The idea was utterly crazy; a tremendous risk for everyone involved. But they insisted and pleaded with him, and even threatened him, until Uncle Tranquillo was forced to promise that on the next trip he would take them along. On this first trip he had to go alone to have a chance to think of a plan that would work, and to study the roadblocks. The date was set for January 12, and the agreement was for Lello and Gino to meet with him back at the mill the night of the eleventh.

We wrote a short note, each of us just a few words to show our handwriting, and gave it to Uncle Tranquillo to bring to our parents. Then we begged him to say what we were afraid of putting in writing: that we were fine and took good care of ourselves and of each other, and that we hoped they would soon be free.

Part 5

RIDING OUT THE STORM

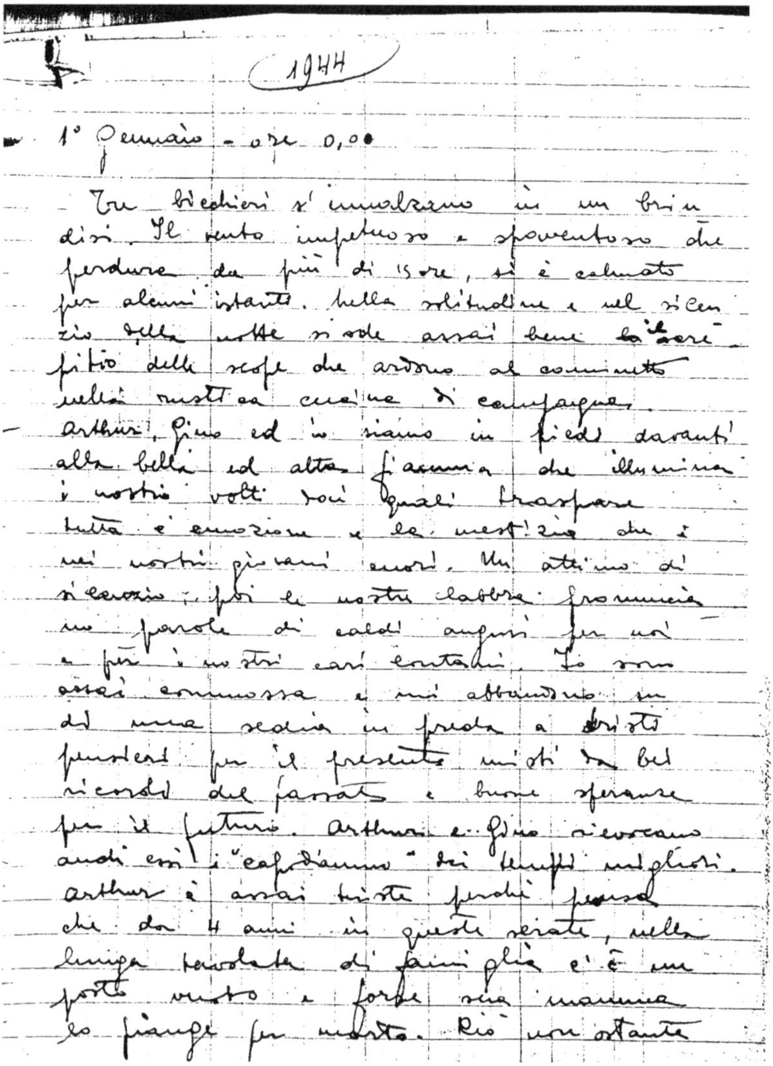
1944

1° Gennaio - ore 0,00

Tre bicchieri s'innalzano in un brindisi. Il vento impetuoso e spaventoso che perdura da più di 15 ore, si è calmato per alcuni istanti. Nella solitudine e nel silenzio della notte si ode assai bene lo scoppiettio delle scope che ardono al caminetto nella nostra cucina di campagna. Arthur, Gino ed io siamo in piedi davanti alla bella ed alta fiamma che illumina i nostri volti sui quali traspare tutta l'emozione e la nostalgia che è nei nostri giovani cuori. Un attimo di silenzio; poi le nostre labbra pronunciano parole di caldi auguri per noi e per i nostri cari lontani. Io sono assai commossa e mi abbandono su di una sedia in preda a tristi pensieri per il presente misti a bei ricordi del passato e buone speranze per il futuro. Arthur e Gino ricordano anch'essi i "capodanno" dei tempi migliori. Arthur è assai triste perchè pensa che da 4 anni in queste serate, nella lunga tavolata di famiglia c'è un posto vuoto e forse sua mamma lo piange per morto. Ciò nonostante

A page from my diary written at the onset of the new year, 1944.

Chapter Nine

Acting and Action

E ver since meeting Uncle Tranquillo, Lello and Gino could hardly wait for the moment to go with him to the concentration camp to see our parents and Mario. We girls were to be left behind, but fortunately, we had other interests to occupy our thoughts when they would leave.

January 1, 1944—Hour 0:00

Three glasses are raised in a toast. The wind, violent and frightful, which has been blowing for more than fifteen hours, has subsided for a few moments. In the sudden silence of the night, we hear the joyous crackling of the twigs burning in the hearth of the country kitchen. The tall flames throw a tremulous light upon our faces. Arthur, Gino and I, standing, look at one another and our eyes express all the emotion and the sadness in our hearts. We remain quiet for a moment, then we click our glasses wishing for a better world. I am suddenly exhausted and let myself fall onto a chair.

Arthur and Gino are recalling the New Year's Eves of times past. Gino mentions our tradition of sitting around the table with our friends and writing poetry while waiting for midnight to roll about and bring us the brand-new New Year. Arthur is very sad because he knows that for the last four years, at the beautiful table full of relatives in his far away Johannesburg home, there has been an empty seat, and perhaps by now his mother thinks that he is dead. However, by comparison with us, he considers himself fortunate. His parents and little brother are not captives in a concentration camp as ours are, and if he survives the war, he is going to be reunited with them. Our chances of this happening seem almost nil.

Arthur, who had come to see me the previous day, had not planned to spend New Year's Eve with us, whereas Lello and Marcella were expected to join us to spend this night—as tradition demanded—together. In the morning of December 31, it was raining a little with some gusts of wind. We were hoping to see the weather improve so that Lello could go to fetch Marcella and the two would come to us as planned. But around noontime, the rain suddenly changed into snow, the wind became furious, and the already bad weather turned into a blizzard. All the hay stacks were blown apart, the terracotta roof tiles were swept away leaving many houses unroofed, huge old trees were uprooted and felled, and the dogs that had not made it in time into the farmhouse were lifted from the ground and drifted like leaves in the wind.

I was sorry that Marcella and Lello could not be with us, but welcomed this horrible weather that kept Arthur from leaving me. Our farmers had provided me with some eggs, flour and honey, and I had made a cake. It was intended for everyone, but in the evening all the people in our household had gone to bed very early, worried and frightened, without even looking at the cake. We moved to the apartment next door, where the people were so poor that they would certainly appreciate sharing the cake with us. But with that dreadful weather, *all* the farmers had gone to bed very early. No one, not even the elders, had ever seen such a violent storm. The three of us, however, were determined to wait up for the New Year. We finished the cake all by ourselves.

There was a skimpy pile of wood and a bunch of twigs for us to use. We had sat in the dark near the fireplace eating the cake and waiting, trying to economize on the wood to have enough for a big flare at midnight. The cake made us thirsty. Gino and Arthur were constantly sending me for water, but this was scarce also and we had to save enough for the toast at midnight. Though there was no wine, we would not give up the toast. We would use water if we were careful enough to save some.

Midnight would never arrive. Waiting for the New Year seemed endless. We were sitting in silence, waiting, overwhelmed by the frightful roar of the blizzard coming through the chimney, the fissures in the windows, the staircase. Finally, when Arthur's watch marked 15 minutes to midnight, I prepared all the wood for the big flame. Gino was supposed to fill the glasses with water, but there was only one glass—the one we had been sharing so far—and how could we toast with one glass? What a misery! What a New Year's Eve! I lit one of the long flax straws and ventured to the adjacent apartment, to our farmer's kitchen, which was separated from this one by the staircase landing from which I had first seen Arthur.

Gino said, "If you find the flask of waterwine bring it here."

Waterwine was made by fermenting the water that had been poured into the machinery with the remains of the pressed grapes, which the farmers drank in place of wine when it ran short.

But no sooner had I reached the staircase landing, when the tenuous flame was blown out by the wind that penetrated violently through the fissures in the window. I shivered with cold and fear, but I didn't go back.

In the total darkness, I quietly opened the door to the neighboring kitchen and groped my way to the sink. I returned to where Arthur and Gino were waiting, with two more glasses and a flask. While I was putting all the remains of wood and twigs on the fire, Gino poured the waterwine for the toast, but what a surprise! Unwittingly I had brought back some excellent red wine. It was a good omen! We were thrilled and very moved. After the toast we were up for another hour talking. By the time we went to sleep—Gino and Arthur on the kitchen floor because they could not descend to the stable—the wind had picked up its strength again and I found my bedmates still awake and trembling with fear.

By morning the blizzard was over. It had left much devastation in its wake. Arthur left by midday of this ugly New Year's Day in his shirt sleeves—his outfit regardless of the weather. I watched him from the window, wishing he could have stayed.

The next few days were spent trying to repair some of the damage caused by the big storm. In our farm we had been lucky that the roof had not been blown away, although it had been damaged extensively. But the main job was to recover as much as possible of the straw and hay that had been scattered all over the fields and drifted in small and large mounds against walls and corners—because without these two staples the big animals in the barn would have neither beds nor food.

Vespina, the dog who knew how to smile, was found almost dead at some distance. We had been watching her from a window, when she was struggling and trying to come home, being lifted by the wind. Each step forward she was able to take, she would be blown back a few yards. Then, in the thickness of the blizzard, we didn't see her anymore.

After we heard that everything was all right with Marcella, Gino left me and went to join Lello.

Arthur and Ivan

A few days later the four of us gathered again at Castellaccio, the farm that sheltered Marcella. She looked radiant this time. At night, when Lello and Gino left to meet with Uncle Tranquillo, I stayed with her. I was eager to talk to her about my feelings for Arthur, but I was still unsure as to whether she was ready. Last time I saw her she was still crying for Mamma. As soon as we were alone, she spoke to me about Ivan. He was a widely read man who loved to talk about his country and his ideals. She felt very proud to be able, at thirteen, to discuss with him the Russian classics they had both read: Tolstoi, Dostoevski, Kolorenko, Pushkin, Gorki. Ivan had the habit of passing his hand through her hair and down her face in a warm, gentle caress. Although Ivan was old enough to be her father, she was moved by a strange feeling that ran through her whole being when he did this.

"Do you think I am in love?"

"It sounds like it," I replied.

It was not the kind of love I had for Arthur, I thought, otherwise she wouldn't have to ask, but I didn't make any comments. I was happy for her. This relationship would help her overcome her longing for Mamma and bring some light into her drab life, just as falling in love with Arthur had made my exile and the dreadful existence I was forced to lead almost desirable.

As she was talking about Ivan, my heart ran wild at the prospect of finally being able to confide in her. Even before she indicated that she was through, I erupted like a volcano, telling her about Arthur, who had instantaneously become the most important element in my life.

"What is he like?" asked Marcella.

"He is tall, blond, has blue eyes, a pudgy reddish nose, and an impertinent mustache."

"I mean, what kind of person is he?"

"I really know very little about him, and the little I know I am not sure I like too much, but it doesn't seem to matter."

Finally I could talk about Arthur. I lit up like a sun.

"When I am with him I forget where I am, who I am, and all my troubles and sorrows."

Marcella looked a little puzzled.

"How can you be so happy when he is not with you?"

"But he is always with me! In my heart, in my thoughts. It makes me so incredibly happy to be near him that my warm feelings last long after he has gone. I feel as if I have always known him and always loved him as I do now."

Marcella said nothing.

Once I started to talk about Arthur, I could have gone on talking forever without pause, but I felt uncomfortable and I suddenly became silent. I realized that all I wanted to talk about were variations on one theme, namely, the million and one nuances that made my heart leap in my chest for him. And this was not very interesting to my sister. Arthur and I had no intellectual interest to share, and how could I ever express in a manner that would be of interest to her this tumultuous torrent of feelings that had taken possession of me?

I kept quiet for a while, thinking of how fortunate I was to have met Arthur and to be able to experience such ecstasy. The world-famous lovers came to mind: Dante and Beatrice, Petrarca and Laura, Paolo and Francesca, Romeo and Juliet...

Arthur and Edda, I thought, just like them. But no! No comparison! Our love was much more powerful than anyone else's.

Somebody knocked at the door.

"Signorina Lili," I heard one of the girls in the household call. "Lieutenant Arthur is here to see you."

I dashed downstairs screaming with joy and flung myself into his arms.

"Ina, Ina," I yelled. "Come down and meet Arthur!"

Marcella and Arthur looked at each other askance without saying much.

"Where are your brothers?" inquired Arthur.

We were not supposed to let anyone know where they had gone, but I could not keep a secret from my love and told him that they had gone to the concentration camp to see our parents.

"I'll stay with you and your sister until they come back," said Arthur. "I need to talk with them."

"About?"

"Never mind. Men's talk."

Some no-good thing was cooking, I knew. But I didn't press to find out. It was enough that he had come. With him near me I would not worry myself to death until I saw my brothers back.

Marcella walked to the shed where Ivan was working.

Arthur and Ivan knew each other and passionately loathed one another. Not only were their birthplaces almost at the antipodes, but their politics and their views in life as well. Arthur was an adventurous and lighthearted young man who tried to get the most out of his disrupted life. Ivan was a deeply committed, ethical man with the responsibility of the entire world on his shoulders. They had one trait in common: they both liked to drink a lot, and it became a frightful experience to be near the two of them when they engaged in competitions such as who would be the first to finish a large copper jug of wine, or who would be better able, afterwards, to shoot at a target standing on one foot. These were not the kind of men my sister and I would have fallen in love with under normal circumstances. As it was, we had suffered from too much rejection, and even without comparing them with the peasants—the few who were not at war—these two, who paid us tender attention, were remarkable and very desirable men.

Infiltrating the Concentration Camp

Lello and Gino arrived at the mill a few minutes before midnight. Not too long afterwards, Uncle Tranquillo arrived too, carrying a bundle under his arm. He gave them the two work shirts and the soiled and greasy overalls he had brought for them and began to explain his plan, begging them to pay careful attention to what he had to say.

In the dreadful event that someone should see them, he concluded, they would pass for his helpers. They had to behave and talk like working people. But, of course, the best thing was not to be seen at all.

While Uncle Tranquillo talked, Lello and Gino changed into the clothes he had brought, and began to imitate, in an exaggerated fashion, the speech and manners of the working classes.

"No clowning around," said Uncle Tranquillo with a shadow of a smile. "Let's get going."

The truck was partially loaded with the wood that was used as fuel for the gazogene, and the rest with bales of fleece. Lello and Gino climbed onto the back of the truck, lay down on top of the bales and tried to get some sleep. Uncle Tranquillo got into the truck's cab and drove away.

There was only one dangerous roadblock near Manciano and it was coming up soon. There was another block on Mussolini Bridge over the Ombrone River near Grosseto, but—strangely enough—the vigilance at that one was much less tight, because no rebels would ever dare travel in that neighborhood. Before they reached their first dangerous spot, Uncle Tranquillo stopped the truck and went to tell the boys to lie down under the bales and stay absolutely motionless and quiet until the danger was over. He returned to his seat and started the truck again. At the roadblock, he was stopped by a German sentry who asked for documents.

From under the bales of fleece, Lello and Gino heard the voice of the sentry reaching them somewhat deadened but still imperious, "Das

189

Papier!"

They held their breath.

Uncle Tranquillo had the papers in good order that explained what he was doing. He had been given a new ID card that did not have *RAZZA EBRAICA* stamped on it, and the name Servi sounded Italian. No one, much less the Germans, would suspect that he was a Jew.

"What's inside those bales," thundered another sentry. "Rebels, huh?" And in so saying he poked at one with his bayonet and split it open. A rush of fleece in the shape of a cloud burst out of the wounded bale. Satisfied, the German soldiers let the truck carrying two *Jewish rebels* go. It took a couple of miles before Uncle Tranquillo stopped the truck again to release the two half-asphyxiated boys who had hardly been able to curb their urge to empty their bladder and bowels.

At dawn they stopped at the edge of a forest to eat the piece of bread and cheese that Uncle Tranquillo had brought for the three of them and to feed the furnace of the gazogene. Afterwards, they went to cut some wood to replace the one just used, and also to get some blood circulating—it was mighty cold! The little food in their stomachs and the physical activity gave them a sudden feeling of well-being. It was great to be alive! Everything had gone well so far, even though the crucial moment, the moment of meeting with our parents inside the camp, the *most* dangerous one, was yet to come. Gino joked, "So far so good, as the man who fell from the sixth floor said on reaching the third floor!"

They resumed their journey.

When the truck was parked at the foot of the long flight of steps that led to the gate of the villa-turned-concentration-camp, Lello and Gino, as instructed, jumped down and pretended to be busy with the motor. They tried to get their hands and faces dirty and greasy, while Uncle Tranquillo had a chance to climb up the steps and warn our parents and everyone who knew them to pretend they were strangers.

"Those of you who cannot control your emotions," he muttered at the end, "please stay away."

Then he called loudly towards the boys, "Come up and say hello to my family!"

Trying to keep in check the tremor of their bodies without appearing too stiff, Lello and Gino began to climb the stairs. Mario, on seeing them, could not resist the impulse to go and meet them. But in order not to create suspicion, he didn't run toward them and didn't even look at them. He began to descend the wide stairs, stopping at each step, as if playing a solitary game, but in reality to curb his own overwhelming emotion. The guards saw him, but didn't stop him, knowing that nine-year-old Mario could not—and would not—run away.

As he hopped down in a zig-zag manner, Mario wondered what went through his older brothers' minds. What had they expected? Were they in any way surprised? Were they afraid of losing their freedom?

When the three reached the same step, Mario, for fear of yielding to his need to jump into their arms, quickly turned around and climbed fast ahead of them. Lello and Gino, after him, entered the gate to the concentration camp and approached the group of prisoners which included our parents.

Father's face bore the stern and dignified expression of solemn occasions. He kept on looking at his boys—who stood several inches above his head—from above the lenses of his tortoiseshell rimmed glasses which were constantly perched near the tip of his nose, and tried to say very little. Later on that day, he entered in pencil on the front page of his prayer book—which somehow he had managed to take with him and was able to hide throughout the period of his captivity—the following:

> Today my two older boys came to see us at the concentration
> camp; for the duration of their visit, I couldn't help envision-
> ing the moment in which they would be discovered and shot in
> front of my eyes.

Mamma had turned fifty a couple of days earlier and looked more beautiful than ever. She had slimmed down considerably, which only became her. Her attractive blue-grey eyes, which were normally ever-ready to pour torrents of tears at the slightest emotional provocation, were now wide open but dry. After the first excruciating moment, she kept on giving the two boys her sweet, reassuring smile.

Mario's head had been completely shaven. Together with his golden locks, he seemed to have lost also the spark that made his intelligent and beautiful face radiant. He kept the corners of his mouth downward, and his sky-blue eyes under a deep frown. He felt very important to be the brother of those two brave young men, and had entered thoroughly into his role of having to behave as not to betray the secret of his relationship. Next to him were his friends Enzo Cava, whom he knew from Pitigliano, and Carlo Nunes, a year or two older than he, whom he had met at the concentration camp. Carlo was the younger brother of Dandolo, the organizer of the talent show. Franca and her parents stood at a distance because Signora Cava was a very emotional person and was afraid she would break down. But Franca kept her beautiful eyes and her ears wide open to catch some news about her friend Marcella.

Our three prisoners, like the rest of the inmates, were dressed in their own clothes, with winter coats on, and if it weren't for those ugly armed guardsmen circling them like vultures, it would have seemed as if they had just come out of their homes for a stroll in the sun.

Uncle Tranquillo introduced Lello and Gino as Nicola Lizzi and Ilio Desideri, his helpers. They shook hands with everybody, repeating absentmindedly, "Pleased to meet you." But when it came to shake hands with our mother and father, whom they were supposed to know from Pitigliano, after having loudly said, "So, how are you?" the four of them didn't utter another word. They kept their hands interlocked for a prolonged time, while their hearts pounded furiously against their chests, and their eyes, looking intently into each other's, spoke of a million messages.

Finally, almost choking, they bent to pat Mario's head and whispered into his ear, "All is well; Marcella and Edda are all right."

To be within reach and not to be able to fall into each other's arms and cry and really talk was a torture beyond endurance, an unbearable experience, perhaps the most heartrending of their lives.

While this was going on, Natalino—a young inmate whom Gino had met once during a business trip—approached the group and pointing at Gino exclaimed, "O Gino! Also you were so stupid as to let them catch you?"

Gino looked at him with eyes full of terror but managed an almost normal voice, "You must be mistaken... My name is Ilio... Ilio Desideri."

The other quickly caught on and said, "Pleased to meet you. For a moment I thought you were someone else."

Natalino Finzi and his wife, Berta, seven months pregnant, together with Berta's parents, Erasmo and Egle Della Riccia, had been taken in their home in Castell'Azzara—where they had moved in order to escape the bombing of their town, Livorno—only a few days earlier. The fascists had burst into their apartment early one morning while the two couples were still asleep. Five weeks after this encounter with Gino on the concentration camp grounds—when Natalino almost gave Gino away—the Finzis' baby was born. Much talk and fuss had been made before the arrival of the baby among the prisoners. What if it were a boy and couldn't be ritually circumcised? Would one of the imprisoned doctors be allowed to perform the operation or would it have to wait until they were free again? What if they had to stay in the concentration camp for a long time? The child, then more conscious of pain, would suffer a trauma!

Fortunately it was a girl. Gigliola became the well-loved mascot of every prisoner.

By the time she was three months old, Gigliola and her parents and grandparents were among the seventy prisoners who were taken by the Germans from the Roccatederighi transshipment camp to the death facto-ries during their retreat northward only a few weeks before the liberation of the camp by the American troops. None of the deportees came back. From the testimony given to Dr. Renzo Cabib by Frida Misul, a survivor of Auschwitz who was deported from Livorno and knew the Della Riccias and the Finzis, it was learned that

> ...at the arrival at Auschwitz, during the selection, baby
> Gigliola is snatched away from her mother's arms and brutally
> murdered in front of the horrified and impotent parents. As the
> child is thrown on the heap of people who had died during the
> trip, the mother collapses onto the rails and there she is left,
> probably dead on the spot. Natalino is selected for work, and
> meets his own, horrendous death after much tribulation later.

Although ten years apart, Mario and Gino looked very much alike. One was the younger version of the other, with similar blond hair, sky-blue eyes, a well-shaped mouth, and delicate, slender hands. There was a grumbling among the prisoners who didn't know what was going on that one of the two young men who had come with Tranquillo was Mario's brother. The guards became suspicious. One of them, out of the blue, began to beat people with the butt end of his rifle at random and badly hurt a few prisoners who had gathered around and were standing close to Mario. Another asked Uncle Tranquillo with a gloomy frown, "How come these two are not in the army?"

"They were declared unfit for the military on account of serious illnesses, but they serve the country the best they can."

At this moment the embarrassing and dangerous situation was saved by Battista, the bishop's butler-turned-camp-cook, who came out with his usual big iron pan, and the large aluminum spoon with which he banged the bottom of it as a gong, to call the prisoners at mealtime. Everybody forgot about the visitors and ran inside the refectory to take their seats at the long tables.

Gino and Lello sat opposite Father, Mamma and Mario. Mamma was afraid that more and more people would become aware of the resemblance between Mario and Gino, and asked Mario to keep his head down on her lap, as sometimes he did while she and Father pretended to eat their rations, which they passed onto Mario's dish after he had lapped up his own in no time. At least once, out of the two meals they were assigned a day, Mamma and Father went without eating to give Mario, a growing boy, their measly portions.

This time it was Uncle Tranquillo's mother, Great Aunt Elodia (deaf as a dormouse, she had not heard her son's announcement that everyone who knew the boys should go along with pretending that they were his helpers) to make some very loud and not too clever remarks: "I am so glad," she said, "that Lello and Gino have joined the family!"

The moment had come to stop tempting fate and cut the visit short. Uncle Tranquillo promptly got up from the table and overpowered his mother's voice by calling Ilio and Nicola to hurry up, otherwise they would arrive at the quarries when it was already dark. Lello and Gino shook hands with our parents again, resisting with great pain the impulse to hug them, but when Mario, realizing that they were leaving, raised his head to say good-bye to his brothers, they did kiss him unobserved.

Repressing the urge to flee at the speed of light, Lello and Gino walked out of the concentration-camp gate and descended the staircase to the truck. They felt a great relief at being free and for having seen their parents and brother alive, but they felt an even greater frustration for having left their dear ones behind the barbed wire.

The Partisans

The truck arrived at the salt quarries of Volterra at mid-afternoon. Lello and Gino looked gaunt. Nobody questioned them. They looked too sick to be in the army. They unloaded the fleece, but let the workers at the quarries reload the truck with rock salt while they joined Uncle Tranquillo and the foreman for some food and a glass of wine. As soon as all the documents were signed, Uncle Tranquillo started on his journey back.

The sad return on top of the hard, cold, salt-filled bales was almost unbearable. The shaking and jolting of the truck over the bumpy road tossed the boys against the sharp-edged salt rocks, bruising them all over. The sky was overcast and it was getting very cold.

Suddenly, from the curtain of grayness above them, a small plane appeared—probably a British *Spitfire*—its buzzing noise hardly audible over the rumbling of the gazogene. It dove close to the truck and a shower of bullets fell on the white, travertine-covered road on the spot the truck had just passed over. The little airplane disappeared above the clouds. Lello and Gino were too exhausted to be affected. The bitter cold of the January evening was so piercing that they were sure they would die of cold anyway. Yet, the physical discomfort, great as it was, was surpassed by the anguish that tormented their souls. They swore to each other, repeatedly, that they would do everything in their power to go and liberate the prisoners.

The block on Mussolini bridge was passed without a search. Salt was so precious that the man who brought it into the region deserved special courtesy. Lello and Gino in the back of the truck were not bothered. The truck stopped in front of the Province warehouse at Grosseto and Uncle Tranquillo begged the workers there to unload it of its precious cargo. Again nobody paid any attention to the boys. However, there was no way they could pass the next roadblock without being seen, now that the truck was empty. A kilometer or so before reaching it, Uncle Tranquillo asked Lello and Gino to get off and walk through the woods to circumvent it. He would wait for them at a distance past the block. If they failed to appear after a certain time, he would assume that they had decided to walk to their destination and he would proceed alone.

Night had long descended upon the countryside. The darkness, the aching, and the tiredness made the walk seem much longer than it was. After a while, thinking that they had walked around the check post, they returned toward the main road. They started to walk hoping to see the truck. After a few steps, however, they realized that they were at the outskirts of Manciano, still on the same side of the road block. They stopped and looked around. While they were trying to decide in which direction to go, they saw an old friend of our father's who was walking home. They recognized the minuscule figure of Fiorlindo Cappelletti.

"What are you doing here? Are you crazy? The Germans are stopping everyone a few yards down the road."

Signor Cappelletti was a tiny man, but in his village he had power. He was neither a fascist nor an anti-fascist. He minded his own business and got along with everyone. Lello and Gino asked him to help them go through the road block, the same block where a German sentry, that very morning, had almost split them open with his bayonet.

They walked a while together like old buddies until they reached the open barrier. A car had been stopped and while the owner was having his papers checked, the three of them walked right under the noses of the German sentries, discussing animatedly about the quality of the new wine. As soon as they were out of sight from the Germans, Lello and Gino hugged Fiorlindo Cappelletti good-bye.

They walked fast without talking until they spotted the truck standing on the shoulder of the road. As they approached it, they saw some commotion and heard several voices shouting: *"Porco! Fascista!* We should kill you, you son-of-a-bitch! This should teach you a lesson!"

They ran toward the small group of men who were beating up Uncle Tranquillo. They tried to stop them yelling that they were making a bad blunder. Finally the man who seemed to be in charge turned around and ordered his men to stop. He had recognized Lello and Gino and they recognized him, Ivan Boris.

They told Ivan who it was that they were beating and what he was doing. Hearing this Ivan went down on his knees to help Uncle Tranquillo and to say that he was sorry. Uncle Tranquillo was bruised all over his face, had a few bumps on his head, and a swollen eye, but he managed a crooked smile: "I am sorry that it had to be me," he said, "but am I happy to see that you people are doing your job!" And they all shook hands. Someone ran to get some water from the nearby creek to wash his wounds, and everybody stayed with him until he was able to resume his trip to Pitigliano.

Uncle Tranquillo reassured Lello and Gino that he was all right and begged them not to go with him any further. The band dispersed, and they joined Ivan to walk back to the farm where Marcella and I had already begun to worry.

Chapter Ten

Encounters

Our safety depended upon our whereabouts remaining unknown to the Fascist authorities. We knew that staying too long at one place was dangerous, since farms invariably had visitors who could innocently spread the news about our presence. Thus, it was necessary for us to move away from any given farm after a few days. However, our present farms, Castellaccio and Capannelle, belonged to our father's best friends among the peasants. We had left them as the last resort, and now we somehow believed that at least Marcella and I could stay at these two places undisturbed until the war was over. These farms were so comfortable for us, and the farmers so trustworthy, that we were loathe to leave them, and stayed longer than we had remained in any other place, and than it was safe for everyone concerned. We started to move around again and met with the most disparate people.

Moving Again

Upon reaching the farm Lello and Gino, emotionally and physically exhausted, went straight to the stable to sleep without answering our anxious questions—saying only that everybody was fine.

Arthur left without waiting for them to wake up. Before leaving he told me what he had kept from me the previous night.

"It is known that you are hiding in these two farms," he said. "You had better move out of here fast."

"Do you have a place for us to go?"

"I'll look all over and get in touch with you as soon as I find something."

"But didn't you say we should move from here right away?"

"Yes, I did. But I'll be also looking. And don't worry," he added half-tenderly, half-mockingly. "I'll *always* find you."

Lello and Gino slept through most of the morning. When they got up, I reported that Arthur said (and they agreed) that lately we had been too lax regarding our safety. Without delay, we packed our things and took leave of the family and Ivan at Castellaccio; then we walked to say good-bye to the family at Capannelle, with whom I had stayed nearly a month. They didn't even try to hide their great relief at seeing us go.

While we walked to Lello's place, Lello and Gino recounted in great detail their trip to the concentration camp. Marcella's nostalgia for Mamma was renewed. Still not feeling well—and now leaving Ivan—she felt that she could no longer endure our harsh fugitive life and had made up her mind once and for all to join our parents and Mario at the concentration camp.

"Wait until we rest at Lello's farm tonight," Gino told her.

"Tomorrow morning," added Lello, "we will get up early and will look for a doctor and a place for you to stay."

This assurance didn't diminish Marcella's misery, but she stopped whining.

When we arrived at Lello's place, we found that while he had been away the farmers had buried all of his belongings. They said they were sure—and no doubt wished—that he would never come back.

"But I *am* back," said Lello, "my little sister is sick and I beg of you to let us stay at least for tonight."

"We are afraid of what might happen to us," they said with a finality in their tone of voice that did not leave room for any insistence on our part. "You'd better find another place."

We dragged our few belongings and our tired bodies and souls all day long going from farm to farm, and the answer to our quest for a little food and a place to rest was always the same negative one. We were famished, cold, overtired, and discouraged, especially Marcella, who was ready to give up. But we had no choice and kept on and on. By nighttime, after miles and miles of walking and five or six rejections, we all were wrecks. Suddenly we realized that in the hamlet perched on the side of the mountain we now faced, lived Quartilia, Aunt Elda's old maid. We made one last effort, and arrived at the place when Quartilia was about to go to bed. She also frowned upon seeing us, but compassion prevailed over fear and she finally asked us in.

She quickly prepared a good supper for us and watched us eat like wolves. After we were well fed and ready to drop anywhere to get some rest, Quartilia made it clear that we had to go. We pleaded and begged and appealed to her sense of decency, reminding her that we were not there by choice. At last she gave in—but only partially.

"Marcella, who needs medical attention," said the woman, "can stay with me for a while. I'll pretend she is my niece from the city and I'll have the doctor take care of her. But the three of you," she added without equivocation, "after resting a bit, *must* go."

We stretched on the kitchen floor and fell asleep in no time at all. We left quietly long before dawn, while Marcella and Quartilia were still sound asleep.

We thought of a stratagem. One of the boys would walk to a farm to ask for a few eggs, or a bit of cheese, or a piece of bread. (Most farmers didn't mind giving refugees food—of which almost always they had some to spare—and they were more than happy to pay such a small price to get rid in a hurry of *outlaws.*) We would then go to the next farm and ask the people to let us eat inside, away from the cold. While eating our food, we would inquire whether we could stay just for the night.

It did not always work, and we lived with the gripping terror of not finding a shelter from the bitter-cold nights. But we were persistent and never had to sleep in the open. Sometimes we even found people who badly needed help on the farm and wouldn't mind letting us stay for a while, as long as we were willing to work for them.

As we finally settled down in one of these farms that traded our labor for shelter and a little of their food, I began to wonder whether Arthur had been looking for us or had forgotten altogether the promise of helping us find a place. Was he aware that we had been wandering around for days and days, sleeping each night in a different and often hostile place, before we had finally found ourselves a farm where we could stay for a while?

Sesto

It was quite by accident that one night Arthur looked for shelter for himself and for two others in our present farm. The two young men with him were good old Spartaco, who had gone with Lello to the rescue of the American parachutists, and an old elementary school friend of Lello's, Sesto, whom we had not seen since before we left home.

Sesto was at first sight an unimpressive youth with shoulders too broad for his average height; a wide mouth, as if fixed in an eternal smile, a thin, off-center nose, and a pair of vivid eyes equipped his roundish face; his straight light-brown hair was smoothly combed back, and his enormous ears seemed to flap each time he moved his head or even opened his mouth to speak. However, his charismatic personality made Sesto stand out from the rest of Pitigliano's youths. With Sesto one hardly ever made small talk. His inquisitive and speculative mind invited people to engage in elaborate debates on existential themes and on the philosophical aspect of politics. Yet, he was never pedantic, as he interjected his discourse with humorous observations and with his uniquely-warm optimism.

Even though it was customary for university students to dress somewhat formally in those days, Sesto went a bit farther than his peers by wearing a formal blue suit with impeccably creased trousers, a white shirt and a burgandy tie at all times—even now, in the middle of nowhere.

Whereas the other students only socialized among themselves, Sesto flaunted his friendship with Spartaco, a simple working boy who spoke the dialect of the peasants and dressed in tattered rags. It seemed an absurdity. However, there was more to this friendship than mere eccentricity. Rather than clashing, their superficial differences seemed to complement each other, and were abundantly compensated for by the boys' fundamental similarities: they were both honest, no-nonsense people, sincere and convinced anti-fascists.

Sesto was perhaps the only one among the students in Pitigliano—of course all of them Catholic—who had maintained a rapport with us. "The students" were a privileged caste. They were the future professionals, quite a few steps above the civil servants and the business people of the village, and way on top of the ladder, near the heavens, compared to the peasants (whose children in most cases they were) who constituted the bulk of the Pitiglianesi.

If not for the racial laws that barred us from getting a formal education, most of us, by merit and ambition, would have belonged to the class of "the students" (but almost certainly without such snobbery!). As it was, we belonged to no class at all and were content to make friends with whoever treated us humanely. Generally, it was the more humble people who felt honored to befriend us.

"The students" ignored us.

Sesto was an exception. A chemist by training, an atheist philosopher by vocation, Sesto had a great respect for the individuality of humans, rejecting all conformity, and therefore fascism, which was the quintessential negation of individual intelligence—in fact the advocacy of mass stupidity. Because Sesto could strike solid friendships with the most disparate people, his overt closeness to Lello was regarded as part of his eccentricity, and the fascists never bothered him for this. It was Sesto who arranged with Don Omero for us to listen to the BBC.

Upon arriving at the farm, he was so surprised and happy to see us that he didn't know how he could best demonstrate his joy. He started by enveloping me in a big bear hug, as if he had found a long lost sister; then he hugged my two brothers; and then, to manifest to us his happiness in an even more graphic manner, he began to roll himself on the floor like a puppy dog, laughing and saying all sort of nice things about running into us, jumping up and down as if he had gone crazy.

What a tribute to us that was! With all the rejection we had been experiencing from all sides, what a welcome relief to feel so well loved and appreciated!

Dancing

On their way up to the farm, our three friends had discovered a place where there was going to be a dance that night. The main form of entertainment for the peasants, and therefore for young refugees, was dancing. My diary of the period is studded with entries that read, "Last night we went to dance at X's, and we had a great time."

We all liked to dance, but it was mainly to celebrate our getting together that we all decided to go.

The place was not the usual family farm, but a large old barn that had been emptied and cleaned up, and was now used only as a dancing hall. The two side walls were lined with wooden benches and the third wall, opposite the entrance, was reserved for the band of three or four players.

When we arrived, the floor was already crowded with young people. Some had brought wine, others tobacco and the much-sought-after cigarette paper. Lia—a beautiful refugee from Rome whom Arthur had spoken to me about and of whom I had been extremely jealous—was also there with a few friends. Although she was even more attractive than I had envisioned her from descriptions, seeing her in person made my jealousy almost disappear and I even felt friendly toward her. In my mind I had seen her as an irresistible *femme fatale*, capable of subduing any man to her will. Now I saw her as just another pretty girl.

We danced, and drank wine, and smoked, and talked and talked and talked. We were having a wonderful time, as only young people are capable of. Suddenly the boy who had been left outside to keep watch burst into the barn saying that two fascist militiamen were slowly coming up toward the barn's entrance. The music and dancing stopped, but we realized that it was impossible for anyone to leave the barn without being seen.

"If they start trouble," shouted Arthur, "we will jump them. Maestro, music!"

The music and the shuffling of feet resumed. We quickly rehearsed our routines. Arthur was from Milan, Lello and Gino from Rome, and I from Florence. The boys were on leave from their army units and were visiting their girlfriends, now refugees from the bombing of cities. The presence of Lia and the other city girls suited the situation.

The two militiamen came to the door and were unable to conceal their surprise at seeing so many of us. They realized that, even though they were heavily armed, if they played a trick on us, they wouldn't have a chance against this mob—possibly also armed—and decided to act friendly. They were offered a glass of wine, and the music and the dancing went on.

With their falcon eyes the two fascists stared around and seemed to have a particular interest in our group. One of them, a loathsome figure who seemed to be the leader, asked me to dance. I was about to refuse, I didn't want to be touched by that nauseating being, but I met Arthur's stare that unequivocally exhorted me to accept.

The fascist slid the rifle from his shoulder and gave it to Gino to hold. Then he took his ammunition belt and his pistol and gave them to Lello. When he held me to dance, I felt sick to my stomach. He told me his name and I realized that this fascist was notorious for his killings of partisans. He asked my name and where I was from, and I replied with a wealth of fake details.

The fascist let me talk, then he said, "You don't have to lie to me. I know who you are."

The dance was over, but as I moved to go back to my group, he held my arm firmly and we both stood in the middle of the floor. He told me not to move before letting go of my arm, then extracted from a pocket a little note book and showed one of its entries to me: *Edda Servi, seventeen, brunette with green eyes, average height and weight, engaged to an English Lieutenant, about twenty-six, tall, blond, brown eyes—two hundred thousand lire for her capture.* I shivered.

"You do not have to fear anything," he said. "See? I gave my arms and ammunitions to your brothers. They are too nice to kill me and they can't afford to keep me as a prisoner because you can't even find food and shelter for yourselves. As for your English Lieutenant—he'll get killed one of these days. But no fear, dear, *I will marry you.*"

I had never been so sick with fear and revulsion. (After the war was over and he had been tried and imprisoned for his war crimes, the repulsive man continued to stalk me obsessively, writing me love letters from jail!)

He went to gather his things, and after conferring a short while with his companion, the two of them left.

Spartaco began to sputter a string of very elaborate and colorful curses, blaming himself for not having killed them. Arthur emphatically declared that if it weren't for the presence of the girls the two fascists would not have gotten away alive. We knew of the reputation of that repulsive assassin and were all very upset, but I was more upset than anyone else, since he had dared talk to me with such impudence.

That same night, in spite of the fact that the people in our present farm had been very hospitable, the six of us left. We walked together for a while, and Sesto found a way to talk to me alone. He told me, just as a brother, that he had heard only bad things about Arthur, and strongly suggested that I stay away from him. I didn't want to believe him and answered, "Don't worry, Sesto, I can take care of myself."

We then parted, quite sad to have to leave each other's company.

Another few days of hardships before finding refuge in three different farms—Gino closer Marcella, and Lello not too far from me.

Little Treasure

On February 22, 1944, my eighteenth birthday, Arthur showed up riding a white horse. As soon as he saw me, he yelled from afar, "It's for you! It's my present to you for your birthday!"

I waited for him to reach the porch and to dismount, then I said, "What a present! Where did you get it?"

He wouldn't say. It could have been a stray horse, but it was more likely that he had stolen it.

"Does it have a name?"

"Sure he does. He is a treasure of a horse, and I call him *Tesoruccio*, Little Treasure."

I had never had any association with horses and in fact I had always been terribly afraid of these unpredictable animals, but I was happy to be remembered on my birthday and said, "I'll learn how to ride it, and it is going to be a lot of fun."

"There is nothing to it," said Arthur. "You'll first take a ride with me and then you will be on your own."

He helped me on the warm bare back of the huge animal and then he climbed on behind me. I was disconcerted at realizing how far from the ground my eyes were. I felt a little dizzy already, but didn't say anything. Arthur held me firmly with one arm around my waist and held both reins in his free hand. His body leaned heavily on me. His breath gave out an odor of bad wine and cheap tobacco.

At first, the horse walked slowly and I felt his hard muscles going up and down under my thighs, while the lower part of my body swung rhythmically from one side to the other. When we reached a dirt path, Arthur warned me that we were about to go into a trot. I tightened the grip of my legs and clutched Arthur's arm with both my hands. I was going up and down on the sweaty back of the horse in a kind of syncopated rhythm. My pelvic bones were beginning to hurt a lot, and my insides were all shaken. I begged Arthur to take me back, I had to get off that animal. But instead he yelled, "Hold on to the mane!" And he spurred the horse to a frantic gallop. We had left the path and were riding through the hilly fields with sharp turns and sudden stops. Arthur was still holding me at my stomach, but I felt as if I was going to fall head down. I screamed and screamed. The fields and the sky were going around in swirls. My heart was pounding furiously, while Arthur was laughing and having the time of his life.

At last we went back and I was standing on my own two feet, but as I started to walk I realized that I couldn't. I was shaking and shivering and weeping.

"Here," said Arthur. "Now Little Treasure is yours."

I collapsed onto the ground on my stomach and moaned, between sobs, "Thank you, I have had enough. I don't want it."

Arthur laughed, "That's exactly what I expected you to say. I had no intention of leaving him here anyway. I'll need this horse when we go into action—and to come to see you."

I didn't care about the horse. My body was aching and my heart was aching even more because of Arthur's cruelty and deviousness. Perhaps Sesto had been right, after all. Yet, hurting as I was, I couldn't help loving this man above anything in the world.

Still lying on my stomach on the cold cobblestones of the threshing-floor, I brought both my hands under my face and closed my eyes. I compared Arthur with the other two men in my life: Engelbert the German soldier, and my cousin Raffaele. Then I remembered meeting with Don Omero and his comforting words.

When Engelbert had come to Pitigliano to warn us against his fellow Germans, risking his life for me, I was touched, but I knew I would never have risked my life for him. Neither would I have given my life for Raffaele. But I would have gladly given my life for Arthur, who, though loving at times, was not even remotely as gentle and as caring as Engelbert and Raffaele had been. Even after what he did to me, I could not bear to be angry with him and readily forgave him his prank.

Lello surprised me in the afternoon with a pocketful of dried figs, my favorite dried fruit. He had walked several hours to find this present and to come and wish me a happy birthday. I was still very upset and in pain from the horrible ride, but seeing Lello made me truly happy and I tried to hide from him my feelings. Lello took a ride on the new horse, and told me that it was a delightful animal to ride. I didn't tell him how much I hated that beast.

Arthur was sobering up and he too seemed happy to see Lello. He told us that he had found a farm that was ideal for me. Laterina was built on the side of a cliff and could be seen from the nearest village, Sorano; but it had the advantage that anyone attempting to reach it would be spotted from the farm while still a distance away. Since for the past few days the farmers with whom I was staying had been hinting that I could no longer stay with them, I was very grateful to Arthur for having found a place for me to move to. I immediately packed my belongings and let the people know that I would be gone that very afternoon.

Arthur warned me that the new farm was quite a distance away, and that I'd better ride the horse. At first I refused, but eventually I conquered my fear, and even though still aching, I found the ride, now with Lello and now with Arthur, to be a pleasant experience. We arrived at Laterina shortly after sunset and, contrary to the norm, got a warm welcome from the people who were expecting us with an eagerness to help.

This was an unusually small family. It was composed of the old widowed woman, her older son with wife and two lovely little daughters, and a younger unmarried son. They seemed more worldly and educated than the farmers I had known so far. Lello was invited to stay with me for a while and he gladly accepted.

"It is dark now," said Emilio the younger son in a gentle and polite manner. "But tomorrow morning I'll show you the vast view we have from this farm. If the fascists find out that we have *guests* and want to come and get you, I'll welcome them with this."

He took from a hook near the fireplace one of the two rifles that were hanging there, and caressed it as if it were his favorite toy.

"Use it in self defence," he said, "if something happens when I am not around."

The rest of the family nodded.

Perplexing Pitiglianesi

We woke up to a very mild and clear morning. Arthur left early, and Lello and I walked with him and Little Treasure for a while. Then Arthur galloped away, and the two of us went back to survey the farm and its surroundings.

It was the most beautiful farm we had yet encountered. Exposed to the sun nearly all day, it was luxuriant with vegetation. The arable land was all terraced; in one of the higher levels, under the frame of a pergola, a round marble table and two semicircular benches about it were inviting. We sat for a while facing each other—two happy young people vacationing at a luxury resort...

White snow-drops, multicolored crocuses, violets, and other early spring flowers were pushing their heads through the rich dark soil all around us. Heavenly. Below the bottom level, a gorge flanked by tall cliffs was the only connection between the farm and the road that led to the village. We felt adventurous and decided to descend into the gorge. We started down slowly, without talking. I was thinking of Arthur. Lello looked pensive.

Finally he broke the silence to ask me, "What was the matter with you yesterday? You seemed to be upset."

I told him of Arthur's practical joke on me.

He listened without interrupting and remained silent for a moment afterwards, as if searching for the right words, then asked, "Have you ever been alone with Arthur?"

"Yes, many times."

"And what's between you and him?"

I stopped walking and looked straight into his eyes. "Love," I said. "Only much, much love."

Lello gently caressed my face.

"Good," he said. "I have faith in you. But I have a tremendous responsibility toward you and Marcella, and I like to be reassured that you know how to behave."

"I know," I said, "don't you worry." And we started to walk again.

We were almost running, now, light-heartedly and happy, when from behind a curve not too distant from us, we saw two armed men in uniform appear. We instinctively stopped and looked around. There was nowhere to go, nowhere to hide. My heart leaped to my throat. What if they were the two fascists who had come to the dancing place a few weeks earlier? I felt a knot in my stomach, and my legs refused to go.

Lello grabbed my arm. "Let's try to walk naturally," he whispered.

As we got nearer, we recognized one of the men as being someone a few years older than Lello from Pitigliano. His older brother was known to have killed partisans, and was a big shot in the new Fascist Republic. His younger brother, Lello's age, was fighting against the Allies. This one had been a barber all his life, and now he was serving in the militia, searching for the outlaws. We didn't know the other man.

I felt a great relief. I knew that we were in danger, but the thought of that vermin with whom I had been forced to dance added to the fear a revolting dimension.

The Pitiglianese, we felt, had two options: to tell his companion who we were and take us prisoners and even shoot us, or to ignore us and continue his dangerous scouting.

We hoped for the latter, of course, but he surprised us with a third choice. When on crossing paths we muttered good morning without raising our eyes, he stopped us by touching Lello on his shoulder and gave us a big grin. Then he hugged Lello, introduced him to his companion as a fellow Pitiglianese, and said, "What are you doing here? I thought you were in the 47th infantry regiment with my brother."

"I still am," answered Lello heartened. "I am on leave for a couple of weeks and came to visit my girlfriend here." And he proceeded to introduce me as Liliana Costantini. I looked very much like Gino and Mario, but nobody would have guessed that I was Lello's sister. The two fascists—including the one from Pitigliano who had known me since my birth—shook hands with me and said, "Pleased to meet you."

The Pitiglianese offered Lello a cigarette and said, "It is not safe for a young man like you to walk around without a uniform; if in my place there was someone else who didn't know you, like this guy here, they might have thought that you were a partisan and shot you."

To which Lello replied, "Actually, it is not safe to walk in this neighborhood in uniform: the partisans may shoot us at sight."

Lello undoubtedly had Emilio in mind, who was certain to be spying upon the scene from the farm above, his rifle leveled at the two men.

The two fascists got the message, turned around, and walked back to the village.

We also understood that we were tempting fate to be walking during the day near a village, and went back to our farm.

After recovering from the astonishment, we couldn't stop talking about this strange encounter. We couldn't get over the fact that this was the second time that after chancing upon two fascists armed to their teeth we were still alive and free.

"The first time," said Lello, "there were many of us, and if the militiamen had started something, they wouldn't have had a chance to get away alive. But these two?"

We kept on speculating over what might have prompted the fascist from Pitigliano to protect us in front of his foreign companion.

"One possibility," continued Lello, "is that when he saw us, he knew that he was near a partisan stronghold, and feared for his life."

We all had a big price on our heads, not because we were considered dangerous, but because we were in contact with, and protected by, the most feared and dangerous of the partisans and escaped prisoners of war.

"The other possibility, the most plausible one," Lello concluded, "is that this Pitiglianese, in spite of being a militiaman and the brother of a killer, did not have it in him to do us serious harm, especially since our father and his were on cordial terms."

This question raised by Lello has, in one form or another, bothered us all our lives. The majority of the Pitiglianesi did increase their harassment of us from the onset of the Racial Laws to our liberation by the Allies, mainly by breaking off all contact with us. We were non-existent, transparent when we met on the streets and alleys of Pitigliano; some abused us verbally, expropriated our assets, and acted in many ways as if we were sub-humans; *but they did not do us bodily harm.*

It must also be said that when our parents returned to Pitigliano three days after they had found refuge in a farm, and were immediately seized to be taken to the concentration camp, one of the *repubblichini* guards that had been sent to arrest them kept on repeating, "What did you come back to give yourselves up for?" And he made sure to distract his companion and to look the other way himself while our parents carried from our house to that of a trustworthy neighbor a large case with the precious temple tapestries and silver ornaments that were in safe-keeping in our home when not in use.

There were individual Pitiglianesi who never lost sight, in such a confusing world, of what was right and what was wrong. Particularly so those who were simple and uneducated but had very clear minds and warm hearts.

A Slap in My Face

Lello left after a week and I stayed for a while longer.

Emilio was constantly teasing me about Arthur. He told me that Arthur had many girlfriends, and I was only one of many. In fact a certain Lia (the girl from Rome I had met at the dancing place and of whom I had been jealous) was more than a girlfriend: she was his lover.

Again, as with Sesto, I didn't want to believe Emilio. Besides, he was interested in me, he made it obvious, and he was jealous of my feelings for someone else. He made me suffer unnecessarily with his accusatory tales about Arthur. I loved Arthur more than life, and I had convinced myself that he was true to me as I was to him, and that his feelings for me were as intense as mine for him. But Emilio insisted that he knew better, and he kept on telling me, at the risk of making a nuisance of himself, that I should stay away from the South African.

One cold March night, three months after we had first met, Arthur returned to Laterina and right away he asked me out for a walk in the garden. He had something important to tell me.

Even though I was beside myself with joy at seeing him again, I didn't like his serious tone.

"I am a bad boy," he said as a start. "I have been lying to you."

A rush of blood swelled my head, but I was able to conceal my pain and preserve a measure of calm.

"When you will know the truth, you will not love me anymore."

"Please, go ahead!"

"I don't know where to start."

"Why don't you start with Lia? I know she is your lover!" I sputtered in one breath.

I felt crushed.

Arthur admitted that he and that girl had been very close at one time, but that was not what he wanted to talk to me about.

What was it, then, that would make me cease to love him if I found out?

"I am not an architect," he finally said. "When I was drafted into the army I was eighteen, and I had not even started college. I am not as old as I told everybody I was, I am only twenty-two."

"Is that all?" I asked repressing my impulse to hug him.

"No, there is more."

Again, a pang of anxiety clutched my chest.

"I am not a lieutenant in the air force. I am just an infantry man."

He paused.

"What else?" I said, expecting the worst.

"I am through," he said.

"And why on earth should I stop loving you?" I almost screamed.

"Because girls only fall in love with officers, not with simple soldiers."

"Silly boy," I cried and laughed at the same time. "I love you more, now that I know the truth." And I kissed his face, and his lips, sweetly and passionately. In turn his kisses made me almost suffer with a new, intense, excessive feeling of pleasure and a consuming desire.

It was getting cool outside, but I didn't feel like going back to the farm. Arthur wrapped his arm around my shoulders and we slowly walked toward the barn, where he had left Little Treasure. We lay on the straw and Arthur fell asleep right away. For a while I watched him sleep. I had never had an opportunity to observe him so closely, but now that I knew, I could see how young he really was.

By the time he woke up my passion had considerably cooled off, and we returned to the house.

Arthur left during the night, leaving a love note for me.

Lello and Gino arrived a couple of days later, and the first thing they were told by the people in the farm was that they expected relatives to come from the city and they no longer had room for me.

My brothers seemed to have anticipated this turn of events, because they had found another place for me and had in fact come to take me away from this farm, which was too close to the village and not at all as safe as we had believed. They didn't tell me or anybody else where we were going. "For our safety," was what they said, but I sensed that they wanted to get me away from Arthur, and make him lose track of me. They had certainly heard, just as Sesto and Emilio had, about Lia, about a fisherman's daughter, and many other girls. Only I was blind and deaf to it all.

I had to believe in Arthur in order to survive.

We arrived at the next farm in the evening. During the hike I had felt—with each step forward—the overwhelming impulse to rush back to the place we had left. I marked in my mind every step of the way. In the middle of the night, while everybody slept, I sneaked out and, gripped with fear and guilt, made my way back to Laterina, expecting Arthur to return there.

Upon awaking and discovering my absence, my brothers went to look for me. It didn't take them long to find me. Once they did, Lello, before saying anything, slapped me right in my face, mainly, I am sure, because I had gone back in search of Arthur, but also because returning to a place our instinct warned us to leave, always constituted an unnecessary risk. This was the only time my brother struck me in my entire life.

Deranged Deutsch

Quartilia could no longer keep Marcella, but eventually we found another place for her, and the three of us moved endlessly in search of a place where at least one of us could stay for a while. We found a farmer that would take only one person and it was decided that Lello would remain there. Gino and I found another farmer in the vicinity who was willing to shelter both of us.

"Could we stay for a few days?" Gino asked as usual.

To our great surprise and joy the farmer answered: "You can stay as long as you wish!"

We had been there only a couple of days when early one morning Gino, who suffered from insomnia, got up and went for a walk in the woods. I had always been a light sleeper, and when Gino left, I also woke up. After a while, when he didn't come back, I got up and looked out of the window. Instead of Gino, however, I saw a German officer climbing up the dirt road on foot. I promptly withdrew from the window and prayed that Gino would see the German before the latter surprised him. I didn't know what to do. Should I go and hide, or stay near the window on the chance of seeing Gino in the distance and somehow warn him of the danger?

I held my breath. From the shuffling of feet on the threshing-floor in front of the house, I knew that the German had reached the farm. The farmers were still asleep. I expected the German to announce his presence by hitting the front door with the butt of his rifle; instead, I heard him say, "Guten Morgen!" and a few other words.

I stuck my head out of the window and saw that Gino was with him! Gino had been sitting on the stoop of the farmhouse when he saw the German approaching and did not have a chance to hide himself. The German had no way of knowing at sight that Gino—blond, tall, and blue-eyed—was a Jew, nor that he was a partisan. He might think Gino was on leave from the army.

Gino saw me at the window and gestured for me to come down.

"I'll explain to you later," Gino said. "He's looking for something. Try to understand what he wants—and *reshud*, get rid of him fast," he added, using a Judeo-Italian word.

I rushed down. On seeing me the young officer, who was holding his cap in his hand, brought it at his chest, made the heels of his boots click sharply and said to me, "Guten Morgen!"

My eyes went directly to his bald head. He was slightly taller than Gino, looking very young, and his precocious baldness caught my attention. He seemed to be self-conscious about it, but he soon regained control of himself and began to ask for something. From his gesturing I understood that he was looking for eggs, and said in English, "Eggs?"

In hearing this English word, the German looked at me with surprise and then asked, also in English, "How come you can speak English?"

"I studied it in school," I said without thinking. "Probably the same reason why *you* speak English."

I worried that he might know that I was lying, since English was forbidden in Italy and not taught in schools. But he nodded and we carried on a brief conversation. He told me that he had just turned twenty-four, that he had lost his hair almost overnight at the front and that war was a horrible thing. I hurried to get all the eggs I could find in the farmhouse and gave them to him hoping that he would leave. But he seemed to be in no hurry. The farmers in the meantime had gotten up, and one of them was calling us for breakfast. Gino and I were hungry, but wanted to get rid of the German first. We said good-bye, we had to go now, but he said, "No good-bye yet, please." We halfheartedly invited him to have breakfast with us, and he promptly accepted.

While we were eating, another two Germans arrived, and after a brief exchange with the first one, they sat at the table with us. They all removed their firearms and put them on the table. For a moment I thought that they might be deserters, since I could not imagine (and to date it remains a mystery to me) their casually coming near partisan lairs, one or two at a time, without a precise order or mission. Gino and I felt extremely uncomfortable, to say the least. Then another three arrived, but they had already eaten. They stopped to rest and to ask directions for a location, which we recognized as being near where Lello was staying. At this point, we got up and simply left the farm. We had to go before they did and try to find Lello and warn him that the area was infested with Germans. It was no place for us, we'd better go and hide someplace else.

But the first visitor got up, took his arms and his bundle of eggs, said something in German to the others and... joined us.

We didn't know what to think. We still had to pretend that all this was natural. We walked together, and on the way the German officer talked about the draft evaders, almost amused at the lack of discipline among the Italians. I gladly became his translator. We were waiting for him to reveal to us that he hated what his country was doing, and would we please accept him as one of ours. As we walked, we met Lello who was coming to visit and almost fainted at the sight of us with a German officer. We said "hi." His face was washed of any vitality and the German, observing his pallor, asked whether our friend was sick. We quickly assented, making sure not to mention that he was our brother.

We turned around to walk with Lello back to our farm, but took a different route in order to avoid the others that were coming up behind us. Our German followed us like a faithful dog. He seemed neither afraid of us, nor suspicious of whom we might be. He was obviously in a good mood, and even sang an English song that spoke of the moon, the night, Hawaii, and you. At the end of his song he offered us a cigarette, and Gino took out of his pocket—where he also carried the *Mezuza* he had torn away from our door post the night of our flight—his old cigarette lighter, almost an amulet which had long ceased to be functional since no lighter fluid had been available for years.

The bald German gave me the eggs to hold and returned his cap on his head. He put one hand on top of the other, palms touching, then he spread them vertically apart to show a tall quantity, and said that he would bring us some gasoline the next day. When we reached our farm, all the other Germans had gone. We were impatient for this one to go too. But he seemed to have nothing better to do than enjoy our company. We asked him about the progress of the war. He was hesitant at first, then he drew a rough map of central Italy with a stick on the dust. He drew a line across it between Naples and Rome, and called it "Montecassino."

"The front," he said, "is right here at this line."

"Is it moving north or south?"

"It is not moving at all."

"What do you think the outcome of this battle will be?" asked Lello as a way of understanding this man's behavior a little. "And the outcome of the war?"

"Why, with a big victory!"

"Whose victory?" I dared at this point, already savoring the sweet taste of discovering that he was indeed one of ours.

"Of mein Fuehrer, of course! As soon as all the Jews, the bandits and the enemies of our Fatherland are destroyed, we will celebrate our big victory!"

Having said this, he clicked his heels, took his egg, and finally said good-bye.

We were shaken. Gino told us that when he had first met this German, as he rested in front of the house, the officer had pointed his gun at him, perhaps thinking that he had stolen his boots from a German soldier. Gino had smiled to hide his fear. The officer had returned the smile, and looking indeed at Gino's German army boots had said, "Gut Morgen! Du bist amico Deutsch!"

We agreed the man was a lunatic, but we would be even more crazy if we didn't leave this farm at once. It was a shame to give up this friendly place, but perhaps it was *too* friendly, and—as we learned later—very close to a main road and often a stop for the Germans in transit. We hastily gathered our things and fled without even saying good-bye. We also gave up Lello's place and began our search again.

A few days later, like guilty people who go back to the site of their crime, we passed through the area and stopped at the farm. On the cupboard there was something for us, the farmers told us. We went to look, curious, and found a huge clear-glass bottle filled with a blue liquid. We opened the bottle and sniffed: and all that liquid was indeed gasoline for Gino's cigarette lighter!

Under the bottle was a piece of paper torn from a note book. It was written in pencil in English. It read,

> Darling!
> I don't know anything about you. I realize I don't even know your name. But I know I love you and if you feel the same about me, please leave a message with these people. I will be

back soon. I was a depressed man when I first arrived at this farm, and I don't know what I would have done had I not met you. But now you have given me the will to live, the will to believe, the will to hope.   I love you!

Gunter

We left precipitously and never set foot on that farm again.

Pesach 5704

Spring arrived by assault. After the most frigid winter anyone could recall, the snow suddenly disappeared and green and yellow patches were spreading arrogantly all over the fields and hills. Every night, as Easter approached, we carefully watched the moon. We knew that when it would be as round as a wheel of cheese, it would be the fourteenth of Nissan, the first night of Passover. With excitement and a great deal of anticipation, we began to make a few matzot with the flour that the farmer who was presently sheltering us allotted to us, and baked them in the rustic stone oven that was built outside, between the farmhouse and the barn. The farmers had never seen unleavened bread before and gathered around us to watch us make these round and oval cakes, cut and trimmed like doilies. But for us not only did they symbolize the festival of remembrance and freedom, they represented home. The commercial square matzot of today had never existed in Italy, and the matzot we made and baked in our community kosher oven each year before Passover were the only ones we had ever known. By being able to make them as we had seen our adults do when we were children, we nourished our souls even more than our stomachs.

With the mild season and with Easter in sight, peddlers from nearby villages began to show up at the farms. Their wares consisted mainly of women's shoes, made with plastic tops and cork soles, and yards of brightly printed rayon material for women's dresses. Each time one of them appeared at the farm where we were staying, we had to run and hide.

One day one of these peddlers arrived pulling a rope harnessed to a live kid goat. The people in the farm he had just visited, he said as he sat on a rock panting, had no cash to pay him and had given him this animal in exchange. Would our farmer buy it from him? What was he going to do with it, going from farm to farm? Having to pull the kid along was a waste of his time and energy. If it weren't for those damned fascists, he explained, he wouldn't have to do this for a living. He had held the local salt and tobacco franchise (in Italy a monopoly of the State) for many years, but now it had been taken away from him because he had been caught speaking against the Fascist regime. Would anyone buy the kid from him? He'd sell it at any price!

When we heard from our hideout that the man was not a fascist, we ran down and told him that we would buy the young goat. We didn't have much money left from what we had brought from home, and offered the small amount we had left: sixteen lire. The animal was worth much more, as the man told us, but he took pity on us and he let us have it for the cost of pair of socks!

Even though we had seen our father ritually slaughter the animals for kosher meat, we had no taste for the job, and begged the farmer to do it for us. It would not be kosher, but it was not kashrut that we were after, now that we had eaten anything to keep alive. Only tradition... and a good meal.

The night the full moon appeared in the sky, the four of us celebrated together the first Seder by reciting excerpts from the *Haggadah* we knew by heart and having a full traditional Passover meal interspersed with laughter and tears. Each bite we swallowed we were reminded of our parents and Mario who were captives and nearly starving. We shared our meal with our hosts who became, for a change, our guests at the festive table.

From Uncle Tranquillo, who kept in touch with us once in a while, we learned that our parents and Mario were still at the same concentration camp and we were thankful that they were alive. After Lello and Gino's dangerous visit, our parents were given a hard time by the director of the camp. They were interrogated daily, first separately and then together, about their other four children. The first of these interrogations was the hardest, because they were taken by surprise and each one lied about us without knowing whether the other's tale corroborated exactly his or her own. They were threatened to be shot if they didn't tell the truth about those fake helpers and didn't give precise indication of where their other four children could be found. Our parents consistently denied that the helpers were their children, and even denied having other children altogether. And as far as the whereabouts of the four of us, anyhow, even if they had admitted to our existence, they indeed knew nothing.

They were not shot and not even physically hurt, as were the non-Italian Jews daily, but were psychologically harassed constantly, and their already meager allotment of foul food was reduced still further. More and more often they went on an empty stomach in order to pool together their three rations and have Mario eat a little bit more.

And we were even celebrating Passover!

During our stay at Laterina, the farm perched on the cliff overlooking a gorge, Lello and I had met Emilio's cousin, Iris. She was a fine young lady who belonged to a well-to-do family and who lived, for the moment, in a hamlet nearby with her mother. On the eve of Easter we received a message through a mutual friend that the four of us were invited the next day to share the festive meal at her home.

"We don't want to be seen in a populated area," we said. "Thank Iris for us, but no, we can't accept."

"I assure you," the friend insisted, "that everyone there sympathizes with you. There is no real cause for alarm."

We were chronically starved and Iris's messenger didn't have to insist too much to convince us to accept, even though we knew there was a risk. We would be watchful. Besides, Easter coincided with Mario's tenth birthday, and it was a good occasion and a good omen too, we felt, not to let Mario's birthday pass without celebration.

As soon as we arrived at the home of our new friend, late next morning, we judged from the aromas that came from the kitchen that we were in for another treat in gourmet food. Twice this week we had a chance to fill our stomachs with excellent food, but this time we were offered indeed the best meal we had had in years, with hors d'oeuvres, elegant trimmings to go with meat and fish dishes, first-rate wines and desserts. We toasted to Mario's birthday, we sang and laughed, and were again filled with sadness.

Not only had the meal been excellent, but the conversation at the table as well. Iris was a conservative, strongly opinionated, traditional school-teacher. She hated technology and progress because she viewed them only in their negative aspects: new weapons, slackening of moral values, and so on. Even though we didn't agree with her one-sided view of such a multifaceted subject, arguing with Iris was as big a treat as relishing her mother's splendid meal.

It was our practice not to linger in one place too long, so as soon as the meal was over, we were ready to go.

"I have prepared a bag with the leftovers for you to take along," said Iris at this point.

We had just finished a sumptuous meal and were quite full. Nevertheless, the thought of those delicacies made our mouths water. During these days of Passover, aside from the two big feasts—the first Seder and this one—we had tried to avoid patently unkosher food and our main meals consisted of a hard-boiled egg, a piece of matza and a dish of wild greens. However, it didn't seem right to us to be taking advantage of these generous ladies and began to timidly decline the offer.

"You gave us the warmest welcome and the most magnificent meal," said Lello. "Thank you, but we can't accept: we don't want to deprive you of the delicious leftovers."

"Please," insisted Iris. "If you don't take them, we'll feed them to the chickens."

"To the chickens?!" we exclaimed in one voice. "We'll take them, we'll take them!"

Ilio Santarelli

We had never stayed at the farm of Ilio Santarelli. He was a committed anti-fascist, we knew, and went out of his way to help everyone in need. But because of this, he seldom had room for more people. By the time we got to know him, he was already hiding a New Zealander and two British soldiers who had escaped from a POW camp. Santarelli had three young daughters, and didn't like to have men staying at his home. He kept the three fugitives in a cave in his property some distance away from his farmhouse. This way he protected his daughters, and the refugees were safer as well.

Ilio Santarelli was the only farmer in that area who owned a radio. As a token of friendship, he once let us gather in his home to listen to Radio London. But after the news was over, we respected his reticence and left his farm to go elsewhere.

Every day, in any kind of weather, Santarelli took time off from his farming chores to go to the cave and bring the men hidden there food and news. One of the two British soldiers was a Jew from Manchester. When he heard of four Jewish adolescents hiding from the Nazi-fascists in the area, he asked Santarelli to take us to see him. We were always on the run, but finally Ilio was able to locate us and invited us to go with him to the cave.

We found the three young men playing cards on top of a rock they used as a table. They were very happy to see us and to find that we spoke English. Lawrence, the Jewish soldier, was especially interested in us and asked us a million questions about our family and ourselves.

We were also curious about him, and he was happy to talk to us. He spoke with tenderness and obvious nostalgia about his wife and his two children.

We all ate together the food that Santarelli had brought, and afterwards we played a few card tricks. I knew a mathematical trick my father had taught me and I played it with Lawrence, an amateur mathematician, and this kept us pleasantly engaged for a while. Then I asked whether they knew the lyrics of a few songs I liked, such as one that began with the words "Lucky, lucky me." Francis, the New Zealander, knew it and wrote those lyrics for me. We sang, talked, laughed, and enjoyed the time together.

To be able to converse in their language was a great treat for the three of them, whose only contact with the world was the farmer with whom they could exchange but a few Italian words, and when Lello decided that it was time for us to part, they begged us to stay a little longer. But Lello—who always seemed to have the feeling of when it would no longer be safe to linger in one place—explained that we had a long way to go that afternoon, and we must leave now. They made us promise that we would come back soon and spend some more time together. For us, too, it had been a great pleasure to meet these three men, especially Lawrence, and we left the cave already looking forward to another visit within a few days.

Santarelli remained behind.

We started walking downhill, and we were soon reached by Francis running after us to return my pen with which he wrote the words of the song. Another hug, then Francis climbed back to the cave, and we began to hop gaily down. We were all smiles and songs. This visit had put us in a great mood!

As we usually did when we walked in broad daylight, we avoided the open space to walk very close to the thicket of bramble. We were halfway down toward the woods when we saw a small group of men in light raincoats climbing up through the bare patch. Since no peasant or partisan would walk around the countryside in such attire, we knew that they were *repubblichini* in plainclothes. We quickly crouched among the thorny bushes waiting for the strangers to pass us by before leaving our hiding place.

A few minutes later, as the group disappeared from view, we were about to resume our walk, when we heard some gun shots. We froze in our position. We knew that Santarelli and his three men were not armed. The shooting had come from the other men. Were Santarelli and our new friends dead? We couldn't get over the fact that but for a few minutes the same fate would have befallen us. We were shattered. So much went on in our minds—all the things we had just done and said, our promise to go back soon to see the three young men again—but we didn't dare to talk. We remained silent and immobile in our hidden spot for what seemed a long time. All of a sudden a group of men appeared in the clearing and we could see the fascists and the Germans walking our four friends down the hill at gun point.

It was not until the end of the war that we learned the details. The fascists went to get Ilio and the three fugitives after a farmer—who knew both Santarelli's habit of going to the cave at a certain time of the day and that neither he nor his men were armed—had betrayed him for a kilo of salt! Salt was scarce and precious, and here was a man ready to sacrifice four human lives for a handful of it! A summary mock trial was held and two days after their capture, on May 5, 1944, barely five weeks before the end of the conflict in that area, the four were compelled to dig their own collective grave, were shot and left the way they had fallen—two of them leaning against the freshly-dug dirt wall—without proper burial. The grave itself with the bodies was not discovered until the end of October, almost five months after the liberation.

All we knew at the moment was that a good man such as Ilio Santarelli and our new friends had been taken prisoners. A couple of days later, we learned that Ilio's farm had been burnt to the ground, leaving the wife and the three girls—who didn't know where their man had been taken, much less that he had been shot—homeless.

Chapter Eleven

Enhanced Danger

After Ilio Santarelli had been arrested and his farm burned, the number of people who were willing to shelter us became smaller by the day. The fascist threats directed at the farmers to prevent them from hiding us—which, until now, few people had taken seriously—began to be heeded, and this had a disastrous effect on us.

Mamma Breaks Down

At about the same time that we began to become discouraged, we heard from our parents that the worst part of being in the concentration camp was not so much hunger and lack of freedom as the periodic rumors that we had been caught and shot. Our parents continued to be interrogated daily about us, but now the Prefect of the Province had expressly come to the concentration camp from Grosseto, the province's capital, to threaten them. He told them that he knew of our existence and whereabouts, and if we didn't give ourselves up to join the rest of the family at the concentration camp, we would be taken and shot without due process.

By now the majority of the camp's prisoners had already been taken by bus, during the night between the 16th and 17th of April, to the enormous transshipment camp of Fossoli di Carpi in the province of Modena, and from there, a few days later, transported by armored cattle cars, in the most horrifying conditions, to the gas chambers of Auschwitz. Our parents, however, were led to believe that their fellow inmates had been taken to a work camp and they thought that in a few weeks when the three of them would be taken there too, the four of us—young and strong—would be able to help them, both with the language and with relieving them should their fatigue become intolerable.

Mamma finally broke down. Uncle Tranquillo brought us a letter from her *requesting* that the four of us present ourselves immediately; but if the boys were not to be found, at least Marcella and I should go. Neither Mamma nor Uncle Tranquillo made mention of the "relocation" that had taken place.

Marcella didn't have to be begged. She had wanted to join Mamma from the very beginning of our nomadic life and welcomed our mother's injunction.

"If Marcella goes, will you go too?" Lello asked me.

"I don't know."

I missed my parents and Mario immensely, but how could I give up my freedom? Yet, if Marcella—who, in spite of being four years younger had psychological power over me—had insisted on wanting to go, I probably would have gone, too.

As we left the outskirts of Pitigliano, where we had met with Uncle Tranquillo, we chanced upon Arthur. I had not seen him for nearly two months and my heart leapt, but I was in no mood for effusions.

"What's the matter with you people?" Arthur asked. "You all look glum."

I told him of our mother's letter and of the possibility that Marcella and I might give ourselves up to be taken to the concentration camp.

Arthur flew into a rage. "Are you crazy?" he said attaching a string of

228

curses to his rhetorical question. "I know that you are sick and tired of knocking at doors like beggars and being rejected—who isn't? But we haven't yet exploited the area of the Viterbese!"

"We don't know the area at all," said Gino.

"Neither do I," replied Arthur, "but we must try."

"Sure," nodded Lello. "I am not ready to give up."

Before taking a step that was not reversible, there were still a few more options, such as moving in another area where we didn't know anybody, as Arthur had suggested. Marcella was utterly miserable and Arthur tried to console her, to little avail. Perhaps Ivan could have convinced her, but we had not seen him in months, and Marcella was sad also about this.

Arthur took us to a farm at the southeast limit of the Lamone Forest (the *real* one, the former hideout of *real* bandits such as the one who had once visited our Grandma Debora!), a zone we had not explored so far. We were told that we could stay at this farm for the night. Arthur continued on his way, making me first promise, no, swear, that I would never voluntarily present myself to the Fascist authorities.

"If you give yourself up," he said lovingly, "I'll go crazy."

Livio Servi

At this farm, although we didn't know the owners, they seemed to know who we were. Here we found someone who told us that another Jewish family from Pitigliano was hiding not too far away, in fact quite close to where he lived. Their family name was Servi, like ours. Although they were not relatives, we certainly shared a few ancestors. In a sense they were more than relatives. As members of the same small community, we Jews lived in close contact from birth to death, bonded to one another not only by traditions, but by a shared history and a common destiny. We got very excited and wanted to go immediately to visit our friends.

We were not sure whether our visit would make them happy or upset them. But the need to be with somebody who was part of our world prevailed over our reticence. We decided to hold off until the next day, and entrusted the person who told us about them to act as our messenger and to stop at their place to announce our visit for the next morning.

None of us could sleep with this exciting thought in mind, and before dawn we were on our way. It was still dark when we reached the lovely little round Lake Mezzano, surrounded by forests. We began to walk around it, since the cave where Livio Servi and his family were hiding was near the opposite bank of the lake. We had walked perhaps ten minutes when we spotted a little row boat a few yards from the shore with a boy fishing.

"Would you take us to the other side of the lake?" we shouted. Knowing that we had nothing to offer him in exchange for his favor, we added, "But we can't pay you!"

"I'll be happy to take you," said the boy pulling his fishing line in. "And I wouldn't want to be paid!"

We felt incredible warmth in our hearts for the spontaneous and generous response of the young boy. We ran down to the shore, the boy hastily rowed to get closer, and one by one we jumped into the boat that for a moment seemed to be on the verge of capsizing. As we took turns at rowing, the sun began to filter through the trees and brighten the water and surrounding trees with colors. The whole scene was enchanting.

We arrived at Livio's cave when everybody was still asleep except for the youngest of the three girls. She hugged us and went to the back of it to wake up the rest of the family. We were stunned to see how this grotto had been transformed into a pleasant, livable place. There were even curtains at the little hole that served as a window!

Livio, a tall, stout man in his early fifties with a stooped posture, came to the front of the cave to greet us. He was touched by our presence and could not hold back a few tears. Signora Olga, a slender and frail-looking lady, was also moved. But the girls, ranging in age from twenty-three to thirteen, and the fiance of one of them—a Jewish refugee from Florence—were as excited and as happy to see us as we were to see them. They offered us a nice breakfast, during which we were asked many questions about our parents and the other people at the concentration camp. We had a lot to talk about. They were astonished to hear that Lello and Gino had ventured inside the concentration camp, but at the same time not too surprised, since they considered all of our family courageous and resourceful. We soon noticed that they seemed to be uneasy, fearing perhaps that we might ask them to let us stay for a while. So we said good-bye and left with our hearts filled with joy.

Although they were all together and their dwelling reflected their neat habits at home, we felt no envy of them. In fact we felt sorry for them, who were much too confined and far more fearful of being caught, and not without reason. For us, in constant movement from place to place, it was much easier to elude capture than for the six of them, all trapped in one place. What was not so easy, of course, was the thought that a segment of our family was already "caught," and for the four of us to be in constant search for shelter and food.

Our joy and excitement were ebbing.

Our peregrination started again.

Rejection and Receptiveness

As we walked without destination in an area unfamiliar to us, we saw a cart pulled by oxen and begged the man who was driving it to give us a ride to wherever he was going. As it turned out, the man knew who we were because he had come to our house a couple of times when our father was helping him with bookkeeping. He said he wanted to help, but in reality he couldn't wait to get rid of us. He told us of a farm where we might stay and stopped the cart to let us off. We headed in the direction that he indicated, but when we arrived, they wouldn't let us stay. They gave us a piece of cheese and some bread, and firmly and with some threats asked us to leave.

We ate our cheese and bread sitting on the ground of a tall-grass meadow, and after resting for a while, we resumed our aimless walk.

We walked and walked.

On our way to nowhere, we met a little old woman who looked and acted a bit crazy. Without our asking, she invited us to her farm, gave us supper, and let us sleep at her place. The next morning, however, the First Communion of her little grandson was going to be celebrated, and the rest of the family wanted us to go away.

Marcella and I told the old woman that we could be of help in tidying up the house and preparing the festive meal. It didn't take her long to persuade the rest of the family, especially those who would otherwise have to remain behind. During the whole morning, while the communicant and his entire family were at the little church for the ceremony, we worked hard—cleaning, cooking, baking, and setting the table. When they came back, we were invited to eat at the table with the family, and everybody praised us for a job well done and for our food; but right after the meal, the old woman begged us to go.

Again, we were on our way to look for shelter and food.

At the next farm, the people refused to help, but told us of another farm. There the scene repeated itself. They told us of a third farm. As we approached the third farm, tired and discouraged, we realized that it was near a main road and in fact, as we consulted with one another as whether to try or not, a German truck stopped in front of the farmhouse. Two soldiers climbed out of the truck and went inside. We turned on our heels and went back to the second farm. The person who opened the door was surprised to see us back, but didn't have the heart to turn us away a second time. She looked like a kind person, and in fact she gave us something to eat, put some straw on the kitchen floor and told us to sleep there.

As we kept quiet, wondering what we would do next, we heard a trampling of heavy shoes and the faint sound of a phonograph reaching us from above.

"They are dancing and have guests," said Gino. "And that's probably why they didn't want us to stay."

Early the next morning, while the whole farm was still asleep, we got up and left before the guests—in case any of them had stayed over—could see us.

We went back to the third farm near the road. There they told us that the previous night two Germans had been there to look for rebels and Jews, and they didn't want anybody to stay at the farm. We had no intention of staying since the location was too exposed and dangerous for us. We were only hoping for some breakfast, but not the slightest hint of an offer of food was made to us, so we resumed our wandering, searching for shelter and something to put in our mouths.

Toward the middle of the day, sweaty and starved, we arrived at a place where we were given some food and were allowed to change our foul-smelling clothes. Afterwards, Marcella and I went to the nearby creek to wash the dirty clothes, while Lello and Gino scouted the area to familiarize themselves with the surroundings.

I did the washing while Marcella, ill and exhausted, sat on a rock. After an hour or so down at the creek, we got an unexpected visit. It was about 4:30 in the afternoon on Monday, May 8. Quite suddenly, a squadron of American fighter planes appeared in the sky right above us. With the noise of the rushing water and our singing and chatting, we had not heard them arrive. They circled around, then suddenly, one by one, began to nose-dive. Even though the war was well into its third year, I had never seen such an occurrence before and believed that the plane coming down over me was actually falling. But as it reached very close to the ground, two objects were ejected from it and the plane soared again. I rejoiced at the thought that those two things were parachutists, like Jack and Jay. But I had hardly had the time to formulate my thoughts when I saw an enormous column of black smoke rise from the ground, not far from us; a formidable roar lacerated the air.

There were more smoke columns and roars, and each time I thought, "Next time it could be us."

I was normally very much afraid of dying, but to my surprise I was filled with an incredible sense of calm and serenity. I thought of Mamma and Father and Mario and Arthur, and prayed to God to let me see them again.

Marcella's reaction was quite different. She seemed thrilled and excited by what was going on as if it were a joyous and long-awaited celebration.

She began to say loudly, "This one is for us! I see it coming!"

"I hope not, I don't want to die!"

"Are you afraid?" she teased me.

"Of course I am!"

"Why be afraid?" she said. "One of these on our heads and all will be over."

"But I don't want it to be over! I love life, I want to live!"*

The bombing and the din had ceased and the little airplanes had left our sky. A fine dust was settling on our laundry, our skin, our lungs. Without even wiping the pasty sweat from my face, I knelt near the running water and began to wash and rinse the clothes again. Marcella, who had come to stand near me during the bombing, went back to perch on top of her rock.

I glanced at her. She looked pretty and bright, and one would assume from the expression on her face that she was ecstatically happy. But her actions and talk showed otherwise. Was she really in such a state of distress that she wished for death? She was a total mystery to me. I could not imagine what went on in the mind of this fourteen-year-old girl. The future didn't exist for any of us, but weren't the memories of the past and even our present struggle to keep alive enough incentive to want to live?

I started to sing again and she joined me.

Lello and Gino arrived out of breath, anxious and frightened. They knew that the airplanes were bombing a bridge on the little river of which our creek was a tributary and that we had gone to wash our clothes not far from the bridge. They were overjoyed and dumbfounded at seeing us unscathed and singing.

Arcangelo Brinzaglia

After six months of wandering around an area of about 500 square miles in Tuscany, Umbria and Lazio, in the vicinity of Pitigliano, Sovana, Sorano, Manciano, Bolsena and countless other towns and villages in search of food and shelter, often separated from one another, we now decided to remain together and to go back to Le Capannelle, the farm where Gino and I had first stayed for about a month.

We made that decision mainly because we didn't know where else to go, but also because we knew that these people were relatively well off and wouldn't turn us down. Besides, the patriarch of the family, Arcangelo, was our father's closest friend among the farmers.

We had to cover a long distance and arrived late at night. We knocked at the door.

There was no answer.

We knocked again, and began to call in whispers, so that they would recognize our muffled voices and not get scared. The dogs recognized us and began to whimper. But no one would come to open the door.

We knocked and called again, and waited for a while, a bit puzzled.

Finally the window on the landing above the entrance door—from which I had seen Arthur for the first time—opened, and one of the women stuck her head out. All we could see was the bright white of the nightgown.

"It's us, please come and open."

"Go away," we heard Agostina say.

We were sure that she hadn't recognized us.

"It's us. Please come and open the door."

"What are you trying to do to us, children dear? Please go away." And she closed the window.

We kept on calling. After a long time the window opened again. This time it was Maria, the oldest of the sisters-in-law. Her large white shape almost filled the rectangle of the window.

"Didn't Agostina recognize us? Please, Maria, come and open the door. We are very hungry and dead tired."

"She recognized you all right. Please go away. We don't want our farm to be burnt!"

We couldn't believe our ears. If these good people didn't want us, whom could we turn to?

Before Maria would close the window again, Lello said calmly, "Only for tonight. Then we have someplace else to go."

"Not in the house," replied Maria. "I'll open the barn for you and you can stay there."

She threw a shawl on top of her nightgown, and came down to open the barn. We didn't dare ask her for something to eat. We slipped into the barn, thanked her, and she locked the door from the outside. We threw ourselves on the smelly straw, but we could not fall asleep. Our stomachs were grumbling. We had never expected to be turned away by these people and the thought of having nowhere else to go frightened us.

The dogs were excited and began to bark. Someone from upstairs tried to calm them down, but they seemed possessed, and wouldn't stop. We tried not to pay any attention to them, but how could we not? They might have a reason for barking so insistently.

The farmers must have been afraid. We were hungry, tired and full of fears ourselves, and all this swelled up into a huge anger for me. Why did we have to go through all this? What had we done to deserve to be punished this way? When people are struck by illness or other calamity, they also question why. But somehow resignation comes because nature, fate, something outside people's power has dealt them an injustice. But in our case there was no possibility of resignation: all our troubles had been caused by other human beings—nasty, beastly, corrupt human beings.

Someone tapped at the barn window from outside. We held our breath.

"It's me," said a familiar voice. "Come and open."

"We can't, we've been locked in ourselves."

We opened the window, and saw Spartaco with two other men.

"We will climb through the window," said Spartaco. And one at the time—with difficulty because the window was very small—Spartaco and the two parachutists, Jack and Jay, joined us.

They too were very tired, and we all tried to get some sleep. But the dogs kept on barking furiously and got all of us scared. Spartaco climbed through the tiny window and went out to look. If something seemed suspicious, he would whistle and we would leave. He was away for a long time, while we planned our fast escape. But as we were all bunched up at the window, we saw Spartaco with Arthur approaching the barn. They climbed through the window and the eight of us were together.

With Arthur near me my anger subsided.

Arthur was out of ideas. Now that the weather had turned hot, the men could sleep under the stars, but for me and Marcella the only thing he could suggest was that we talk the matter over with the old patriarch.

At dawn Arthur, Spartaco, Jack, and Jay left and the four of us got a little rest.

When someone came to open the barn to feed the animals, we said that we would like to talk to the old man.

"No use," the man replied. "You'd better get out of here before he gets up."

We insisted while we helped to feed the animals and change their beds, and finally, reluctantly, he went to ask his father whether he would receive us. Shortly after, we were called to the kitchen. The patriarch was sitting near the window, looking outside. He slowly turned his head toward us. He seemed to be uncomfortable, as if ashamed of the way his women had behaved with us the previous night. He first asked Giuditta, his wife, to give us some food, then he listened to us.

We promised that we would look for another place, but in the meantime could the four of us stay together at his farm?

He didn't have any objections, but the others did. Nobody liked what had happened to Santarelli. Besides, he said, their resources, too, were beginning to run low.

The Italian front had been at a stalemate in Montecassino, southeast of Rome—the place mentioned by the bald German officer—for over four months. After the Allies' landing in Sicily on July 9, 1943, and the armistice of two months later, everybody expected the war to be over soon, at least in our region. Instead, what had appeared to be the last quick battle before the liberation of Rome, had gone on for much longer than anyone had anticipated.

We were not the only ones the farmers were feeding: There were the many Italian deserters and the escaped POWs as well. Under normal circumstances, when the supply of staples did not last until the new crops, the farmers could count on the factor—their manager and foreman—to help them from his own overflowing granaries. But because he was a fascist, the factor for the farmers in this area could not be trusted. To let him know that a given farm was short of corn and wheat in the middle of May was equivalent to admitting that a whole lot of fugitives had been fed and given shelter during the winter months—and that spelled trouble!

Arcangelo, however, simply could not turn Signor Azeglio's children away, and told the women of his decision.

"Giorgio and Libero will sleep in the barn. Lili and Ina will share the large bed with Angelina and her boy." (This man knew our real names, but never once did he mention them in front of anyone, including his own family.)

Lello and Gino went immediately out to look for a place to stay, while Marcella and I began to help with the household chores—she inside the house, and I in the vegetable garden.

Stealing

The first staple our farm had run out of was charcoal. During the winter, cooking was done directly over the flames of the huge hearth. But when it was too hot to be standing in front of the fireplace, cooking was done on a charcoal range, and feeding all these extra people meant cooking much more every day. One night, after the recitation of the rosary, while everybody's eyes were cast down and hands still joined in silent prayer, Angelina—normally quiet but cantankerous—declared that stealing from thieves was no sin.

"Tonight I am going to steal some charcoal from the foreman who has mountains of it in the Valle del Tufo," she said simply, and made again the sign of the cross, looking askance at her mother-in-law.

Her mother-in-law and the rest of the women, without raising their heads, said, "Amen!"

"Is anybody going with me?"

I didn't particularly like Angelina. She was too taciturn for my temperament and I never could guess what was in her mind. But she had shared her bed with me when I first arrived at this farm six months earlier, and now both Marcella and I slept with her and her son. I volunteered to go with her.

We waited until eleven o'clock, then we took two burlap sacks and began to walk furtively toward the Valle del Tufo. At the fence that surrounded the area, we stopped to look around. There was no sign of life. With great effort Angelina went over the fence, managing not to tear her dress or break a leg. I, younger and more agile, went over it quickly and without difficulty.

As we drew near the enormous black pile of charcoal, we heard a rustling of leaves. Startled, we ran to the road, without realizing that we had crossed the big fence again! The noise might have been a snake. Brrrr, we shivered with fear. We wouldn't go back there. Angelina knew of another charcoal deposit a bit further, near the factor's mill. We were on the road a couple of minutes when the droning of a motor made us hold our breath. Luckily it was only an airplane, and we started our march again. But no sooner had we reached the site of the charcoal deposit, that we heard dogs barking. Those damned animals were barking so loudly that we were afraid someone might come out to meet us with a gun. Again we turned on our heels and walked away fast, painfully aware of having failed in our purpose.

Suddenly we began to laugh immoderately. We laughed at the ludicrous situation we were in, we laughed at ourselves for not being capable of stealing.

Our good humor and our need for charcoal rekindled our courage. We decided to return to the first deposit. There might be snakes, we agreed, but nothing would deter us this time: we were determined not to go back without bringing some. Silently we filled our sacks, then ran back to the road. At this point I realized that my golden fountain pen, a Bat Mizvah present from my aunt Rita in Rome and a faithful companion throughout my vicissitudes, was missing from my shirt pocket. Sadly I recognized that there was no use trying to look for it. My diary would have to be written with a pencil from now on.

A sudden foreboding that Aunt Rita might have been among the deportees from Rome appeared in my consciousness for a few seconds. But in a sense I felt relieved. I had stolen and sinned. Now with the loss of my cherished pen, I had paid for my sin.

We arrived back at the farm when everybody was asleep, except for Lello who had been waiting up for me.

"Were you worried?"

"Yes, a little. But I stayed up also because I wanted to talk to you."

I sat down. I hoped he wouldn't want to talk about Arthur. Last time Lello had talked to me about Arthur, it was in anger.

At that time, Arthur had arrived galloping towards the farm with twelve other men. They were all heavily armed. Arthur's face was covered with a three-day beard, and he looked wistful. I prepared the food for all these men, and after eating, they left for what obviously was a guerrilla action. It was staged against a German convoy that was due to pass soon on a road nearby and was supposed to carry valuable documents.

Of the thirteen young men who had participated in the action, including an adolescent who had become Arthur's orderly, only nine had returned. The boy rode with Arthur all the time, in front of him. He was an easy target and had been the first to fall. When I saw Arthur riding back on his white horse with a bleeding arm and without the boy, I knew. One

German had been killed and his truck with some ammunition had remained immobilized in a muddy ditch. But the rest of the Germans got away alive, and not only did they manage to kill four partisans, but reported to their command the exact location, Casasbraci, where they had encountered the rebels who had killed one of them. Casasbraci was a cluster of houses where Aunt Argia, Uncle Augusto, and Cousins Giorgio and Lida had found refuge. The next morning a convoy of about seventy SS storm troopers arrived and invaded the hamlet. As a show of force, and as a reprisal against those people who sheltered the outlaws, they began to throw hand grenades at random through the windows inside the houses. When Lello learned of the Germans' raid and bombing, he came to pick me up, and we both ran toward Casasbraci to ascertain whether our relatives were all right or needed help. But from the top of the hill, we could see that the SS troopers were still there.

Lello had to remain in hiding, but I decided to go anyway. As Lello tried to stop me, I jerked myself free of his grip on my arm, and began to run downhill. At the entrance to the village, I assumed a calmer composure and moved slowly, as if returning from a walk.

I stopped the first German officer I encountered, and with brazenness I shouted into his face, *"Was wollen Sie?"* The officer must have thought that I was a Nazi collaborator because he put on his face a stereotyped smile and began to address me with a river of German words which I didn't understand but which included *Juden* and *Banditen.* I told him in Italian that there were no Jews or partisans here. We all hated those people and wouldn't have them in our village.

"The *bandits* you are talking about," I added, "came from far, far away, and now *we* have to suffer because of them."

I said *Auf Wiedersehen* and calmly walked to the home where our relatives were staying. A hand grenade had in fact been thrown into this house and had left a big hole in the middle of the kitchen and other minor damage caused by shrapnel. However, on seeing the Germans approach, they and their protectors had moved to the back room, and no one was hit. A German soldier had then gone in scaring them almost to death. But all he wanted was Giorgio's gold watch!

I quickly hugged them and went back to Lello, making a detour so that no one could see where I was going.

I found Lello frantic. He had seen me talking with the German officer and had thought that he would never see me alive again. He was so angry that he said, "It is your friend Arthur who's responsible for all this tragedy. It is because of his foolhardy action that so many innocents are paying with their lives!"

It was true, but I still loved Arthur and could not get angry at him.

From our post we saw the SS troopers moving away from Casasbraci, leaving behind clouds of dust and smoke. What we didn't see was that they took with them six young men, including a dear friend of our friend Iris, to make up the ten they "needed" for the ten-to-one German reprisal rule.

Provisions

This time Lello did not talk about Arthur and the disaster he had provoked with his ill-planned action.

"Listen," he said. "These people are not only out of charcoal; they are out of almost everything else."

"I know, and we are partly responsible for this."

"I was thinking of Pecorella," Lello continued. "Last time we went to his mill to see Uncle Tranquillo, he solemnly promised me, `As long as I live, you kids will not starve'."

Lello paused for a moment, pursing his lips, then he continued, "I had asked him whether one of us could stay at his mill, but he had answered, `That's the first place the fascists would raid if they suspected that I was hiding a Jew! Believe me, Lello, it is not safe. But whenever you need flour, come by night and you will not leave empty-handed'."

The time had come to take advantage of his offer, for sure. But now it was late, I was tired and didn't want to prolong this conversation.

"I just wanted to know your opinion on that. Marcella and Gino have already approved and I don't want to waste any time. Good night, now."

I went to bed relieved that he didn't mention Arthur. I truly didn't want to hear anything bad about the young South African I loved unconditionally.

Early the next morning, Lello spoke to the old patriarch of the possibility of getting some flour from a friend of ours, but he needed the donkey to bring the flour back. The old man called a big family meeting to discuss the matter. There were a few men in the household, and many women—some already widowed and others with husbands or sweethearts in the army or prisoners somewhere. They all weighed carefully the pros and the cons of Lello's proposal. The risk involved was considerable. If Lello got caught, they would lose their donkey—the only means of transportation on the farm. On the other hand there was the hoped-for possibility that Lello would come back with the flour.

The vote was almost unanimous: they should take the risk.

At sunset Lello mounted the donkey and was off riding bareback toward Pecorella's mill.

"Don't expect me back too soon," he had told us. "I might stay overnight and come back tomorrow morning before dawn."

We watched him and his donkey leave until they disappeared into the shadows of the night.

The next morning Lello had not yet returned. We thought that he had overslept and was hiding somewhere to wait for nightfall.

By supper time, we were all nervous, but days were longer now and he certainly would come later, in the heart of the night.

The next day and the day after, nobody talked anymore. Everyone knew what was going on in the minds of the others. Only at night, at Rosary time, after the mention of their men at war, did they add the name of Lello to their prayer.

Gino, Marcella and I didn't expect to see him alive now any more than we did to see our parents and Mario. We did not refer to him in front of the people on the farm, but in private we couldn't talk about anything else, and wept until we could no more. Lello had just turned twenty-two, but being the oldest of the children, he had taken the place of our father. Without him we felt insecure and once again orphaned.

We tried to work harder than ever, partly in the hope that fatigue would take our minds off what fate might have befallen our brother, but also because we felt responsible for the loss of the donkey and wanted to show our consideration by multiplying our efforts. The gloomy silence of the farmers made us feel even more downcast.

The fourth day since Lello had left, we decided to move. We didn't know where to go, but we could not bear the tension at the farm, we wouldn't spend another night there. We would leave by nightfall.

Marcella remained at the farmhouse all day to help with the chores and to put together our few belongings; Gino worked in the fields as usual; and I went to hoe the minuscule vegetable garden in a plot the farmers had assigned to me. It was beginning to yield lettuce, cabbage, beans, and zucchini.

Although it was not yet noon, I was already dripping with perspiration. Who would take care of my little garden after I left? Would they think of me with some affection when they ate the vegetables I had worked so hard to grow? How could I think of such irrelevant matters, I scolded myself, when I might have lost my older brother?

Tears ran down my face and mixed with sweat, and I tasted the salty bitter mixture. Bitter, I thought. That's what I really feel—bitter. Bitter! Angry! Furious!

I flung the hoe down to the ground with force and straightened myself up to wipe my face. I kept my burning eyes closed for a long moment, thinking confusedly of my parents and Mario, of Lello, of our dreadful situation....

When I opened them again, I could hardly believe what I saw: in the distance, a human figure was pulling with all his might the reins attached to a dinosaur whose feet were obstinately anchored to the ground.

I ran into the kitchen to call Marcella, we both ran to the fields to call Gino, and the three of us ran toward Lello, who immediately relinquished the reins and dropped to the ground, completely worn-out.

What had looked like a dinosaur was the poor donkey, so burdened with provisions that it refused to move one more step until we had lightened its load a little. A 50-kilo sack of flour was set astride its back, and hanging from all over, dangling with every move, were heavy prosciutti, bunches of salamis, strings of sausages, wheels of cheese, bags of dry beans and much else.

Without even tying the donkey, we ran to hug Lello, and cried, and laughed, and danced. Then we made a procession toward the farmhouse to bring all the bounty that Lello had been able to collect and the good news about the donkey. The women came out with big smiles to bring their precious animal some water, and to pat it and to hug it.

Not only had Pecorella kept his promise, but he had also suggested that Lello go to some of the wealthiest landowners who, in the past, had employed our father as a bookkeeper. Almost all of them held high positions in the Fascist Party, and it was not easy for Lello to knock at their doors. But his sense of responsibility toward the people who were now in bad shape for helping us, gave him the courage he needed.

Some gave willingly to help the children of Signor Azeglio survive the persecution. The majority gave out of fear that Lello had come backed by partisan bands who would raid their provisions if they didn't give spontaneously. When the donkey had been loaded to capacity, Lello had started his journey back, but the animal could not walk for long with that weight on its back. All those days had been spent in different hideouts, unloading the donkey and taking it to a brook to water it, then resting; and the nights were spent reloading the animal to start walking again.

Part 6

THE STORM BREAKS

My father wrote the above in his prayer book listing the people taken in the second bus from the concentration camp near Roccatederighi to the camp at Fossoli near Parma and from there to Germany and death. Also listed are those who remained behind and were saved.

בְּטוֹב אָלִין וְאָקִיץ בְּרַחֲמִים חַיִּים טוֹבִים ׃
אָמֵן ׃

תֹ"ו יֹשְׂ"ל כ"ע

The bottom portion of a page in Father's prayer book where he noted our arrival at the hotel in Roccatederighi on June 18, 1944

Dante Lattes, my grandmother's first cousin

Internment Camp: Risiera di San Sabba, Trieste. Permission to publish from Fondazione Centro di Documentazione Ebraica Contemporanea.

Internment Camp, Bolzano-Gries. Permission to publish from Fondazione Centro di Documentazione Ebraica Contemporanea.

Chapter Twelve

The Front Moves Up

U nbeknownst to us, the Allies had managed to capture the German stronghold at Montecassino and started to move north. This step enhanced our danger even more, as we would soon learn.

D-Day:
Rome is Liberated

It was great to see Lello and to know that we and the farmers would not have to worry about food running out for a while. However, Lello brought a piece of bad news. The Fascists were about to take more drastic measures against the partisans and the Jews who were still at large. They had announced that this May 25, 1944, was the deadline for the "enemies of the country" to present themselves voluntarily. They made no promise of leniency for those who complied, but threatened those who didn't with death by firing squad as soon as they were caught. And this time they would comb the countryside with German-trained dogs.

Fascists were unpredictable and almost never were their threats taken seriously, but after having witnessed the capture of Santarelli and the men he protected, we wouldn't take a chance. Lello and Gino knew of a small hut in the middle of a forest on top of a nearby hill, and made plans to move there. It was ironic that now that we had an abundance of food, we had to leave it at the farm to go and hide for our life. We took with us the bare essentials—a frying pan, some sausages and cheese, and a few books—and buried the rest of our belongings, including Gino's accordion, to leave no trace of our presence at the farm.

When Lello and Gino had joined the Resistance, they were given two guns. But none of the partisans actually carried their weapons with them at all times. Lello and Gino kept theirs hidden in the hollow of an old tree not far from this hut we had moved to, and nobody—not even Marcella and I—knew about it. Their plan was to retrieve and use their guns at the last possible moment, if it became necessary to help the advance of the Allies.

The first day in our hideout, we were full of joy for our newly-found freedom. It was good for a change not to have to beg. We climbed to the tops of very young and tall trees, and as they bent down close to the ground under our weight, we jumped off them and started to climb them all over again. We sang all the songs we could remember, and integrated the few notes of a singing bird into one of our songs. We laughed, we read, we talked, we made a little fire to fry the sausages for the only meal we allowed ourselves, and we went to a nearby creek to drink and to bathe.

The next day, however, much of our joy dissipated. During the day the heat was unbearable. The boys had stripped to the waist and Marcella and I wore sunsuits we had made at the farm out of old shirts. At night it was humid and chilly. We slept on the bare ground, but all sorts of crawling creatures kept us from resting. Days were long, and, without anything specific to do, time didn't pass fast enough for us. We became very edgy and argued with one another for nothing. The third day things were even worse. Not knowing what to do with ourselves, we began to fight, and realized that if we had to endure this kind of isolation for much longer, we would end up hating or even hurting one another. After one week of utter misery, we finally agreed on one thing: that almost anything was better than this non-life, and we descended once again.

To our surprise and relief, we found out that the Italian front, after months of stalemate at Montecassino with heavy losses for both sides, was now rapidly moving north. As the Allies advanced, the retreating Germans were combing the cities, the villages and the countryside for Jews. If the Fascists sometimes didn't carry out their threats, the Germans always did, with obstinacy and great efficiency. We had been without news of our parents and Mario for over a month—since the time our mother had begged us to give ourselves up—and if they were still alive, we assumed that they would soon be deported to Germany. Not yet knowing what this meant, we were concerned that they did not know the language and they might be too weak and unfit for heavy work.

Since my brothers' trip to the concentration camp, Lello had never given up the dream of going to liberate them and the rest of the Jews who were kept prisoners there. But he could not convince any of the partisans in our area to act with us. It was a risk they would not take. Moreover, through Sesto we had been able to arrange a meeting with our friend Don Omero. The meeting took place in the outskirts of Sovana. We were happy to see Don Omero and he seemed happy to see us, but when we begged him to make a trip to the concentration camp to assess the situation, he too had refused.

The morning of June 7 the news reached us of the Allies' landing in Normandy, and also that Rome had been liberated a few days earlier. It was great news. But once again we became aware that this also meant that with the front advancing north the chances of our loved ones being deported to Germany increased. There were in fact rumors that they had already been transferred to the concentration camp of Fossoli di Carpi in the province of Modena, the last stop before crossing the Brenner Pass to Austria and Germany. But nobody knew for sure. It might be too late for us to do anything. On the other hand, they might still be in the same camp of Roccatederighi praying for help.

What could we do? How would we reach them? Moving away from the area where we were known was incalculably dangerous. But could we let them be taken away without even attempting to do something about it?

We decided that the first thing to do was to talk with Uncle Tranquillo. He was the only one who might know the situation at the concentration camp. And there was no way we could get in touch with him in a hurry other than going to Pitigliano ourselves. We would stop at the outskirts and hope to see someone sympathetic to us to go and fetch our uncle before the fascists saw us. That same afternoon of June 7, Lello and I began to walk toward Pitigliano, while Marcella and Gino remained at the farm. At about six, Lello and I stopped at Valle Rotonda—a farm overlooking one of the valleys that surround Pitigliano—to eat our sausages and bread. The farmers gave us a glass of wine, and we all toasted the liberation of Rome and the approach of the Allies. At long last the war would come to an end in our region.

Dichotomy of Feelings

After our quick meal, we resumed our walk, and when a few minutes later we saw on the horizon the familiar skyline of Pitigliano rising in front of our eyes, we stopped for a moment to contemplate the beauty of that medieval fortress.

I had mixed feelings about my native village. I loved it because there I had roots that had been branching out over the course of many centuries; there my ancestors had lived, loved and been buried; there I was born and had spent all my life. But, I mostly hated it, because as a Jew—and as a girl—I suffered many abuses and humiliations. Moreover, for a person of my exuberance, the limited opportunities and the lack of freedom of a small village were tantamount to clipping my wings. And finally, because I was forced to run from it for my life.

Its beauty, however, was indisputable and we stood there with a smile on our faces, as if we were discovering it for the first time. The sun, setting behind us, reflected its copper-and-golden light on the windowpanes so that all the buildings were brightly illuminated. Before the war, some of the Catholic religious holidays were marked by the burning of oil lamps at every window with an extraordinary effect of flickering flames. But what we saw now was much more dramatic.

As we watched the spectacle, we heard a droning noise coming from far away. We thought it was distant thunder, but there was not one cloud in the sky. The noise continued, and became more and more audible as we paid it attention. We kept scrutinizing the sky, unsure which direction the noise was coming from. Finally, as we looked in a south-easterly direction, we saw in the distance a swarm of "liberators" in formation coming toward us. We had no doubt, now. They were the four-engined American bombers en route to an air-raid. What city were they going to bomb? Orbetello and Porto Santo Stefano were desirable targets. The first was renowned for its arsenal and powder magazine, the other for its port and the German fleet stationed there. But those two towns were slightly southwest of us, and the bombers, coming up from the Rome area, we presumed, didn't have to go so far. Besides, it was still light, and didn't they wait until it was dark to bomb places where the anti-aircraft could spot them and shoot them down?

Now the formation was in front of us, almost at our eye level, and before we even noticed that the bombers were directly above Pitigliano, we saw a hail of bombs being ejected from them, obliquely falling in the direction of the main piazza. A big roar and a flash—as bright as the reflection of the sunset—and the skyline of Pitigliano disappeared, enveloped in an enormous cloud of dark smoke, rubble and dust.

We remained standing, without moving or uttering a word for a long time, shaken beyond telling by the event. Pitigliano had nothing that would classify it as a military target; and the population, because of the heavy emigration to the New World, was generally sympathetic towards America. We didn't know at the moment that it was the Americans' strategy to bomb every village's bridge and main road on the way as they advanced north, partly as a show of force against the retreating Germans, but mainly to make the latter's attempt at readvancing more difficult. Those bombs were in fact directed at the little bridge over the Meleta, right under our house's windows.

All our concern was for the human loss. Who had been killed by those bombs? We knew everybody in Pitigliano, and among the dead there surely were many of our friends. It was the time in the evening when nearly everybody was out for walks in the Corso, or lingering in the main piazza before supper time. Whom had we lost? We kept looking until the big cloud settled uncovering the bell tower that was, to our surprise, still standing intact. In fact, the entire skyline, as seen from our viewpoint, had changed very little.

I was disappointed. Our house was adjacent to the Cathedral and if the bell tower was up, it meant that our house was still standing also. I would have liked for it to be destroyed by the bombs, as part of my hostile feelings toward my village, and also because when we returned home we would *have* to move to the *case nuove*, the new buildings where my wealthier cousins lived. But then, if our house had been destroyed, so would be the Temple, the Hebrew School, our rich libraries, and all the dear places of my childhood. I blushed at my own angry thoughts.

We didn't go to Pitigliano, after all. We walked back to where we had left Gino and Marcella, our heads spinning with a sense of urgency and impotence—and the unsettling thought that if not for our stop at Valle Rotonda to eat our supper, we could have been among the over 100 victims of the bombing we had witnessed from a safe spot. Gino and Marcella had already heard the news, and were relieved to see us back. They had also heard that Uncle Tranquillo had moved with his family and was no longer in Pitigliano.

We went to sleep, totally prostrated.

We spent the next few days trying to make up our minds on what to do next.

"The life of our parents is at stake," said Lello solemnly on the fourth day of discussions. "They are the givers of our life, and we must at any moment be ready to risk it in order to save theirs."

It was finally decided to separate again, not only to diminish our risk, but also so that someone would be in the neighborhood, when and if our parents and Mario came back. We agreed that the best thing would be for Gino and Marcella to join the partisans in earnest to enter our village and to take possession of our home again. Lello and I would walk to the site of the concentration camp.

Venturous Voyage

Lello and I left on Sunday, June 11, toward sunset. We hugged our brother and sister and I begged Marcella to tell Arthur, in case she saw him, that I loved him more than ever. She nodded, her eyes full of tears.

We walked briskly since we had more than 120 kilometers to cover. The cool evening air made our walking easy. Our first stop was Monte-vitozzo, the hamlet where the families of many of our former maids lived. As we approached the outskirts, we came across a great number of people carrying bundles, mattresses and other household items, hastily walking in groups away from the village. We stopped a man and asked what was going on.

"Don't you know?" he said. "Tonight the English (which in the jargon of the time meant any of the Allies) will destroy the village with bombs; then the SS storm troopers will come to round up all the young men and women they will find. But," he added with a spark of malice in his eyes, "they will not find anyone: we are all running away!"

We nodded. What we gathered was that the front had almost reached us.

He gave us a curious look, then he said, "I don't know where you think you're going, but my advice is that you go back to where you're coming from."

We thanked him for his kind suggestion, but continued to walk in the direction of the home of our last maid Eda's parents.

The door was locked, the lights were off. We knocked. No answer. They had left the village like everyone else.

When we were children, both Lello and I had spent many summers here with one or the other of our maids' families, and we had fond memories of the village with its unevenly cobbled streets, the square, the fountain. Now it all looked unreal, like a ghost town enveloped in darkness, its dreary silence interrupted only by the occasional wailing of a stray dog. We felt cold and lost.

We walked away from this cluster of houses, and in the darkness we met someone who directed us to a cabin where a few young people were hiding. We walked toward the cabin fearful of what and whom we would find there. As we peered inside we felt relieved. A number of noisy youngsters were drinking and joking and laughing, as if they were at a party. Here we spent the night. We all lay on the wooden floor, but no one could really sleep because of the firing of the cannons which were getting closer and closer, and, down the road, the rumbling noise of the German trucks retreating north.

Lello and I left early.

We had no food with us, but wherever we went we met hundreds of people who had fled from the front line, and those who had some food generously shared it with those who didn't have any.

The second night, after marching all day without resting or eating, we knocked at a door with no idea of whom we might face. We were immediately invited in. Upon learning that we were from Pitigliano, they told us that they had relatives in Pitigliano, and had a son who was prisoner in Germany. After this warm welcome and a decent meal, they offered us two beds. Two real beds, one for each one of us! During supper they asked us about the purpose of our trip and we told them of our intent to free our parents and brother. They expressed skepticism about the feasibility of our plan and felt strongly—like the man we had met the night before—that we should go back to our brother and sister and wait there for the front to move up.

Before going to bed, we all listened to the free radio and learned that Pitigliano had just been liberated!

"Why are you waiting to go home?" said the man of the house excitedly. "You are free now. Instead, you are going north, with the Germans! It doesn't make any sense, if you ask me."

We thanked the man for his concern, but told him that nothing and nobody would change our minds.

For seven days and seven nights, we moved caught between two fronts—the German one in retreat, and the advancing Allied. We walked through the woods and slept in huts or grottos, trying carefully to avoid highways. The Germans were recruiting all able-bodied people, and more eagerly than ever were hunting for Jews, while leaflets of the Allied Forces, constantly showered all over the countryside from reconnaissance planes, were warning that anything moving on the roads would be system-atically machine-gunned from the air.

One morning, however, we had no choice but to walk on a stretch of a winding main road. Suddenly from nowhere a British Spitfire dove so close that we could see the pilot. We jumped into a ditch near a wild cherry tree and hugged one another in an instinctive need for protection. The small craft fired a shower of bullets, then soared in the sky and disappeared.

There were gleaming shells all over. It took us a while before we could gather enough courage to resume our walk on the road. As we reached the other side of a big bend, we saw a German truck parked on the left side of the road. We were about to turn and run, when the driver descended from the cabin and hailed us with a quick gesture urging us to get closer. There was no use in trying to escape, so, quite shaky, we obeyed. He was not injured, but his companion was. The latter was riddled with bullet holes and bleeding heavily. Lello helped the driver place the wounded man on the ground. I looked on, feeling compassion but not knowing what to do. The driver took out a first-aid box and began to give his comrade injections. The wounded man opened his eyes and, looking at us imploringly, said, *"Wasser."* We saw a farm on top of the hill and Lello and I offered to go up and bring back water. We were amazed that the driver let us both go.

We found a woman and told her that there was a dying man in need of water at the road, would she please bring some down. While she went to fetch the water we fled into the woods.

Crossing the Bridge

We had another close call that same day, as we walked toward the bridge near Santa Fiora. Near the bridge's entrance, we ran up against two boys and four or five German soldiers running in the opposite direction. Instinctively, without giving much thought, Lello grabbed my arm and pulled me faster toward the bridge. The Germans and the boys turned toward us and yelled something we couldn't hear and gestured that we should walk back. This made us run even faster away from them, and they gave up. We had not gone twenty meters when a formidable explosion paralyzed us. The Germans had mined the power station at some distance and the bridge in front of us. Within a few minutes, two other explosions, this time even louder, followed the first one, and there was no more bridge to cross. The two of us were flat on the ground, all covered with rubble.

We got up, and when we realized that we were all in one piece, we hopped down to the river bank and walked along the water hoping to find a way to wade across. But as the night closed in upon us, we found ourselves exhausted, hungry, and still on the same side of the river. We soon heard human voices, and moved in the direction of their source. We arrived at a huge cavern crowded with refugees and we were fed, no questions asked. We inquired about the possibility of crossing the river, and someone told us that he knew of a bridge of sorts a few kilometers upstream. But it was difficult to cross, he warned, and wished us luck.

Another person gently called us aside and asked us what was the real purpose of our dangerous trip. His last name was Corsi, he said; like the secretary of the Fascist Party in Pitigliano—the man who had catalogued and signed the list of the goods confiscated from the Jewish-owned stores. He was a kind of caricature, going around all dressed up with a black suit and the hopelessly out-of-fashion white gaiters. But of this one we had a good impression, so we took a chance and told him the truth. He was an anti-fascist and was eager to be of help. He gave us a list of people he knew who shared his sentiments and said that they might be able to help us along the way. We spent the night at the cavern.

The next day—it was Wednesday, June 14, the fourth day since we had started our march—we climbed for a long while, then moved along fjord-like cliffs. The valleys were covered with bright green vegetation that looked black on the shady sides. After a steep and uneven descent, we reached a narrow dirt path halfway down the valley and walked some distance on it. We arrived at the bridge about 2 o'clock in the afternoon. The river at that point was very narrow and deep, with turbulent waterfalls and rapids a long distance down from where we were. The "bridge" consisted of a tall tree that had been felled so that it spanned the gorge. The bark was almost all gone and the trunk was damp with the drizzle of the rushing water and slippery with moss. How could we ever do it? Not even the most skilled and agile of acrobats could walk on top of that trunk without slipping and falling.

"The only way to go through it," said Lello, "is to hug the trunk with both arms and legs. We'll crawl forward, inch by inch, pressing our chests against the trunk. If you look carefully, you can see that the trunk still has stumps of branches here and there: that should help us too. It is not going to be easy, I know, but we have no choice."

Lello went first to show me the way and to encourage me. It took him a long time to move a few feet, and I couldn't help letting out a scream each time he seemed to lose his balance. I was wearing a silk dress and a pair of worn-out dress shoes, which were the only summer things I had with me from when we left our home seven months earlier. Lello was taking across both our small knapsacks. I placed myself astride the trunk, then I bent down and hugged it. The rushing of the water underneath gave me vertigo and I began to scream that I couldn't do it. I was paralyzed with fear. I was locked in that position without being able to move. Lello kept on going, slowly, without turning or talking in order not to lose his grip. When he finally reached the other bank, he began to shout over the roar of the water, "Have courage, Edda! If I have done it, there is no reason why you shouldn't be able to!"

I hardly heard him. I felt myself slowly slipping toward one side of the trunk, and it was only because of the many broken branches that got stuck to my dress that I didn't fall down. Lello kept yelling words of support, and I finally began my laborious crawl. Each move made a new tear in my dress and bruised and scratched my skin. I closed my eyes. I was only halfway across, exhausted and discouraged more than ever. I felt as if I were going to remain in that position forever. I could not move forward, and I could not go back. The only part of my body that moved furiously was my heart. The more I stayed over the roaring water, the more difficult it became to move. Lello now watched me without saying anything. After a while, I found a new spurt of energy and began to move again. The pain on my chest had reached such an intensity that I could hardly bear it. When I finally made it to the other side, I was trembling with fatigue and emotion. Lello murmured a few words of praise, and we shook each other's aching and bleeding hands.

As we sat down to rest before resuming our journey, we stared at the bridge and at the turbulent water in awe; then we looked at each other with disbelief. We had made it! Having overcome this obstacle gave us a great feeling of achievement. From now on, no barrier would stand in the way of our reaching our goal.

We wondered what might have happened to Marcella and Gino. They were the first members of our family to be liberated—if they were still alive! We prayed that they were and that we would soon find out that they were all right.

You Are a Partisan!

The night Lello and I took off on our journey toward the concentration camp, Marcella and Gino slowly directed their steps back to the farm in silence. As they were walking, they thought they heard a faint sound of thunder. Thunderstorms were not a rarity in our region at the beginning of summer, and at first they didn't pay much attention; but as the thundering got closer and closer, the sky remained clear of clouds and the air dry and fresh—nothing like the gathering of menacing clouds and the muggy, still air that precedes summer thunderstorms. They thought of an air raid, but air raids would only last a few minutes and then there would be silence again. This thundering, however, kept on and on, and became more and more distinct.

Suddenly, a thought flashed into Gino's mind: could it be the Allied front advancing? He and Marcella now ran to the farmhouse to share the good news, but found everybody in a pitiful state. The farmers knew it was not a thunderstorm or an air raid since the noise was too relentless. But the advancing of the front was the last thing they wanted to admit to, and when Gino suggested that that was the only logical explanation, they were panic-stricken. Although their farm was far from any important or even country road, they feared the passage of the front because they had heard stories of soldiers spreading into the countryside, attacking women and looting. They didn't know what to do.

Nobody slept that night. The noise was frightful. Early in the morning Gino wished good luck to the family, and leaving behind everything that belonged to us, took Marcella by one hand and ran toward the hollow tree in the forest where he and Lello had hidden their guns.

He gave one rifle to Marcella, and also a practical lesson on how to use it, while reminding her of the importance of the moment. Marcella, to his surprise, handled the heavy gun as if she had dealt with one all her life. Gino congratulated her and said, "Now you are a partisan!"

For the first time since we had fled our home, Marcella was happy not to have joined Mamma at the concentration camp.

"Always stay near me," said Gino as they began to walk.

"Where are we going?"

"We are going to join the partisan unit that operates near Sorano. Should something happen to me during the battle, you go and live with Aunt Lidia until Mamma comes back."

The thought that Mamma might never come back had occurred to both of them. But it was our strength not to give in to gloomy thoughts, and especially not to express them.

Aunt Lidia was the wife of Uncle Tranquillo; the latter, after a few dangerous trips to Volterra to transport the precious salt back to Grosseto, had been rewarded by the Fascist Authorities of the Province by having his family freed from the concentration camp. They had not returned to their home because as Jews they were still subject to arrest by the local fascists, but Gino knew that they were residing on a farm between Sorano and Pitigliano, only half in hiding. Gino had no idea of what might have happened to our family in the concentration camp, nor what fate Lello and I had encountered. To go and live with Aunt Lidia seemed for the moment the only solution. Marcella was too excited in her new role of active combatant to acknowledge the danger that awaited them during the passage of the front, and didn't pay much attention to what Gino was saying. She felt that she was strong and ready for any event.

And so they marched toward Sorano, rifle on shoulder, as the rumbling of the cannons became louder and louder.

They stopped at an old abandoned farmhouse where Gino and Lello had often gathered with other partisans. There they found a handful of armed men all excited and hardly able to wait for the arrival of the Allies. The *English* were moving very slowly northward, Marcella and Gino were informed, and were expected to arrive in Sorano by the next day.

Bread and cheese and some wine were distributed. The remainder of the day was to be spent cleaning the arms and preparing their spirits for action, while waiting for other Resistance fighters scattered in the area to join the band.

"This is the moment we have all been waiting for," said Lieutenant Solera, the commander of the unit. "We will liberate Sorano during the first hours of the morning, before the English arrive, and then we will make ourselves ready to meet them."

At night everybody bivouacked in the empty barn without getting much sleep, and before dawn, the partisans (some two dozen) were marching toward their final action.

By the time the band arrived at the gates of Sorano, the Germans—if any had ever been stationed there—had already been sent to the front, and most of the local fascists had fled without firing one shot. The only shots that were fired in the air were those of the overjoyed partisans, and just by dint of a miracle Gino didn't get killed by Dova' who was so excited that he didn't pay attention to what he was doing!

Of the fascists who remained, some locked themselves in their homes in fear, and others readily gave themselves up, since by now all they wanted was to save their skins and pretend that they had never been *true* fascists. The partisans' first stop was at the village jail where they liberated the political prisoners and locked up the few fascists they had rounded-up on the way. Then they occupied City Hall and other key office buildings. Relatives and friends joined in: a group went to destroy all the fascist flags and symbols, and another to whitewash all the black on white graffiti and slogans that had been stenciled on flat walls throughout Italy during the twenty years of fascist rule.

It was decided that those who spoke English should give the Allied fighters a warm welcome in their native tongue. A small group of people, including Gino and Marcella, stood ready to welcome the liberators, and someone even prepared a moving little speech. However, as the sun began to rise behind the valley, French troops entered the village, and Gino was the only one who was able to communicate with them!

Marcella was the only woman among the partisans. She was wearing a torn summer dress, a pair of worn-out wooden clogs (which Ivan had carved for her five months earlier), a Russian military cap with a big red star in front, and Lello's gun, which was almost heavier than she. When the nuns saw fourteen-year-old Marcella showing so much of her skin among all those tramp-like, unshaven and dirty young men, they ran to look for some decent clothes to put on her. They couldn't come up with anything better than a *Giovani Italiane* fascist uniform. Marcella had never worn one because by the time she was of an age to be obliged to wear it to school, she, as a Jew, had been banned from public school for several years. Now she had no choice but to accept the offering. So, her first days as a free citizen, free from the yoke of Fascism, were spent—wearing a fascist uniform!

After an emotional morning, with people shouting and hugging one another in a state of total euphoria, a big meal was prepared by the nuns in the nursery-school grounds for the liberators. The meal went on for the remainder of the day among expressions of jubilation, moments of silence for the fallen, emotional speeches, and much rhetoric. At night, those whose homes were in the village or not too far from it, walked home; the rest slept on the floor of the nursery school. Marcella and Gino were invited by family friends to stay over in their house.

Going Home

Of the seven members of our family, Marcella and Gino were the only ones who were liberated. The war for them had at last come to an end. But although they were free citizens again after the tyranny of fascist dictatorship and life-threatening persecution, the sweet taste of freedom—the kind of freedom they had never known during their entire lifetime—was poisoned for them by the lack of news about the other five members of the family.

Pitigliano had been liberated about the same time as Sorano, but Gino and Marcella were in no rush to go home. During our forced peregrination, we all had missed our home, our beds, our comforts, the familiar objects that had surrounded us all our growing years; we dreamed of, and were eager for, the moment of our return. However, now, without our parents and Mario and the two of us, their return home seemed to them much less desirable. Yet, they also felt a need to regain possession of our home and our belongings, and to let our fellow Pitiglianesi know that they had survived and were eager to become productive members of the new free society.

They had moved to the farm with Aunt Lidia, and Marcella, of the two, was the first one to push to go home, even without Mamma there. Gino was very protective of her, and knowing how Marcella had missed our mother, feared for her to return to an empty home. But Marcella had done some growing up in the last few days, and she could not wait to start her new life.

"Our family might still show up, after the North has been liberated,"

263

said Marcella, "and we must not become discouraged. In the meantime, we'll have to make our home a welcoming place for them."

Gino was surprised at her display of maturity. Only a couple of weeks earlier she was ready to give up and go to the concentration camp!

"Think, Gino," she finally said to convince him that she was ready to go on with her life. "Think of the many books we can read. We'll have the library (the only library in Pitigliano had been established by the Jews and was located practically underneath our apartment) all to ourselves!"

This time Gino was touched. The thought of the time they would be able to spend browsing in the library and reading to ward off the gloom that would certainly set in, gave him the confidence that Marcella would be able to withstand the reality of the situation.

They had to cover the nine or ten kilometers' distance on foot. With all the bridges either bombed by the Allies or blown up by the Germans mines, the roads were not in any condition to be traveled by motor vehicles. But this long walk, without the fear of being chased, was a new and exhilarating experience. Gino was still wearing his torn German boots and Marcella her worn-out clogs, so that the walk took a great deal longer than it would have normally taken. Their mood fluctuated between excitement and dread, but in a subtle and persistent way they began to absorb and savor their recently acquired freedom, even though for the moment it was hard to know what to do with it.

As they approached the first few houses on the outskirts of Pitigliano, people began to recognize them, and depending on where their sympathies rested, and the degree of past closeness, they greeted them either with just a smile, or with hugs and effusions. After the first few encounters, they started to grow weary of these welcomes, and wanted to hurry home. But the thought of home was also a dreadful one. They heard that a foreign fascist family had been living there all this time, and they would have the thankless task of evicting them. Neither Gino nor Marcella—angry as they were with the fascists—felt up to it. They stopped at the house of a friend and sent someone to warn those people that the rightful owners were back. Luckily the fascists had already fled and nobody had to meet with them.

Entering our home became a soul-stirring event when they faced the near total devastation. The piano, a bed, and other pieces of furniture had been stolen, and the few pieces that had been left were ruined. The closets were emptied of clothes, the linens were gone, and so were the typewriters, one sewing machine, and many other furnishings that at a first glance escaped their survey. The apartment looked dirty and quite desolate. Marcella cried for the family that was not there, for all this destruction, for her own sense of helplessness. She wanted to run away. But there was no place to go. This inhospitable, squalid wreck *was* home. She forced herself to accept this fact, and after having exhausted all her tears, she rolled up her sleeves and began to make the place decent for her and Gino—and hopefully for the whole family. As she and Gino worked hard at getting the apartment in shape, the hope of our return appeared to them to be a certainty.

But a few weeks went by, and with each day that passed without bringing any of us back and without any news about us, they saw their hope of a total family reunion recede mercilessly.

Signora Nunes

Meanwhile Lello and I, after having overcome the difficult crossing of the river Fiora, continued our irrational march north, between the retreating Germans and the advancing Allies. Moments of hope were soon replaced by moments of hopelessness, in an incessant, tiresome emotional see-saw. It was almost impossible to make contact with the people who were supposed to help us in our search because, as if on schedule, we arrived at each village or hamlet on our way just hours after it had been bombed by the Allies. We found ourselves among mounds of rubble and dust, and all we heard were laments and cries from survivors who had lost family members and farm animals, and stories from people, who bore hallucinated looks on their faces from fear and despair for the atrocities that the Germans were committing as they retreated. For the first time in our lives we fed abundantly on horse meat.

By the fifth day of our journey, the advance of the Allied forces had a setback. At night we saw the dark sky crisscrossed, as in a display of fireworks, by the luminous trajectories of the projectiles exchanged by the two fronts, and believed that by the next day the Allies would reach us. Instead, between Bagnore and Arcidosso—roughly three quarters of the way toward the concentration camp—we came upon large chestnut woods, the grounds of which were covered with thousands upon thousands of German armored vehicles, horses, and an unimaginable amount of war material of all kinds, together with entire units of every branch of the army. It was an impressive sight, one that made us fear that the Germans were invincible. We had taken to the woods to avoid the roads, and here we were, facing almost the entire Wehrmacht! With pounding hearts we skirted the area unseen and went to walk on the open road, dripping with sweat, vulnerable to attacks from the air.

In Arcidosso we were finally able to locate one of our contacts and learned through him that our mutual acquaintance, Signora Nunes, who had been an inmate at the concentration camp with our parents and Mario, was free and hiding in a hut in the nearby forest. We entered the forest, and after an hour's walk we reached a village-like conglomeration of huts, hundreds of them, where city people, fearing the air-raids, the German violence, and the approaching fronts, had taken refuge.

Finding Signora Nunes—if indeed she was there—would not be an easy undertaking. Lello had met her briefly only once during his hazardous visit to the concentration camp five months earlier. I had never met her, and Lello's description of her characteristics (middle-age, thick-set, dark frizzy hair) was not much help, since there were hundreds of women who corresponded to such specifications.

We peered into countless huts calling her name, until, hours later, we finally did come upon Signora Nunes sitting on a low stool outside, talking with a neighbor. As we called her name, she was startled. She didn't recognize Lello and at first she thought that we were fascists coming to get her. But upon learning our true identity, she hugged us affectionately and emotionally, as if we were dear relatives.

We immediately asked her the question that was in our hearts, "Where are our parents and Mario?"

"I wish I could tell you more," she said apologetically, after informing us that she alone had been released because the director of the camp, a man she had known from Grosseto where they both lived, had managed to let her free on the basis of her poor health.

"All I know," she continued, "is that when I left, your parents and

266

Mario were still at the camp with some other twenty people, including my children."

"What happened to all the rest?"

"They were taken away. I heard that they were taken to Germany."

"Why not all of you?"

"Because the bus that came from Pitigliano was too small to fit everybody in it. The guards called people in alphabetical order and only those whose names started with "A" through "G" were pushed into the first bus."

"Then the Cavas, with their beautiful children, Franca and Enzo, and the Finzis, with the new baby... "

"Yes. In fact Elda Cava was happy to be among the first to be called so that she could choose a good seat in the front of bus since she suffers from motion sickness."

"Did you say 'first bus'?"

"Yes. They came back a few weeks later and they fit into the second bus all those people whose names started with "H" through "M". The rest of us were waiting for the third bus, when I was told that because of my asthma I could go free. But evidently before the third bus arrived my children had managed to escape, together with a couple named Pollack. I got a note from them just this morning that they are free and the concentration camp has been dismantled."

Dismantled?! If the concentration camp didn't exist anymore, then our parents and Mario were taken to Germany! Or...

We felt fear and hope gripping at our throat.

"Where are your children now?"

"They are hiding at the farm of the butcher Baldassini."

The person who had brought her the note from her children was M., a school teacher. We hugged her and quickly left in search of the teacher. Again, it was almost an impossible task, but eventually we did find Signor M., who readily volunteered to take us to the butcher's farm. The teacher was a short but strongly-built young man. We walked, as usual, through the woods, exchanging notes about our most recent experiences. M. talked fast and gesticulated a lot with his arms up in the air, as if his hands above his head made him feel taller. Suddenly we heard a few shots very close to us. The teacher let out a scream, lowering his hand over his right ear, which was now bleeding profusely. With his left hand he grabbed mine and began to run, yelling, "Let's get out of here, dammit!"

We ran, hunched, until he felt that we were safe. A sniper had recognized him and had fired a round of bullets, hoping to get the three of us, but he had only succeeded in hitting our companion very superficially in his earlobe. We stayed with him until the bleeding stopped.

"I am known too well here. You'd be better off without me," said the teacher with a discouraged tone of voice. "I am all right and can easily find my way back," he added, seeing our reluctance to leave him alone. "You will be able to continue by yourselves."

We arrived at the farmhouse after dusk. We didn't find the Nunes boys, who were hiding in a safer place, but we were given something to eat, and again each of us had a chance to sleep in a real bed. When the people in the farm found out the reason why we wanted to see the Nuneses, they had a better suggestion: we should go to see another farmer who had been smuggling eggs into the concentration camp and knew more than the Nuneses did of what had been going on there.

In a direct line, we were told, this farm was not too distant, but to reach it was a little complicated, especially for people who didn't know the area. They gave us directions the best they could, and we carefully annotated them in our minds. We had come so far without getting lost, we would not have any problems now that we were so near our goal.

Lucky to be Alive

We walked and walked all day, resting only during the hottest hours, when we took cover from the sun under a large tree. We then resumed our march. As we proceeded, we realized that the dirt path had ended and the forest was becoming thicker and thicker. Believing that we were on the right track, we kept on going, even though we had difficulty making much progress because of the clumps of briars and bramble bushes. The more we advanced, the thicker the forest became. In addition, the terrain began to go downhill, steeply and unevenly. In order to advance we had to leap down, sometimes blindly, with the height of the jump unclear. The thorny branches were ripping our clothes and making deep scratches in our skin. Suddenly we realized that it was completely dark, and very humid. It was June 17, almost the longest day of the year. To be so dark, it must have been late at night. We concluded that we could not possibly go on. Lello, who had had pneumonia as a child, said, "I'm afraid that if we stayed here all night, we would surely catch pneumonia. Let's get out of here!"

We turned around and began the difficult climb back through the barriers of thorns, until we reached the flat land we had left hours earlier. Bleeding and exhausted, we dropped to the ground and almost immediately fell asleep.

We were awakened by the first sunlight. The air was already warm and it felt good after the mist and the dew that had chilled us during the night. We resumed our walk away from the forest, and eventually we chanced upon a farmer and asked him for directions. We told him of our adventure during the night, and he said, "You're lucky you're alive! I'll take you to your man, but first I want you to see something."

We were in a hurry to find the man who could give us news about our family, but didn't want to be rude to this one who was being so kind. So we followed him. We walked downhill on a long and tortuous dirt road, and suddenly the man told us, "Turn around and look up, look where you were last night. You had reached that ridge. Another few steps down, and good-bye you!"

We shuddered. We were looking at a very tall bluff surmounted by a thick forest.

"Nobody, not even wolves, ventures in that forest at night!"

Now we knew why he wanted us to see it. It was a sight we were never to forget.

After another hour's walk, we were knocking at the door of the chicken farmhouse. Our escort left us there. The man who opened the door was so distressed by the sight of these two dirty ragamuffins, scratched all over, that he almost slammed it in our faces. With obvious repugnance, he asked us what he could do for us.

Lello, generally circumspect, had by now lost any shred of caution and simply asked him, "Please tell us what you know about Signor Azeglio Servi."

The man's instinctive response was to deny that he even knew a person by that name.

"Please," insisted Lello. "We are his children, we walked a long distance to find out about our parents and little brother. If you know anything, bad or good, we must know."

The man still looked suspicious.

"We were directed here by the family of the butcher Baldassini... "

At these words the man finally relaxed. His face lit up as he told us that they were free and living in the house of the *Federale del Fascio* in Roccatederighi!

The head of the Fascist Party? We were not sure that we had heard him right, and we made him repeat that it was *our* family that he said were alive and hiding nearby.

The man said, "I was about to go and bring them some fresh eggs, as I used to do when they were locked up. Come along, I'll take you."

"How did you manage to bring eggs inside the camp?"

"One of the fascist guards was in love with your cousin Bianca, and through him I was able to smuggle the eggs."

On the way Lello begged the man to go ahead of us and cautiously prepare our parents for our arrival.

As we walked our legs were shaking. The man stopped in front of a tall building that looked more like a hotel than an apartment building.

"Here we are," he said.

Lello and I remained at some distance. The man knocked at the big door and after a while someone came to open it. We could not see the person inside.

"I came to bring you some fresh eggs," the man said in a loud voice. "And also some good news about your children."

"What?"

I thought I heard my father's voice.

Father did not understand why the eggman, generally very quiet, was now so talkative, and called out, "Sa' (his affectionate diminutive for Sara), come here and listen to what the man with the eggs is saying."

This time I heard my father's voice all right! It had been such a long time since I had last heard it!

"Babbo, Babbo!" I screamed.

Mario from the kitchen began to yell, "Mamma, I hear Edda's voice!" Mamma in turn yelled that he was dreaming, it was only the man with the eggs outside.

At this point Lello and I could no longer hide. We ran to hug our father who was so confused by our sight—our hair tangled and dusty, our cloths thorn, our bodies scratched all over, covered with dried blood—that he almost didn't recognize us. (Later he entered in his prayer books, where he noted the most important events since his arrest, "Roccatederighi, June 18, 1944: Lello and Edda arrived in a piteous state after walking 9 days and nights in search of us.")

Meanwhile Mario and Mamma had come to the door screaming and crying. We all began to hug and kiss excitedly, and lots of confused and tearful talk filled the room. Mamma looked at us questioningly, and we blurted out that Gino and Marcella were all right. We wanted to give her some peace of mind.

In reality we knew nothing about them. A week during the movement of the front could mean anything.

The German Headquarters

After we all calmed down a little, Lello and I looked around, hardly believing our eyes. We were indeed standing in the hall of a hotel! A marble staircase to the right led to a dining room on the mezzanine and to the bedrooms on the upper floors. On the left was the kitchen, and between the kitchen and the staircase a small metal door led to a cement patio for outdoor dining. We thought we were dreaming.

We learned from Father that when the second bus had come—contrary to what Signora Nunes had told us—people were not called in alphabetical order: all the foreign Jews were taken with the exception of a couple from Vienna, the Schechters, because Mrs. Schechter had become the lover of the camp director; and the remaining Italians—after some bribing of the director and of the bus drivers—were left behind. After this, there had not been a third bus. The director of the camp and the guards had fled in fear of the Allies and of the revenge of the survivors. The bishop, his sister and his butler had also vanished, and the few Jews who had not been deported were left to their own wits. Not knowing where to go, they remained at the camp, planning to wait there for the arrival of the Allies. No sooner had they agreed on this than they saw a garrison of the Gestapo stopping at the foot of the large flight of steps outside. The Jews immediately split into two groups, locked themselves inside two of the three bathrooms in the building, and waited for the worst. The Gestapo men looked in the dormitories, ransacked the place, and with their rifle butts sprang open the door of the one bathroom where nobody was hiding; then they stole whatever food was still in the pantries and left. At this point no one wanted to remain in the camp one more minute, and they all fled in different directions in search of safer shelter.

Father remembered that he had had a customer in Roccatederighi from the time when he had been a salesman. The three members of our family set off on foot to look for him. As Father inquired of his whereabouts, they found out that the man was the head of the local Fascist Party. Not knowing anybody else, Father had no choice but to go and face him. Leopoldo was a bachelor and lived with his mother in this hotel, of which he was the owner. Father then made a deal with the *Federale del Fascio.*

"The Allies are about to come," he told the man. "If you give me and my family shelter until then, I will intercede with them and with the partisans in your favor when they come to kill you."

The man must have been guilty of some crimes, because at these words he gave Father the keys of the hotel and permission—no, orders— to use anything he found. He then fled with his mother.

The hotel was furnished with an abundance of everything conceivable. Three frightened and semi-starved people freshly escaped from a concentration camp could not get over the fact that, while ordinary citizens were near starvation and the Jews were being deported, the fascists lived and ate like nabobs.

It was midday by the time we arrived, and we found Mario eating a raw onion—something he had learned in the concentration camp and not normally done in Italy. For us, however, Mamma began to prepare a real meal. While waiting, we went upstairs to wash and I changed into one of the couple of dresses Mamma had. We then stepped outside to look at the patio and take a deep breath. A volley of bullets brushed past us. We hid behind a square column, but as soon as the firing ceased we ran indoors.

We had just reentered the hall when the frightfully familiar knocking of rifle butts was heard at the front door. Being of draft age and knowing that his presence would jeopardize also our safety, Lello jumped through the kitchen window without having had a chance to put anything into his mouth, and vanished. Mamma pushed me toward the kitchen suggesting that I, too, go and hide. Instead, I promptly went to open the door and found myself in front of a dozen SS storm troopers. Without giving myself a chance to think, I yelled in their faces, *"Was wollen Sie?"* And then, since this was about the extent of my knowledge of German, I sternly added in Italian, "What manners are these? Can't you behave when you go to someone else's home?"

There was a loud grumbling among the men. An old army officer stepped forward and yelled some orders which made all those SS men turn and leave. In good Italian, he apologized for the soldiers' behavior, and said that from this moment this hotel was requisitioned for the officers' headquarters. There were only five of them, and we didn't have to fear anything. We wouldn't be bothered: they knew we were good fascists.

Pretending to be the host, Father took him to the cellar and showed him the vintage wine that had been preserved just for the occasion. Another four men arrived shortly after, and Mamma casually ordered me to make some coffee, as if we had been waiting for their arrival. Mario looked on, trying to say the least for fear of betraying himself. I would have liked to put poison in that coffee. But what good would it do? For the five of them, fifty of us would be killed, and perhaps more because these were high officers and were "worth" more than ordinary soldiers.

For about a week, with terror and anxiety in our hearts, knowing nothing about Lello, we hosted the German military command! There was a general with four other high-ranking officers. Mamma was doing the cleaning, Father and I the cooking, and Mario helped us all. The officers went in and out without telling us anything of their comings and goings, but at supper time they were always back, and after supper they would spread huge maps on the dining table and discuss in German their plans. Father, at these moments, would leave the dining room and we would do the same: he had told us to stay away, because those officers were certainly discussing war secrets and it was dangerous for us to know too much.

Every day one or more of them would come with some loot— generally food that they liked. Once one of them arrived with a live goose.

Father was convinced that they suspected that we were Jews and the slaughtering of the goose would be the proof. But he would outsmart them. Instead of killing the animal the way he had ritually done all his adult life—to quickly cut the throat of the animal with a very sharp knife at the jugular vein to minimize the suffering and to eliminate all the blood, which the Jews are forbidden to eat—he would kill the goose with a big hammer. This was the way he usually did it, he said. The officer who had brought the goose laughed, and said he had never seen anyone using a hammer. Father began to feel on tenterhooks. The officer then ordered Father to hold the goose firmly on the butcher block and me to hold the head with the neck stretched. The animal was squirming and, in spite of my firm grip holding its beak shut, tried to bite me. The officer drew his sabre and with one stroke decapitated the animal. Blood spurted all over us, but we all felt relieved.

One night, when they were studying the maps more carefully than ever, we silently walked away as usual. As we were about to mount the staircase to our bedrooms, the older man called us in. Our blood froze in our veins. We were eager to know where the front was, but we were afraid of betraying our joy if we found out that the Allies would be coming within the next few days. The general was in a mood to talk. Without our asking anything, he told us that the front was very near. Father did his utmost to make a long face instead of a happy one. We avoided looking at one another and still kept quiet. Finally the officer addressed our father directly: "You're as old as I am; you have seen more than one war. What do you think of wars?"

Father hesitated, searching for an uncompromising answer. The man didn't wait for an answer. He told Father that he had been fighting for five years now, and did Father know what *he* thought of wars? Father shook his head.

"I think," the general began, "that all wars should be fought in an arena. Mussolini, Hitler, Stalin, Churchill, Roosevelt should be standing in the middle of it, killing one another, and we—all of us—should be seated all around the arena, clapping hands and shouting, 'yeah, yeah!'"

Father was flabbergasted, but did not comment. He limited himself to repeat, *"Ja, Ja."*

The next day the officers arrived with a truckload of wheels of pecorino cheese. God knows why they had to steal from someone to bring things here where there was abundance of everything: cheese, oil, wine, flour, pasta, preserves, sugar! Perhaps they were stealing from farmers who were known to help partisans to bring the booty to the home of a fascist. Who knows. Whatever the reason, we had no choice but help them unload the truck and carry those heavy wheels of cheese down into the cellar. That same night, they announced that they were leaving the next morning and that they would take me along since I was such a great cook.

Mamma's face grew white but she said nothing. She had feared all along that this might occur and had prepared for the eventuality. Father changed the subject, and Mario instinctively grabbed my hand and wouldn't let go. I wasn't scared because I had the feeling that they were joking: they had ignored me all this time, they would not become interested in me now that they had to run for their lives. But I didn't like that remark even as a joke, and remained aloof all evening.

When we went to bed, Mamma said to me that they might have noticed where I normally slept; she accompanied me to an attic room with a little bed, told me to sleep there, and locked me in from the outside.

"If they look for you before they leave," she said, "I'll show them your bedroom and say that you had been scared by their talk and fled."

During the night I had one of my terrible nightmares and woke up screaming at the top of my lungs. Mamma saw her little scheme ruined, and ran up to help me quiet down. On the way up she ran into the five German officers who were fleeing precipitously, without even noticing her.

The Lucky Star

By dawn we began to hear the rumbling of the cannons. Then the sirens announced an air raid. Only then was I finally freed from my prison because we all had to go down into the shelter that was right underneath the cellar of our hotel. At the shelter we found many people, some hopeful and happy, the majority bewildered with fear. The shells from the cannons flew over our heads with ominous whistles. I knew that if we heard a whistle the shell would fall far from us. But, at times, instead of the whistle we heard a shuffling, and that meant that the shell was so close it could fall right on us. I had come a long way from that May afternoon at the creek when I was in panic for the bombing! Now the close shelling did not bother me. Somehow I felt very courageous and cheerful and tried to cheer and distract my shelter companions as well. I told them stories of funny moments that had occurred to us. I also told them that my nickname was "Lucky Star," and nothing bad would happen wherever I was; and they all loved to hear this and told my father that I was a remarkable girl.

Pretty soon everybody was laughing, and in fact I had a hard time being excused for a while to go and make some coffee. I promised that I would be back right away and went upstairs to make a big pot of coffee, which I served with sugar and cheese and bread.

Father made friends with a young man and passed the time talking with him. Mario found a playmate. Mamma was worried for Lello, who had disappeared through the kitchen window the day we arrived and not heard from since. She was also worried about Marcella and Gino, and kept quiet and to herself. I enjoyed my popularity, but I could not stay trapped inside a shelter. What difference would it make being here or upstairs? Should one of those shells fall on the building, it wouldn't help much to be underneath it: we would die the death of trapped mice. I went again up to the hotel, and began to tidy the rooms and prepare some lunch. From up there the noise was much louder and frightening.

I had been in the house only minutes when I heard a gentle tapping at the kitchen window. I ran to see, and found Lello emaciated and very dirty, his cap lowered down over his forehead. I let him in and gave him some coffee and something to eat. He told me that he had spent all day and part of the night hiding in a waste ditch the day that the Germans had installed their headquarters inside our hotel. Then, starved and exhausted, he had tried to get in touch with the local partisans, but it was hard for him to ask anybody, since he didn't know whom he could trust. He had spent the days hiding and resting and the nights walking from place to place hoping to locate a partisan formation. He had finally found one and had joined it. Through the partisans he had learned that the Germans had left, so he had come to see what had happened to us.

"We are all right, well fed, and we will tell you more later. But let's go down now and show the rest of the family that *you* are alive."

"No, you'll tell them later. Now I must go. I have been assigned to the main bridge. The Germans mined all the bridges, and we have to find the mines and clear them before the liberators arrive."

I reluctantly let him go. When I told Father that Lello had shown up and had gone with other partisans to clear the main bridge, Father became angry.

"We have suffered enough and are alive by dint of a miracle," he said. "You should have told him to stay with us and let trained people do the job."

I told Father that Lello *had* become an expert at defusing mines, and not to worry. In reality I was very worried myself. Lello was so weak and battered he might indeed make a mistake.

We went to bed early that night, and Mamma let me sleep in my room, even though she was still very much afraid that the Germans might come back for me. In the middle of the night, unable to sleep, I heard the gentle tapping at the kitchen window that I had heard that morning. Without telling anybody, I went down to open the door for Lello who was so excited he could hardly speak.

"What is the matter?" I asked, a little anxious.

"The English are here! Let's wake everybody up!"

We ran upstairs and woke up the rest of the family.

"Let's go up, come up!" yelled Lello as he climbed the stairs to the roof terrace two by two.

We all followed him, and from up there we could see a long, long snake of lights slowly making its way up the tortuous road that led to Roccatederighi. The convoy was still so far away that all we could see were the front lights like tiny round eyes shining in the night.

"How do you know they are the English?" inquired Father still sceptical. "Couldn't it be the Germans coming back?"

"No, *Babbo*. If these were the Germans coming back, there would be fighting. But all is calm and the English will be able to come through the main bridge because *I* have helped save it!"

He said this with unconcealed pride.

It was apparent that the liberators were not arriving at the village quite yet. We'd better get some rest. But who could rest? We kept on lying down and getting up immediately afterward to watch the progress of the march. They moved so slowly! The few hours that went by before dawn seemed eternal.

Soon after the sun rose, we began to hear the rumbling of hundreds of motors coming uphill. We went down to the cellar, each one of us grabbed a flask of wine in each hand and went out into the street to be the first ones to welcome the English. When the first tank appeared at the end of our street, our hearts leaped at our throats. We cheered and lifted the wine, but the tank didn't stop. Another tank filed past us, and another and another... Strange little uncovered cars also passed by with men almost reclining and with their feet on either side, or even on top, of the low windshields. We eventually learned that those curious little cars were called *jeeps*.

Finally the whole column came to a halt. Men with khaki uniforms began to peer out of their tanks, others jumped out of their strange little cars shouting and cheering. They didn't look very English to us, but they did speak an English dialect. We said Hello! Welcome!! And above all we kept repeating, THANK YOU!!!

They hugged us, drank wine early in the morning, gave us cigarettes and chocolate bars. They were extremely happy that we could understand them and speak their language. They were warm, sloppy, generous, friendly. They were Americans!

We lived the days that followed our liberation in a state of psychological intoxication. We couldn't get over the fact that we were truly free. Twenty years of dictatorship and tyranny, of oppression and harassment—which for our generation meant a lifetime—and the senseless persecution and killing of the Jews, had been replaced by total liberty, and it was hard for us to fully savor the meaning of this reversal. Only a few days earlier our very lives were at stake as we unwittingly hosted the German military command!

Among our parents' former co-inmates, the Schechters—the Viennese couple who had been spared deportation by the director of the camp—showed up at our hotel one day and became almost part of our family. So did Clara Piperno, a colorful character from the Roman Ghetto; and the Pollacks, who had escaped the camp with the Nunes brothers. There was enough of everything (and especially of cheese!) to feed everybody for months, and it made us happy to share this abundance with our fellow sufferers. We befriended some of the American liberators who had been stationed in the neighborhood, and they also came to share a meal with us from time to time. I especially remember with fondness one of them, a funny young man nicknamed Duke (or Duck, I am not sure), who had a marvelous voice, and sang for me all the latest American hits and the beautiful *Stardust*.

Of course Gino and Marcella were constantly on our minds, and the impossibility of knowing whether they were safe was a tremendous strain on our psyches. But our general spirits were high and we never lost hope of hearing from them.

The Mine

By this time, on the other hand, Marcella and Gino had serious doubts whether any of us were still alive. As it were, all the bridges and the main roads had been destroyed or rendered impassable by the mines of the retreating Germans and by the bombardments from the air of the advancing Allies. Telephone communications were practically non-existent even before being totally destroyed by the movement of the front. The result was that there was no way of getting in touch with anyone outside the immediate vicinity.

Marcella and Gino kept on going to Uncle Tranquillo's to see if through some of his many acquaintances he had been able to learn anything about our parents, but the answer was always negative. The two of them had managed, without anybody's help, to make our home a livable place, and continued to make progress and improvements on it with admirable tenacity. Their daily discovery that more and more of our personal belongings and books were missing, however, inevitably caused depression which made their task more difficult.

Finally, one day, Uncle Tranquillo had a piece of news for them which could be very good.

"Someone I know," he said to them, "came from San Lorenzo, near Arcidosso, and brought me the news that the numerous members of the Nunes family have survived and are all living in that village waiting to go back to their Grosseto home."

"How about our family?"

"He didn't know anything about anyone else, and not even the circumstances of the Nuneses' escape."

The news that someone had been able to go free rekindled in Marcella and Gino the hope that our parents and Mario might also have escaped deportation. Without deluding themselves with false expectations, they immediately decided to go and pay a visit to the Nunes family.

In addition to the coveted certificate of participation in the Resistance, Gino and Marcella had received from the newly-established Partisans Association a modest sum of money which enabled them to eat and to purchase two second-hand pairs of shoes. They set off on foot, with their old knap-sack containing some food on Gino's shoulder, and felt excited, almost elated to be walking again in the familiar countryside—without the fears and anxieties of being chased. Whenever the roads were passable, they hitch-hiked on American military vehicles, but mainly they went on foot.

Unlike the hike that Lello and I had taken on the same route a couple of weeks earlier, in which we faced destruction wherever we set foot, the trip Marcella and Gino took offered the positive spectacle of immediate and feverish reconstruction activities. There were no new buildings going up as yet, and thousands of people were still displaced and living in hastily constructed huts. But rubble was being carried away, roads were being repaired, temporary raft bridges were being put together. Whereas we met with the Germans in defeat, destroying nearly everything and everybody that was in their way, Gino and Marcella met with victorious Allied soldiers, generous and ready to help in any way they could.

Yet, their trip was not devoid of anxiety. They were, like us, marching toward the unknown. The Nuneses could either give them wonderful news, or destroy forever their tenuous hopes.

It took them only two days to reach San Lorenzo, and it was not difficult to locate the Nuneses, since they were a very outgoing and noisy clan (especially Dandolo, who had had the guts to organize a talent show inside the concentration camp!) and everyone in the village knew of this family of survivors with a real zest for life.

Marcella and Gino climbed the stairs to the apartment where the Nuneses were staying, feeling weak in their legs and heavy in their hearts. When they knocked at the door, Marcella had a fainting spell. The door was opened by cheerful Dandolo, the second youngest of the brothers, who immediately recognized Gino. In seeing Marcella almost lifeless with Gino sustaining her, he guessed the object of their visit and screamed with joy, "Hail the Servis! Your parents and Mario will be very happy to see that you are alive. Come on in!"

Marcella came immediately to and found herself crying and laughing at the same time, and hugging and kissing everyone near her.

"Have you heard anything about Lello and Edda?" asked Gino not without trepidation.

"I saw them on their way to Roccatederighi," promptly answered Signora Nunes. "They seemed quite determined to make it. I am sure they did."

Marcella and Gino were given all the known details on the circumstances of our family's escape from the camp and where they could be found.

Signora Nunes, who was preparing a delicious stew—judging from the aromas coming from the kitchen—invited Gino and Marcella to stay for lunch. The temptation to accept was great; however, they were so anxious to go and see for themselves what had happened to the rest of the family that they declined—albeit reluctantly—and said good-bye to the lovely Nuneses.

"On your way out of the village," said Signora Nunes, "stop at the park in front of the church and tell Carlo and my adorable grandchildren, Renata and Pier Luigi, to come home for lunch.

Carlo was the youngest of the Nunes boys. He was a couple of years older than Mario, whom he had met and become friends with in the concentration camp. Unlike his older brothers, Carlo was a rather quiet boy, and had found in gentle Mario the perfect companion. The other two with him were his niece and nephew, the children of his older sister, who were almost his age.

Marcella and Gino, though in a hurry to reach Roccatederighi, were happy to stop and say hello to Carlo, who for many months had shared Mario's fate. The other two, being children of a mixed marriage and raised Catholic, had never been in the concentration camp.

Marcella and Gino left the Nuneses' apartment in a state of total elation. They tried to walk in the shade away from the direct rays of the scorching sun. However, although the tremendous July heat reflected on them from the concrete buildings, they hardly felt it. Everything around them seemed so beautiful—the trees, the sky, the people...

Gino spotted the three children squatting over a toy and called out, "Hey, Carlo-o-o! Your mother wants you to go home. Lunch is ready!"

Carlo raised his head for a few seconds as he heard someone calling his name, but quickly returned to his activity. Marcella and Gino got near the little group and saw that the toy they were playing with was a strange aluminum box shining in the sun. Carlo was poking it with a piece of rigid wire with the intent of opening it while his nephew and niece were looking on with great curiosity.

"What kind of toy is that?" inquired Gino.

"It's a treasure," said Carlo still working at trying to open the box. "We'll soon find out what's in this box. As soon as I open it."

"I wouldn't play with something you found, if I were you," cautioned Gino. "Besides, your mother is waiting for you!"

But Carlo insisted that inside that box there was a treasure and it wouldn't be long until he was able to open it.

Marcella and Gino left the children at their play, eager to be on their way to join our parents and Mario, and hopefully Lello and me.

"Tell me the truth," said Marcella to Gino. "Do you really think that Lello and Edda made it?"

"I am positive, I just know it in my heart that they did!"

"Then why all of a sudden you have a frown and look so serious?"

"It just occurred to me that that box could be a mine."

"I have thought of it myself, but haven't they all been deactivated by the partisans?"

"Yes, they supposedly have. But what if *that* one is still fused? We must go back and get those kids to stop fidgeting with that thing."

Before they had a chance to turn, a tremendous detonation reached their ears and made them sway on their feet. They turned to look. A big cloud stood between them and the church; but after the rubble and the dust settled down a little, they saw that the whole side of the building had been demolished and there was nothing left of the three children in the crater that the mine had excavated.

Marcella stiffened and without looking at Gino uttered only three words: "Take me home."

It took Gino and Marcella quite a while to recover somewhat from the shock. A mere few seconds had separated them from sharing the fate of those children. And what a tragedy had befallen the Nunes family a few days after their liberation!

To this day Gino and Marcella shudder each time they remember that episode. The mines remained a danger long after the war was over. A few weeks after the Nunes tragedy, Pietro Casciani, a well known partisan from Pitigliano, was also blown apart while trying do deactivate a mine.

Two weeks after Marcella and Gino's sad encounter with the Nunes children, most of the roads had been made passable, and the most urgent traffic had been allowed to resume. Gino was trying to persuade Uncle Tranquillo to lend him his gazogene truck to go to Roccatederighi and get the family, but to no avail. Gino didn't even have a driver's license.

Brutality & Brutality

We, in Roccatederighi, were not aware of any of the misadventures that Gino and Marcella had gone through. In fact we didn't even know whether *they* were alive, and if they were, whether they knew that we were all safe and sound. We kept on living amidst all this luxury, but it didn't do us much good, and we waited impatiently for the opportunity to go back to our home.

One afternoon, while our parents were taking a rest, a hard knock at the door reminded us of the Germans. Lello went to open and found himself facing two huge American military policemen. Without ceremony the two entered and one of them, the heavier and taller of the two, asked Lello with a menacing voice, "Are you Leopoldo?"

Lello couldn't help a smile and shook his head.

"We have this address as the home of the head of the Fascist Party. Where is he?" thundered the man with a deep frown and a rising anger in his voice.

"We have no idea," said Lello, and proceeded to explain who we were and why we were living there.

The Americans softened a little, "He must be among the fascist suspects who are being held at the school. Would you recognize him if you saw him?"

"No, I never met the man," said Lello. "But my little brother knows him."

Lello was very protective of our parents and avoided mentioning them at all.

The two MPs ordered Lello and Mario to go with them. I was curious and a bit apprehensive, and followed them to the school building, where the two Americans were directed to one room guarded by an armed partisan. The room was small and bare. About a dozen people were either standing or sitting on the floor.

"Is he here?" asked one of the MPs to Mario.

Mario timidly looked around and pointed at the corner of the room where a little old woman was standing hugging protectively a younger and slightly taller man. As these two saw us entering the room, they began to kiss each other, fast frantic small kisses on the mouth, as if they were expecting to be executed on the spot.

Billy, the bigger of the two big Americans, got near the couple and did in fact brandish his pistol very close to their faces. Then he broke into a sinister laughter, and separating the two, began to punch the man, interspersing his blows with, "So, you were the big shot in the Fascist Party! Take this, and this..."

Lello, Mario and I were shocked at the sight of such brutality. We tried to stop the military policeman, but we too got hit in the process. We looked at the old woman with shame. She was trying to put herself between the short man and the huge American in a pathetic attempt to protect her son.

We left. Even though we knew that Leopoldo, as the head of the local Fascist Party, must have been responsible for more than one crime, we couldn't bear to be witnesses to such uncivilized behavior on the part of someone who personally had nothing to do with his victim. We decided not to tell our father, who would not condone such behavior. After all Leopoldo had given his home to us and had not reported to the Germans that the people who lived at his place were Jews who had escaped deportation. This we made known to the partisans and to those who now administered justice. Whether his trial would reveal that Leopoldo's action was dictated by generosity or merely by cowardice, we wanted our deposition to be considered and help mitigate his sentence.

We had not expected the behavior of the two Americans. It came as a blow to our love for our liberators whom we had romanticized. Another disillusion followed when we learned in Pitigliano—which had been liberated by the French and Moroccan troops—that our washerwoman Lucietta, a very tiny and unattractive middle-aged woman, was found dead after having been raped. The crime was attributed to a colossal Moroccan soldier, who had been seen running near the site where the body was found.

However, horrifying as these acts of brutality were, we could not even compare them with the atrocities that the Germans had perpetrated against the Jews, the extent of which we would learn bit by bit.

Chapter Thirteen

Return

O n the morning of July 15, 1944, exactly four weeks after Lello and I had first arrived in Roccatederighi, we heard a gazogene truck puffing up the street. We ran out to see, thinking it might be our uncle Tranquillo. What a surprise and joy to see Marcella and Gino jumping from it! Uncle Tranquillo had lent them the truck on condition that Gino hire a licensed and expert driver. We stormed our brother and sister with a million questions and then we ran to call our parents. Mamma and Marcella hugged each other as we stood around in silence, our eyes moist.

Packing for a long trip was never so simple and quick. We hardly had any possessions and we were eager to go back home. By now Leopoldo's sister-in-law had come to live at the hotel and we couldn't wait to get away from there.

On our way to Pitigliano, we stopped at the site of the concentration camp. It was guarded by American soldiers and we had a hard time convincing them to let us in. Mario gave us a tour of the place showing us, first, the two bathrooms where they had been hiding the morning that the Germans had come to take whoever had been left behind. Then he took us to the dormitories—first to the women's barracks, where he had slept until his 10th birthday near Mamma, then to the men's, where he shared a bunk bed with Father. Mamma kept on shaking her head, talking to herself, naming each of her companions, asking herself, "What has ever happened to poor Signora Baba... And Elda Cava... And baby Gigliola... When will they come back?..." (She had no notion at that moment that her own mother, our good Nonna Fiorina, and her sister Rita, and her uncles and cousins and old friends in Rome had also been deported, and like her fellow captives would never come back.)

On seeing the place where our father had slept, Marcella became very emotional and dramatic. She looked at it from a distance, she slowly approached it, she touched and kissed it. Then she climbed onto it and began to hop up and down. One of the guards who didn't know who we were peered in, and, seeing what was going on, began to yell at Marcella with such a frightful voice that she, who had never shown fear during the whole period of our escape from the Nazi-fascists, got frightened. We were ordered to leave the camp at once or else!

Our parents sat inside the cab with Nicola Lizzi—the driver whose name Lello had assumed on his venturous trip to the concentration camp six months earlier—and Donna Clara, as we called Clara Piperno, who came to live with us in Pitigliano until she was able to go back to her home in the heart of the Roman Ghetto. The five of us stood on the open back holding onto the rail. The wind ruffled our hair and made our clothes adhere to our bodies.

We raised our voices above the noise of the truck to ask each other questions and to tell of our different experiences, but eventually we kept quiet: there was no rush to tell everything that had happened to us; now we had plenty of time to do that. Facing the wind, we rode with our hearts filled with contentment. Once in a while Marcella would bang on the roof of the cab to let the driver know that he should stop. She would jump over the back of the truck onto the road and go to hug Mamma.

It was a beautiful Saturday afternoon, that July 15, 1944, when our family reunited. The war was still going on in the north of Italy, in the rest of Europe, and in Asia. But for us it was finally over.

As the truck jolted along, we noticed that the sides of the road had been planted with hundreds of saplings. In a few years these shaky little plants running by below us would become tall and strong trees.

In Pitigliano the news got around that the entire family of Signor Azeglio had survived and was coming back. A small crowd of relatives and friends came to meet us, and as we walked from the Piazza, others joined the group and we arrived at our home surrounded by people.

As the seven of us walked into the house—the house that had been our paternal grandparents'—our father recited a special prayer; then, in the vast kitchen where we had seen each other for the last time before the flight (from that moment on, we referred to time and events in terms of *before the flight* and *after the flight)*, he gathered us under his stretched arms to give us his *b'racha.*

We went all over the house trying to get used to the place and to make it ours again—Marcella and Gino acting as the proud *hosts.*

A knock at the door startled us. We had seen everybody that counted. Who could that possibly be? We went to open the door and couldn't believe our eyes. Ivan and Arthur stood there, each holding one arm around the other's shoulder.

Marcella and I screamed with surprise, "What are you two still doing here?"

They said that they had not been able to reach their respective regiments until now but were leaving today. Hearing that we were back, they had come to say good-bye.

We asked them in and offered them a glass of wine from the flask we had brought back from Roccatederighi. They accepted, although they certainly didn't seem to need it.

As they were leaving I asked Arthur, sobbing, "You're not going to marry me before you go?"

"No, bambina," he said. "You deserve better than to marry me." And without hugging me, he followed Ivan through the door.

I was shattered, although even his coldness could not attenuate my love *usque ad mortem* and the passion I harbored for him. The illusory certainty that he would come back at any moment to marry me stayed with me for a long time to come. But for the moment, the fact that overrode any other consideration was that the seven of us were together again.

We resumed our questioning one another and our roaming from room to room, with Marcella pointing out what she and Gino had done.

There was a lot to be done before we could return to a normal life. And there was a lot to be told to each other and to the world. All this would take time. For the moment we had accomplished the most important feat: we had survived.

From the very first moment of our return, we considered our survival not only a gift to be cherished forever, not merely a link in the long historical chain of Jewish survival, but also and above all a responsibility bestowed on us. With the conclusion of the war, we felt simultaneously elated and numb. Many years had to pass before we would be able to translate our sense of responsibility into actively bearing witness and remembering and communicating to others both the unspeakable cruelty committed by millions, either actively or by default, against millions of innocent people, and the unsuspected compassion found in some during the monstrous collective madness that swept most of Europe—the heart of Christendom—in the heart of the twentieth century.

The Neophytes of San Nicandro

Even though our house in Pitigliano was in danger of tumbling down into the valley because of the deep cracks in the rock foundation caused by the recent bombing (and eventually it did!), we continued to live there for several more years before we were finally able to move to Florence and start our new life there.

In the meantime we needed food and practically everything else. From clothing to linens, from cooking implements to tableware, from beds and other pieces of furniture to my rickety piano, most of our belongings had been stolen during our absence and we had to replace them. We did receive one C.A.R.E package with some sugar and other imperishable foodstuffs, and one package from the Joint Distribution Committee of America with some clothing—both of which uplifted our spirits and were a great help. Moreover, a few months before she had been taken to the concentration camp, Mamma had inherited some money, a few pieces of furniture, and an apartment in Livorno which had been damaged by bombings, and now she was finally free to take possession of her inheritance.

Neighbors also helped. So, for the moment, we managed.

But we needed steady income, and while waiting for better opportunities, my two older brothers rose to the occasion. They temporarily took jobs helping to rebuild the bridge on the Meleta River (the real target of the bombing). Marcella and I put the skills we had acquired at Lida's atelier to work, and became the most sought-after fashion designers and seamstresses in Pitigliano not only for fine dresses—especially Communion and wedding gowns—but for men's dress shirts as well. And after fixing my old sewing machine (which had been stolen and later found under the rubble of the bombing at some distance from our home), Mario—ten—began to tutor children his age and older.

Now that our most basic needs were met, we had only one burning desire: to get together with other Jews our age. Youth groups were forming in every city among survivors, and gatherings were organized in one place or another. We went to all of these conventions and always returned from them full of excitement and enthusiasm.

One of these meetings was held in the *Hachsharah* of San Marco di Cevoli in the province of Pisa. *Hachsharot* were training centers that had sprung up after the liberation to prepare people to make *Aliya* to the land of Israel, and for life in a kibbutz.

Here, in addition to the usual mingling with young people from all parts of Italy, we had the honor of meeting for the first time, and talking at length with, the renowned philosopher Dante Lattes—a first cousin of our grandmother Debora Lattes—who was invited to deliver the keynote address to our Congress. The strongest memory I have of this encounter—in addition to the fact that I shared with him a great pride in being Jewish—was the humility of this extraordinary man. Even though he was a relative of ours, we began to address him with the formal *Lei*, since we were in awe of him for his worldwide renown as a scholar, as a Zionism theorist and leader, as a discerning and sensitive multi-lingual translator of important Jewish texts, and as a journalist and prolific writer of important original works. But he insisted that we use the familiar *tu*, since in Hebrew, in the land of Israel where he now lived, everybody was addressed with *tu*—even God.

We also had the singular experience of being introduced to five young men, all strictly orthodox, who were there not for our Congress but actually to prepare to move to the land of Israel. What was so singular about this encounter was that whereas throughout our lives we had met many people who had converted from Judaism to Christianity, the reverse had never occurred. However, these young men had all been baptized Christians, born of peasant parentage in the small cluster of houses called San Nicandro Garganico in Puglia, on the *spur* of the *boot*. But on their own, together with some 70 others—including the sacristan of their church—they had taught themselves how to read and write, had systematically read the Bible, carefully studied the Mosaic Law, and spontaneously embraced the Jewish religion, despite having been repeatedly discouraged by the leaders of the Italian Jewish community in Rome. Now, fifteen years after the first of the group had made the spiritual conversion—at the apogee of the *Era Fascista!*—all the thirty-nine males, from the oldest man to the smallest child, had undergone the *Brit Mila,* the ritual circumcision (performed by Dr. Ascarelli of Rome who had operated on my brothers), and with their women and children were ready to move to the land of Israel. These five young men we met at the *Hachsharah* were the first ones to go to establish their community in the northern region of Galilee, and the rest of the converts followed shortly after. It must be emphasized that they did not choose to become Jewish after the war, when being Jewish had become almost fashionable, but at a time when being a Jew was disadvantageous and downright dangerous.

Their story has been documented by the first soldier of the Jewish Brigade—a division of the British Eighth Army—who came into contact with them during the advance of the Allied front in 1943.[1]

After our encounter with Dante Lattes and with these remarkable young men, we felt that we no longer could live in Pitigliano where there was no Jewish life left. Most of the Jews who had escaped deportation had already left the village that had betrayed them to move to larger centers. Like the neophytes of San Nicandro, who first sent a small contingent to explore the situation in Galilee, Gino and I were the first members of our family to move to Florence to get the feeling of how we would fare in that city. Eventually our father—for forty years the devoted head of our Jewish community—and the rest of the family moved too, ending our centuries-long dynasty there and closing thus the long and glorious chapter of Jewish history in Pitigliano.

---

1. Phinn E. Lapide, *Mosè in Puglia,* Longanesi & C., Milano, from the English original *The Prophet of San Nicandro*.

Epilogue

A gainst tremendous odds, the seven of us survived. It took me half a century of partial silence to be finally ready to share with the world my personal experiences as an Italian Jew—from my birth under fascism, through the persecutions of the Jews, to the end of World War II and with it of the abuses of dictatorship. I close my story with additional information about some of the people encountered in it.

Uncle Guido

After his disappearance from Pitigliano, we didn't hear from Uncle Guido until well after the end of the war. Initially he had moved to Florence, preferring the anonymity of the city to the frustration of being harassed and ostracized in the village where he had once been well-known and esteemed by all. After the armistice of September 8, 1943, like others who had the economic wherewithal, Uncle Guido had been able to buy himself a ticket to freedom by escaping to Switzerland. However—contrary to the belief of those who sought shelter in that neutral country—Switzerland was not kind to the Jews who knocked at her door, and accepted them only under the most restricted conditions. Jews were not able to open bank accounts and were interned in refugee camps, isolated from the rest of the population; moreover, men and women, even when newly-wed like two of my cousins, were kept apart, and severe punishments were inflicted upon the transgressors of the rules. Everyone had to work, and this would have been actually a blessing had the jobs been more consonant to each person's ability to perform.

Uncle Guido, a man of enormous capabilities, was assigned to peel potatoes eighteen hours a day. Not just for a week or two, but for all the period he spent in the refugee camp—twenty months!

Upon his return, he went back to Pitigliano with the possible intent of starting his business again, but he found that not only was all the merchandise confiscated by the Fascists stolen, but so was everything else, including the furniture and even the shelves! He went to Florence where—because of his past reputation—he was able to borrow money from banks to start his wholesale business again. Gino and I, as the first two in the family to move to Florence, went to work for him again. Soon we noticed that Uncle Guido had suffered a tremendous transformation, even more dramatic than our father's. From being parsimonious he became extravagant; from a man with realistic goals to be achieved a small step at a time, he became a megalomaniac with delusions of grandeur.

Because of his new personality, which included a fanciful life-style with a suite at the Baglioni Hotel and every meal consumed at Sabatini's and teas at Doney's in our company (and often offered to other members of his staff), we felt very uncomfortable in his presence. The business flourished, but quickly the borrowed money ran out, because no matter how prosperous his business, he would spend more than he made. We who had known him closely could hardly recognize him.

Soon his old ethics began to play a role. He began to judge himself very harshly. His manic behavior was suddenly replaced by deep depression, and one night he was found lying across the railroad tracks. To his rescuers who questioned his suicidal act, he only replied, "My life has all been a big mistake." Typically, he blamed himself for his bankruptcy instead of recognizing that as a Jew he was a victim of his ungrateful country.

He was committed to a mental hospital.

At the beginning of his hospitalization, every Thursday morning I went to see him and brought him a homemade meal, which he ate with the same elegance that had distinguished him all his life. But he would not talk to me or anyone else. He was known among the caregivers for being the easiest of patients. I would talk to him, trying to bring to memory some of his glorious past. But no sign of recognition ever came from that impassive face, not even when I reminded him that he had been a proud and outstanding Bersagliere during World War I.

But one day in the spring of 1955 (I will never know why, since the subject had not come up in more than a decade), I mentioned the German soldier who had so much upset him in Porto Santo Stefano, perhaps to trigger his anger and hopefully make him come back to life. What a shock that was for me! For the first time in months, I saw blood coloring his face. As I, encouraged, kept on reminiscing, he flushed some more, then he began to talk, at first a few disconnected, unintelligible words, then with more and more clarity, until he became loquacious using, as in the past, a chosen and rich vocabulary. But with a difference: his old gentleness was substituted by fury as he accused me, cursed me, verbally abused me, for having befriended a German soldier.

I wasn't sure whether I was happy for having succeeded in awakening him to life, or upset to see his tremendous anger and frustration surface, and to be made the brunt of his pain.

Eventually I got scared and ran away from that dreadful place, and never went back.

The German Soldier

As I arrived home from my last visit to the mental hospital where

Uncle Guido would waste away the remainder of his life, the telephone rang. Norma the maid answered and called me, "Signorina Edda, it's for you. It is a man but I couldn't make out his name."

I went to the telephone, emotionally exhausted, and in no mood for conversation.

"Edda, Edda, don't you remember me?"

The voice on the other end of the wire was unfamiliar. But the accent...? Yes, the accent reminded me vaguely of someone I once knew... No! It couldn't be! Too much of a coincidence! Finally the man ended my suspense by saying, "I am Nino, Nino the German soldier!"

Twelve years had passed since I had last seen him or heard from him. And that was only for a short while in my home and a few more minutes in a cell of the Carabinieri Headquarters in Pitigliano on the day of Corpus Christi, 1943, when our lives had not yet been shattered by the rages of human madness. Now it was June 1955. Important, mostly tragic events had occurred in the interim that had dramatically changed my views, and most of my memories of the German soldier had faded into oblivion until being revived a little earlier as I was talking to Uncle Guido! The name that I had remembered, though, was Engelbert, not Nino.

We decided to meet at four o'clock in the tearoom of a fashionable café in the center of town.

I begged my sister to come with me. We dressed elegantly and went to meet the man—by now in his mid-thirties—not without some trepidation and, quite frankly, irritation. The word *German* evoked horrifying images, and even though he had behaved humanely and uncharacteristically, he had now, most unfortunately—as I had with Uncle Guido—identified himself as "the German soldier."

In the semi-dark tearoom of Torricelli's upstairs balcony, we were greeted by a thick-set peasant in his best Sunday clothes, awkward, and prematurely balding. Nothing had remained of his youthful arrogance and of his Leslie Howard look. Only his accent and his adoring glance reminded me of the young man who had once risked his life in trying to save mine.

We tried to make conversation, but we didn't find much to say to each other. I wanted to let him know *how much* I had appreciated his generosity in coming to warn my family about his fellow Germans, and how much his action had contributed to my conserving some faith in humanity, but all I could come up with were a few stereotyped words of thanks.

We sat for a while, then we got up, shook hands and parted.

A few days later I received a poem (reminiscent of the many he had written to me when I was sixteen, before he knew that I was a Jew) in which he declared himself still in love but unworthy of the love of this "beautiful flower." This poem, the only one left of the many he had composed for me, was the last he would write to me.

After the visit of Engelbert, I reflected upon my ambivalent feelings toward him, as well as others who had been sympathetic and helpful to us. I realized that my sense of gratitude was poisoned and neutralized by the resentment I still harbored for what I had been put through in the first place, and by the huge anger I guarded inside for the senseless loss of many beloved ones (we had not known any of our four biological grandparents and Nonna Fiorina, our beloved step grandmother, was the only one we had to love and be loved by, and they took her away from us and murdered her!) and the immense number of my brethren.

It was my husband, years later, who made me aware that I had underestimated the action of Engelbert and that my anger and resentment would only hurt me and my new family—not undo the past or solve anything. Perhaps recognizing that in the cataclysm and collective madness there had been a few sane people of good will could help me overcome my unremitting resentment and anger.

During one of our trips to Italy, my husband insisted that we look up this man who had been righteous to a Jewish family: he wanted to shake his hand and thank him personally. But again, I could only remember his German name, Engelbert Berner, and we couldn't find it in the telephone books in the area where, forty years earlier, he had told me that his mother lived.

Only recently, as I was digging up some of my memorabilia to help me write these pages, I found his last poem to me, and realized that after the war was over, Engelbert Berner had chosen to use his Italian name, Nino Bernabè.

Signora Maddalena

The beautiful lady who had moved into the apartment above ours—where I, the twins, and Mario were born—and had come to our home the night of November 27, 1943 to urge us to flee because the fascists were coming to get us, turned out to be a noblewoman who had come to Italy with her mother to escape the frigid winter of 1928 in her native Estonia. In the pensione where the two women were staying in the north of Italy, young Maddalena noticed a very handsome young Major of the Italian Army. After a few *"occhiate assassine"* (her words—which I call as "rapturous glances," for lack of a better translation), the two met, married, and had three beautiful daughters. With the entrance of Italy into the war, the major was called to the front and promoted to colonel. Eventually, when large cities began to be bombed, his family sought refuge in Pitigliano.

After the war, Signora Maddalena, Colonel Bellandi (who after the armistice of September 8, 1943 was said to have been missing in action, but had in fact deserted the new Fascist Republic's Army to join the Resistance), and their three daughters moved to Florence. We moved to Florence too, and we kept in touch from time to time. After a while, as often happens, we totally lost track of each other—although we did hear at one point that Colonel Bellandi had died.

Two years ago, during one of my research trips to Italy, I called Signora Maddalena on impulse and asked her if she was willing to grant me an interview. She responded enthusiastically and immediately invited me, my husband, my brother Gino and his wife Metella to go to her villa in the outskirts of Florence for an after-dinner drink. We found her alone, although she told us that she lived with the oldest of her daughters. The first thing that struck me in seeing her after so many years was that—in her eighties—Signora Maddalena was still beautiful, erect, and as vivacious as I remembered her. She greeted us with her magic smile, and made us feel immediately at ease.

We reminisced for a while, and it was amazing how the stories she told us were exactly the same as the ones I had told my husband and my children. But I had not come to her to be reconfirmed in what I already knew and remembered. I had a specific question for her and I finally got around to asking it: How did *she* know that the fascists were coming to get us that precise night? We all knew that the success of their wicked operations depended on secrecy. So, why was she so well informed? Her answer was very simple and I don't know why none of us had thought of it before.

"I was playing the double game!" she said with a mischievous little laughter. "With the fascists I pretended to be a loyal fascist, and this gave me many advantages (do you remember the ricotta pudding I sent down with Bassano? How do you think I could get sugar if I were not a fascist?). But my heart was with my husband who was fighting *against* the fascists, and my helping you Jews was one way I was fighting alongside with him."

"Do you realize what you risked?"

"I know what you mean. But I really didn't risk much. My position among the fascists was very strong, and I might have come to you, a neighbor, just to borrow something."

Fat chance! What could a well-to-do fascist borrow from poor Jews? She knew what she was risking, but chose to listen to her conscience rather than remain silent about what she had come to know and let us be taken to the German slaughterhouses.

Her good humor at being with us came through her smile and through all her being! We enjoyed every minute we spent with her.

The Bombing of Pitigliano

When Lello and I became spectators to the bombing of Pitigliano, the first thought that occupied our minds was, "Whom did we lose? Who died among our friends?" We knew nearly everybody, and among the victims of the bombing there certainly were some of our close friends, but we wouldn't find out until we were free and went back home. Now, after half a century, many names and faces have faded from my memory. But I still remember Alfiero Agresti, a jovial disabled veteran of World War I, who could predict the changes in weather according to the degree of pain from his old wounds; he was our good neighbor and the father of Rosina, the young lady who had sewn my Bat Mitzva dress; I also remember Carla Coppi, a young pianist from whom I had taken a few piano lessons when, at sixteen, I had a little money of my own; Enrichetta Paggi, known as Richettozza, a poor Jew, old and obese, who remained in her home in Pitigliano unbothered and unharmed for reasons unknown while we were in hiding; and our good young dentist.

The dentist was in fact the one we missed most. He had been taking good care of our mouths for the past two or three years with skill and the latest technology. But even more than that was the fact that in spite of his being a foreigner he had shown us more warmth and friendliness than the majority of our fellow Pitiglianesi. He, a foreigner like Signora Maddalena, had been among the few people who had warned us of the evil-doings of the Germans and had insisted that we go into hiding.

Only years later—when a member of his family came to Pitigliano to reclaim his remains—did we learn that the dentist was a Polish Jew, who had come to Pitigliano with false documents and had been able to pass for an Italian because of his perfect command of the language. The irony of his fate was that he had been able to avoid deportation only to end his life under the bombs!

Arthur and Ivan

We never saw nor received word from either Arthur or Ivan since the time they came to our home the day we returned to Pitigliano after our liberation. Of Ivan, in fact, we never heard anything further. However one day—I don't remember precisely when—I came to know, quite abruptly, that Arthur had died.

I was taking a course to become a fashion designer given on the premises of the nun-operated nursery school of my early childhood by a technician who had expressly come to Pitigliano, when I was summoned by two carabinieri to go with them to their headquarters. I took the summons jokingly, convinced that it was a case of mistaken identity. I stretched my arms toward them as if to say, "here, put manacles on my wrists!" But I had no choice but follow them. Besides, I was curious about the real reason for my being called.

I wasn't prepared for what awaited me. At the headquarters the lieutenant told me that they had received notice that the South African soldier Arthur Osborne Moss had become a casualty. My name had been given as the person closest to him in Italy, and he asked me whether I wanted to know the circumstances of his death. The news came to me as a tremendous shock and I couldn't help showing my emotions in the presence of those young men. But I saw no point in learning the details. I composed myself, I thanked the officer, and told him that I preferred not to hear what he had to say.

Quite shaken, I slowly walked back to the nursery school.

The Man with the Swastika

One day, soon after our return to Pitigliano in July 1944, the postman called our name. A piece of mail in those crazy days was a rarity, an unexpected event. Father went down to pick up the mail and was given a large manila envelope addressed to him from an indecipherable provenance. He began to open it with deliberation. We all made a circle around him, curious as to what the contents might be. Father extracted from the envelope two colored enlargements of his portrait and Mamma's taken in Rome the day of their engagement twenty-four years earlier—and the two original brown ones. We were dumbfounded and ashamed for the way we had treated our father when he had trusted the stranger with those precious photographs, but ecstatic at the outcome. Obviously the gentleman who had claimed to be a Jew *was* a Jew, *had* survived, and our father had helped, not only with the much-needed material support, but also with his giving a fellow Jew confidence that he would make it. Unfortunately the man did not enclose his name and return address, so we never found out who he really was except for what he had told our father the day he presented himself at our door wearing a band with a swastika on his arm.

301

The two enlargements were framed after we moved to Florence and are now hanging in the living room of my American home—a precious reminder of Jewish survival.

My Parents

Both my parents reached a ripe old age and died of natural causes. After our liberation from the twenty-year period of fascist oppression, Father lived another quarter of a century. In 1943, two days after his sixtieth birthday—unaware of the atrocities committed by the Germans against the Jews in the rest of Europe, much less that death camps existed also in Italy—he was taken (half-voluntarily!) to an Italian concentration camp, where he stayed for only seven months, and was among the fortunate fourteen who were spared deportation. Had he had the slightest inkling of what he would risk—and make Mamma and Mario risk—by letting the fascists take them, he would have been foolish not to go into hiding and do everything in his power to avoid capture. Far from being foolish, Father was a knowledgeable, wise, talented, and giving man who, as a true Jew, was compelled to love and trust all people. Even when more than one person warned him that the Germans were doing bad things to the Jews, his benevolent mind could only translate *bad* into *make people work at jobs for which they were not trained*. That the Germans were actually starving, torturing, mutilating, murdering and burning millions of innocent people, regardless of age, gender, status, level of education, degree of contribution to society, and that a large number of Italians collaborated with the murderers, did not, in his wildest of nightmares, enter his consciousness.

During the sixty years that preceded his traumatic experience at the concentration camp, Father had been an outgoing, jovial and gregarious human being, leading an intense and interesting life. For a man of his time, he was widely traveled, and counted among his friends people who ranged from the most humble of peasants to notables, philosophers, writers—Italian and foreigners, Jews and non-Jews alike. His demeanor, equanimity, friendliness, and generosity made him the lovable person he was. Perhaps all these qualities were tools that helped him survive. As a veteran of World War I, who had been awarded two medals for his courage—a bronze one on the field during the conflict, and a gold one, which was delivered to Mamma after his death—he had certainly witnessed the gore of battle.

However, his awakening to the brutal reality of the gratuitous murdering of millions of unarmed innocents, redefined his outlook in life. He became taciturn and introverted, spending the succeeding twenty-five years mostly reading about the atrocities that had been perpetrated by the Germans and their collaborators against the Jewish people. Although he retained some of his previous ebullience, he emerged an altered man. Until the day he died, he could hardly talk about anything but these atrocities and his experiences of the seven months he had spent in the concentration camp. He who had never been a Zionist—believing in his heart of hearts that Jews had long ceased to be a nation and were instead one religious group among others in their native countries—became a fervent supporter of Israel; he who had been a peaceful, loving soul became convinced that the only means of fighting fire was with fire itself.

Mamma lived another thirty-four years after coming back from the concentration camp. Having never trusted people unconditionally the way Father had, she did not succumb to severe shock and continued to be, above all, the mother-par-excellence she had always been. However, when she thought that she could not be heard, we often caught her talking to herself, "I am sure that my mother died of a heart attack the minute the SS dragged her out of her bed at five o'clock on that chilly morning."

She could not bear the thought that her beloved sweet mother had gone through the atrocities of the inhumane beatings, the starvation, the psychologically and physically dehumanizing trip in the cattle cars to end up gassed and burned after much unimaginable suffering, preferring to think that she had died before all this. (How else, if not for this mechanism, could she preserve her own sanity?)

Her soliloquies included her compassionate wondering of what had happened to her fellow inmates at the concentration camp. "How did gentle and very neat Elda Cava, who suffered from motion sickness, endure the long bus ride to Fossoli di Carpi, and the seven-day and seven-night atrocious cattle-car ride without food, water or air, and the screaming, the vomit, the excrements, the stench...?" [....] "What happened to Signora Baba who used to lament that she had cried so much in the last five years, that she didn't even have the comfort of tears anymore?" [....] "And baby Gigliola? When her mother was pregnant, we worried that if the child were a boy he might be conscious of pain for late circumcision. Was she conscious when she was thrown up in the air and met with a bayonet on her way down? And what went through her mother's mind when she had had to witness this atrocity before she collapsed lifeless herself?" And 18-year-old Rita, whom Mario adored because she reminded him of his sister Edda, did she make it?...."

We never once heard Mamma talk about her own suffering and of hers, Father's and Mario's narrow escape from sharing the same fate as her mother, and many other beloved ones, as if her altruistic and self-effacing demeanor would not allow her to indulge in recalling her own personal discomforts and terrors.

One good thing came out of this tragedy for our parents: their relationship—which as in all long-lasting marriages had had its rocky moments—mellowed remarkably, and the remaining quarter century of their lives together was spent in perfect harmony.

The Five Children

In spite of the fact that when we had been forced to be separated from our parents we had sworn that if we came out of the nightmare alive we would never be separate again, we in fact dispersed across three continents: the three boys remained in Italy; Marcella went to the United States of America and then to Israel; and I came to visit my younger sister in New York and here I still am.

The oldest of us, Lello, not having had a chance to go through regular schooling, gave himself an education studying by correspondence while working. However, in spite of the highest marks and all the praise he received from his invisible professors, this method of self improvement did not make up for the lack of formal education which, in an academic environment, would have helped to fulfil, to a far greater extent, the enormous potential in him. This dichotomy (superior intelligence and great potential versus the impossibility of achieving his goals) frustrated and afflicted him all his life. He was the one most adversely affected by the limitation of opportunity due to the racial laws and our lack of means, and by the full disclosure—at war's end—of the atrocities committed by the Nazi-fascists.

Immediately after the war ended, he joined the Partito d'Azione—an extension of the movement *Giustizia e Libertà,* which was founded by the brothers Carlo e Nello Rosselli (after the motto *Non Mollare,* Do Not Give In), and adhered to by a group of liberal intellectuals among the staunchest anti-fascists.

Having been compelled to go to work as a bank teller when he was not quite twelve, he went on to become a manager at a very early age. However, this did not satisfy his intellectual needs and in his spare time, in addition to his studies by correspondence, he dedicated himself to the demands of his creative mind. His many talents included writing, drawing and painting. He became an accomplished painter without ever having had a single lesson in the subject.

At age forty-eight his life concluded tragically when an army truck that ran a red light hit him while he was crossing on his bicycle a street near home, in Florence. The talented and sensitive man he was, Lello left a legacy of numerous poems and essays, and many masterful drawings and paintings.

Gino—also a victim of the impossibility of becoming the professional man he aspired to be—never abandoned the pursuit of his intellectual interests whenever and however he could. To make a decent living, however, he didn't have many choices and—following in the footsteps of Uncle Guido, who had been his teacher and mentor—became a successful and well-respected businessman. Upon retirement from his business, he dedicated much of his time to the betterment of the Jewish Community of Florence of which he is a prominent member. A few years ago, the Board of Education of the city of Florence decided, as part of the curriculum, to send groups of Christian children, from elementary to high school, to visit the Jewish Temple of the town and begged the Rabbi to answer any question on Judaism the children might have. These informal lectures were given inside the Sanctuary.

Gino was once called to substitute for the Rabbi. He was so well liked that he became the preferred—and eventually the sole—lecturer. Today, students and their teachers (often including a priest) come from all corners of Italy to hear him talk—in excess of five thousand a year. I have had the opportunity of attending some of his lectures and learned a great deal from him.

Mario, who was still young when he was liberated from the concentration camp, was the only one of us who was able to—thanks to Gino's honoring of his early pledge to finance Mario's studies—complete at a normal age his higher education. Because he had the opportunity to match his potential with his achievements, he is the most well-balanced, level-headed of all the children. For the past thirty years, he has been a respected and beloved Mathematics Professor at the University of Parma.

His experience at the concentration camp, rather than making him a bitter person, taught him compassion for all humankind and sharpened his innate sense of justice. His optimistic outlook in life is very refreshing. I immensely enjoy a daily electronic-mail exchange with him on a variety of subjects. Thanks to him I continue to grow, both intellectually and morally.

Marcella and I, upon returning to our home after our liberation, took over most of the household duties, and continued to work as fashion designers and seamstresses. Suppressing our aspirations for a loftier profession, we hoped for a good Jewish man to marry us and to raise a family. However, neither in Pitigliano nor in Florence did our dream come true, and although in Florence we were able to take advantage of the art and culture that surrounded us and to advance our studies of the English language, our need for a formal education was not met. Eventually, first Marcella then I moved to America, and not only did our dream for a fine husband and family come true, but as adults we were finally able to go to college and obtain our degrees with high honors, removing thus some of the frustration we had endured when we were denied our formal education as children. Marcella went on to graduate school to get the degree of "Master of Social Work". After a quarter of a century in America, she and her family made *Aliya* to Israel, where she worked as a volunteer with the handicapped children of ILAN in Jerusalem. Marcella became a prominent member of the Italian Community of that city and the co-founder and active member of the *Friends of the Italian Temple* foundation.

With the exception of Lello, who in spite of his uniquely warm ways with children was himself childless, we are all blessed with outstanding spouses and children.

Reproductions of the photographs the man with the swastika mailed back to us after we had returned to Pitigliano.

My brother Lello at the age of about 40

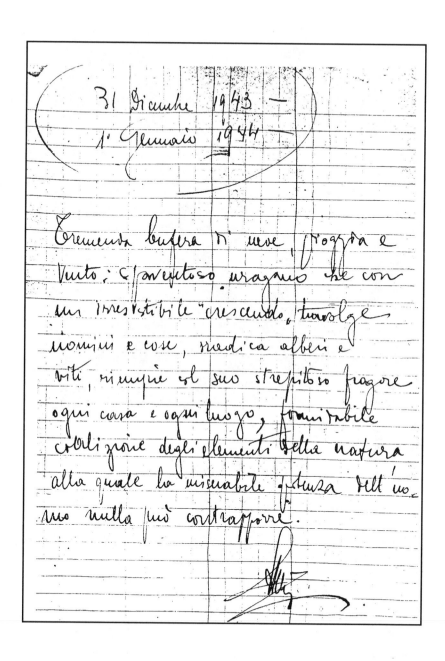

Written by Lello in my diary describing the storm on New Year's Eve. An example of Lello's style of writing, which we all envied.

FIORELLINO MIO.

Diletto fiore, che sei sbocciato
nella furia del vento,
il cui sole ostacolato
da un manto di nuvole
tentò il riscaldarti.
In quell'immensità
ritornò pace e giustizia,
guardasti quella
infinita solitudine
e trovasti te sofferente
e l'orrenda realtà,
molte tue consorelle
non erano più.
Indur tenacia che ha dato
al tuo esile stelo
la forza di sopravvivere
a sì vitale tempesta.

Gridai vittoria nel rivederti,
soave e dolce come
quel tempo burrascoso
che impedì al mio volere
d'avvicinarmi alla tua bellezza,
ma avranno ora queste
mie povere mani il coraggio
o potranno esse raccoglierti
e sperare ancora
al tuo possente profumo
il quale potrà darmi
l'unica radiosa felicità?

Nino BERNABÈ

310

Formal notes prepared by my father for the first Yom Kippur service after the liberation to be held in the Temple in Pitigliano. Among these notes are a list of former Rabbis and Heads of the Community to be read in the Kaddish. Also mentioned is that the prayer for the King, who having sustained il Duce had become his accomplice, would be replaced by a prayer for the Armies of Liberation.

336) - WOLF IZHAQ E SHIMON = PIRQE SHIRAH

      Venezia - Bragadini - 1664 - 16°   Cat. U. XXXI   287

337) - === ZOHAR AL HA-TORAH

      Amsterdam - Props - 1715 - 16°   " " XXIII 86

338) - ==== ZOHAR AL HA-TORAH

      Constantina - ----- -- 1736 - 16°   " " XXIII 90

339) - ==== ZOHA AL HA-TORAH

      Livorno - E/Sadun - 1791 - 8°   " " XXV 133

340) - ==== ZOHAR AL HA-TORAH

      Amsterdam - Props - 1705 - 16°   " " XXXI 278

M A N O S C R I T T I

1) - JEHUDA HA-LEVY = CUSARI (Cz . Cardinal) Cat. U a 1 cc 116 sec. X

2) - MUSAFIA BENJAMIN = MUSAF HA-ARUCH sec.XVIII° U a 2 cc 26

3) - ==== == ==== == = TIQQUN 7 BEADAR Sec.XVIII° U a 3 cc 26

Calola Levi

The last page of an inventory of Hebrew books found in the Temple library at Pitigliano after the war that I prepared at the time. Note that the first of the three manuscript is on the Khazars by Jehuda Ha-Levy.